Reading Faulkner
THE UNVANQUISHED

READING FAULKNER SERIES

Noel Polk, *Series Editor*

Reading Faulkner

THE
UNVANQUISHED

Glossary and Commentary by

JAMES C. HINKLE

and

ROBERT MCCOY

University Press of Mississippi   Jackson

Copyright © 1995 by the University Press of Mississippi
All rights reserved
Manufactured in the United States of America
98 97 96 95   4 3 2 1
The paper in this book meets the guidelines for
permanence and durability of the Committee on
Production Guidelines for Book Longevity of the Council
on Library Resources.

Library of Congress Cataloging-in-Publication Data

Hinkle, James.
Reading Faulkner. The unvanquished : glossary and commentary /
by James C. Hinkle and Robert McCoy.
p.   cm. — (Reading Faulkner series)
Includes bibliographical references and index.
ISBN 0-87805-784-6 (alk. paper). — ISBN 0-87805-785-4 (pbk. :
alk. paper)
1. Faulkner, William, 1897–1962. Unvanquished. 2. Faulkner,
William, 1897–1962—Language—Glossaries, etc. I. McCoy, Robert.
II. Faulkner, William, 1897–1962. Unvanquished. III. Title.
IV. Series.
PS3511.A86U537   1995
813'.52—dc20   94-43863
                                                              CIP

British Library Cataloging-in-Publication data available

CONTENTS

CONTENTS

SERIES PREFACE

This volume is one of a series of glossaries of Faulkner's novels which is the brainchild of the late James Hinkle, who established its principles, selected the authors, worked long hours with each of us in various stages of planning and preparation, and then died before seeing any of the volumes in print. The series derives from Jim's hardcore commitment to the principle that readers must understand each word in Faulkner's difficult novels at its most basic, literal, level before hoping to understand the works' "larger" issues. In pursuit of this principle, Jim, a non-Southerner, spent years of his scholarly life reading about the South and things Southern, in order to learn all he could about sharecropping, about hame strings, about mule fact and lore, about the Civil War, about blockade running, duelling, slavery and Reconstruction, Indian culture and history. When he had learned all he could from published sources, he betook himself to county and city archives to find what he could there. He was intrigued by Faulkner's names, for example, and over the years compiled a fascinating and invaluable commentary on their etymologies, their cultural and historical backgrounds, and, not least, their pronunciations: Jim is the only person I know of who listened to all of the tapes of Faulkner's readings and interviews at the University of Virginia, in order to hear how Faulkner himself pronounced the names and words he wrote. In short, for Jim, there was no detail too fine, no fact or supposition too arcane to be of interest or potential significance for readers of Faulkner: he took great pleasure in opening up the atoms of Faulkner's world, and in exploring the cosmos he found there.

It was my great fortune and pleasure to be Jim's friend and colleague for slightly more than a decade. In the late seventies, I managed to tell him something he didn't know; he smiled and we were friends for life. Our friendship involved an ongoing competition to discover and pass on something the other didn't know. I was mostly on the losing end of this competition, though of course ultimately the winner because of what I learned from him. It was extremely agreeable to me to supply him with some arcana or other because of the sheer delight he took in learning something—anything, no matter how large or small.

On numerous occasions before and after the inception of this series, we spent hours with each other and with other Faulkner scholars reading the novels aloud, pausing to parse out a difficult passage, to look up a word we didn't understand, to discuss historical and mythological allusions, to work through the visual details of a scene to make sure we understood exactly what was happening, to complete Faulkner's interruptions, to fill in his gaps, and to be certain that we paid as much attention to the unfamiliar passages as we did to the better-known ones, not to let a single word escape our scrutiny; we also paused quite frequently, to savor what we had just read. These readings were a significant part of my education in Faulkner, and I'm forever grateful to Jim for his friendship and his guidance.

This series, Reading Faulkner, grows out of these experiences in reading Faulkner aloud, the effort to understand every nuance of meaning contained in the words. The volumes in the series will try to provide, for new readers and for old hands, a handy guide not just to the novel's allusions, chronologies, Southernisms, and difficult words, but also to its more difficult passages.

Jim's death in December 1990 was a great loss to Faulkner studies; it was especially grievous to those of us embarked with him on this series. Absent his guidance, the University Press of Mississippi asked me to assume editorship of the series; I am happy to continue the work he started. The volumes in the series will not be what they would have been had Jim lived, but they all will bear his stamp and his spirit, and they all will try to be worthy of his high standards. And they will all be lovingly dedicated to his memory.

Noel Polk

PREFACE

to *The Unvanquished*

The late Jim Hinkle, Founding Editor of the Reading Faulkner Series, and I "did" Faulkner together for over a quarter of a century; that is, we exchanged ideas, information, interpretations, and shared the collegial joy that perhaps can come only from a joint admiration of one of the greatest writers of the western world. When I first met Jim in 1961, he was already established as a Hemingway scholar. I had been told that he could recite *The Sun Also Rises*: one merely opened the book at random, read a line or so, and he would pick it up from there. I challenged; he performed. But he quickly perceived that I had reservations, not so much about the achievement, but about the selection. He was so unauthoritarian, so open to others' ideas, that when my opinion emerged that it was not only a greater challenge but vastly more important to be able to read and understand Part Four of *The Bear* than to know a Hemingway novel so well as to be able to recite it, he immediately found a copy of *The Portable Faulkner* and began to read.

Several years later, by the time Jim was teaching far more Faulkner than any other author, we attended a lecture on *The Bear* by its foremost explicator. We sat toward the back of a steeply-raked auditorium with many of our students between us and the podium; from time to time a face would flash back in our direction, marked with a quizzical look, checking us out, but our attention was mostly given to the pieces of paper we were passing back and forth, noting the expert's errors in fact and in interpretation, which totalled sixteen by the end of the talk. Jim, ever a gentleman in the best sense of that word, asked no embarrassing questions, but ever a scholar, again in the best sense of the word, reviewed what had been said with great care, then wrote the explicator a polite letter suggesting with quotations from the text that he perhaps might wish to reconsider some of his pronouncements.

That was Jim, through and through. He believed that careful reading, exhaustive inquiry, and thoughtful interpretation just might allow one to slip inside Faulkner's incomparable genius for a bit, to return a different—a better—person, and it really bothered him when anyone, a first-year student or a Ph.D., missed that opportunity through laziness, inattention, or presumption. Some of what Jim wanted to tell us about *The Unvanquished* was incomplete when he left us and it has been my task and my pleasure to have inked in his tracings; the vision and design are his, the errors and omissions mine.

Robert McCoy

How to Use This Book

The line-by-line entries are keyed to the page and line numbers of the Library of America Edition of *William Faulkner: Novels 1936–1940* (1990), edited by Joseph Blotner and Noel Polk. Running heads in bold type will locate passages in this text and, following the abbreviation VI, in the Vintage International paperback text (New York, 1990). Cross references in the entries themselves will be identified by page and line numbers to both editions separated by a double virgule (e.g., 358 : 22//58 : 11). All line counts start with the top line of text on each page. A reliable locating guide can be made as a bookmark by simply preparing a numbered slip of paper that fits your edition.

We believe that the entries will be of greatest service if they are consulted immediately after reading the story itself; we are confident that a subsequent reading after the entries have been reviewed will provide a manifold increase in a reader's understanding and appreciation of the art of William Faulkner.

Reading Faulkner
THE UNVANQUISHED

CHAPTER I
Ambuscade

"Ambuscade" takes place during the summer of 1862 when Bayard and Ringo are twelve. It is the second summer of the Civil War, the year the Northern Army first reached north Mississippi where the Sartoris plantation is located. The war began in the spring of 1861 and ended in the spring of 1865.

Title: **Ambuscade** the Civil War term for a surprise attack from a concealed position. As a military term it is now obsolete but it is still sometimes heard in Southern speech in the sense of a disagreement or a not-too-serious confrontation: "Him and me had a little ambuscade." The word 'ambuscade' is different from 'ambush' in that 'ambuscade' does not imply anything cowardly or unfair—as 'ambush' (with its suggestion of 'bushwhack') does. Dumas, Balzac, and Joel Chandler Harris had used 'Ambuscade' for a story or chapter title. It rhymes with 'lemonade' and 'escapade.' (Boatner 51; Edson viii; Dwyer n.p.; Dollard 354; Skaggs 124)

321:1 **smokehouse** an outbuilding on a farm or plantation where meat is smoked over a smoldering fire to prevent spoiling; also a building where food is stored.

321:2 **a living map** Bayard's and Ringo's backyard battlefield, big enough for them to stand within it and act out their war games on it. 'Living map' is a variation on *tableau*

• 3 •

vivant (living picture), a popular diversion of the time where people posed in imitation of well-known paintings.

321:2 **Vicksburg** Civil War Mississippi's second largest city (after Natchez), on the Mississippi River, about 250 river miles above New Orleans and 250 below Memphis. News reports (rumors?) in late May 1862 say the Northern assault on Vicksburg will soon begin (has already begun?). The Union Navy already controls the river above and below Vicksburg and, if the North could take Vicksburg too, all Southern forces west of the river (Texas, Arkansas, much of Louisiana, and Indian Territory) would be cut off from the rest of the Confederacy. Also Union ships would then be able to take advantage of the uninterrupted length of the Mississippi for troop transport, supplies, and commercial shipping. Thus the defense of Vicksburg is a matter of considerable importance to the South. (Fiske 138; Silver *Retrospect* 37; Long 213; Cash 70)

321:2 **a handful of chips from the woodpile** The boys stand the chips upright to represent the buildings of Vicksburg.

321:5 **possessing even in miniature that ponderable though passive recalcitrance of topography** 'topography' refers to the surface contours of land; 'recalcitrance of topography' to the resistance of land to humanity's attempts to work its will on it, its noncompliance with efforts to overcome its natural inertia; thus, 'passive recalcitrance of topography' means that land does not deliberately *try* to resist efforts to affect it but that it is simply the nature of land to resist and nullify such efforts; 'ponderable' has two meanings and both fit the sentence: 1) having weight: land resists being modified because dirt is heavy; 2) worth thinking about: it is instructive to contemplate the fact that land itself is relatively unaffected by humanity's most ambitious actions upon it.

321:6 **outweighs artillery** 'outweighs' picks up the two meanings of 'ponderable': 1) land literally *is* heavier than an artillery piece resting on it (we would have to dig down only a few feet under a cannon before we had displaced enough dirt to outweigh it on a balance scale); 2) in the long run land will always prove to be of more consequence than artillery, because (as the sentence goes on to tell us) 'the most brilliant of victories and most tragic of defeats are but the loud noises of the moment'—of only fleeting significance measured against the land itself which will remain, essentially unchanged, after the actors upon it have strutted their own brief hour and then disappeared.

Bayard Sartoris as Narrator of The Unvanquished

We are at only the second sentence of *The Unvanquished* but already we have a sample of an exuberant barrage of words which only Faulkner could have written. Bayard Sartoris is telling the story, but Bayard is twelve when "Ambuscade" takes place, so the words of "Ambuscade" are clearly not those of any twelve-year-old boy. What *The Unvanquished* must be, then, is a story-telling performance by an adult Bayard Sartoris (a story-teller with a vocabulary and style equal to Faulkner's) looking back in his mind on his experiences during and after the Civil War, filtered through the haze of memory which, without necessarily deliberately distorting, perhaps sometimes shades the way things actually were to the way they might have been, or should have been, or sometimes simply in whatever ways that will make a more interesting memory and story. See entry at 463//211 for *when* Bayard is telling his story.

321:8 **To Ringo and me it lived, if only because** The preceding sentence told us first what those who called their battlefield a 'living map' presumably meant, and then the sense in which Bayard as an adult now understands that it truly *was* a 'living map.' The beginning of this third sentence tells us what Bayard and Ringo as twelve-year-olds understood 'living map' to mean: it must be 'living' because, like other living things, it drinks water.

321:13 **wellhouse** a roofed shelter over an open well

321:15 **a common enemy, time** Literally this refers to the sunparched ground's absorbing water faster than they could fetch it from the well, but in another and more ominous sense it reminds us of the loss of innocence which time inevitably brings. Bayard and Ringo, a white boy and a black one, are playing together as friends and equals. Soon they will be older, and their friendship must inevitably go the way of that, say, of Roth Edmonds and Henry Beauchamp in *Go Down, Moses* (1942).

321:16 **engender between us** create, the two of us working together

321:16 **recapitulant** This word, a Faulkner coinage not in standard dictionaries, combines the similar but not identical meanings of 'repeating' and 'recapitulating.' It means something like 'a summing up, over and over again.' Compare 'triumphing,' an upscale synonym for 'winning,' with 'triumphant,' which defines not the act but the manner. The boys' fighting the Battle of Vicksburg each day behind the smokehouse results in a Southern victory every time (as we learn in the next line). Since they believe *all* battles of the war ought to (and therefore *will*) result in Southern victories, their repeated acting out a victory at Vicksburg is for them a summing up and demonstration of that assumed truth.

321:17 **like a cloth, a shield** 'cloth' goes with 'pattern' of the preceding line (a pattern of victory like a pattern on a cloth) but then Bayard apparently realizes that 'cloth' is too unsubstantial to suggest how completely he and Ringo were insulated from reality (cloth can too easily be pierced) so he substitutes 'shield,' an appropriately more formidable barrier protecting them from 'fact and doom.'

321:18 **fact and doom** The truth, of course, is that the South eventually loses the battle of Vicksburg, the war itself, and a way of life Southerners believed fine enough to be worth fighting a war to try to preserve.

321:20 **there had not even been dew in three weeks** This is a small bit of corroborating evidence that "Ambuscade" takes place in 1862, not 1863 as some readers have believed, for the summer of 1862 set new records in the South for scarcity of rainfall. At times Faulkner seems to have known *everything.* (Foote I 546)

321:22 **we could begin** playing war, acting out the Battle of Vicksburg

321:23 **Loosh** a slave, the only not-aged or not-still-a-child male (black or white) currently on the Sartoris plantation. His name is short for Lucius.

321:24 **Joby** an elderly house-servant, Loosh's father, Ringo's grandfather, Louvinia's husband

322:2 **fierce, dull early afternoon sunlight** Most of the time the sun in Mississippi is not obscured by a haze. But on some days even the normally blue and clear Mississippi sky does have a haze. The sun is no less hot (fierce) on such days, but it does appear to be duller.

322:3 **his head slanted a little** bent forward and down—perhaps in an habitual attitude of subservience, more likely in mockery of subservience

322:4 **like a cannonball** round, black, hard, smooth (very short hair). That the comparison of Loosh's head to a cannonball should occur to Bayard at this moment perhaps says something about the intensity of the illusion of war that the boys with their backyard battle have created—although we should not make too much of this suggestion, since Faulkner in *Soldiers' Pay* (1926) and in *Sanctuary* (1931) describes male black heads in non-war contexts with the same image. (Nilon 60)

322:5 **his eyes a little red at the inner corners as negroes' eyes get when they have been drinking** Cheap whisky is sometimes called 'red-eye,' but Bayard at twelve seems to believe drinking produces this eye-reddening effect specifically with black persons. At 334:12//22:23, however, we learn that as an adult Bayard no longer believes this: there he describes Loosh 'with that look on his face again which resembled drunkenness but was not.' (Hundley 227; Rose 58)

322:16 **something curious in her voice too** two possible explanations for 'too': 1) something curious as there was in the way she was looking at Loosh; 2) something curious as there was in Loosh's laugh. Both of these meanings fit the context and maybe both are intended.

322:16 **urgent—perhaps frightened** Philadelphy realizes Loosh is about to tell Bayard something he should not, since it is the primary rule for all servants that they should at all times protect, not disturb, the innocence of the master's children.

322:21 **with his hand he swept the chips flat. "There's your Vicksburg"** Loosh is reporting, charade-fashion, that the battle of Vicksburg is over and Vicksburg has fallen to Northern forces. Because that well-known Civil War event occurred in the summer of 1863, many readers have assumed "Ambuscade" must take place then too. But Loosh is mistaken in his report. *The Unvanquished* does not make this explicit but history does. The siege of Vicksburg began and the first demand for its surrender was made on 18 May *1862* by Admiral Farragut, who arrived at Vicksburg with a good portion of the Federal Navy. Farragut had already forced the river cities of New Orleans, Baton Rouge, and Natchez to surrender in one day each (29 April, 8 May, and 12 May, all 1862) and he assumed the superior firepower of his guns would give Vicksburg no option but to surrender too. What Loosh reports as having already occurred at Vicksburg was a reasonable expectation from news reports which reached north Mississippi in early summer of 1862: Vicksburg would fall any day. In fact, however, Vicksburg held out for more than a year. Farragut found that Vicksburg was at the top of such a steep bluff (250 feet straight up from the river) that when he aimed his big guns high enough to clear the bluff the shells flew over the defending Confederate guns at the crest and hit only non-military targets well inside the city—truly an instance of 'topography outweighing artillery.' After two months of intermittent shelling Farragut gave up the attempt to subdue Vicksburg from the river. It took another year for Grant and Sherman to maneuver their armies into position to take Vicksburg by land. Vicksburg finally surrendered on 4 July 1863—for which reason the Fourth of July for more than fifty years after the War was a holiday celebrated in Mississippi only by black people. (Long 213; Greene 19; McPherson 421; Hamilton 251; Cash *Letters* 66, 70; Stone 108, 126; Rainwater 174; Wiley *Embattled* 143; Matloff 63; Hildebrand 270; Foote II 384; Rowland I 279, 853, 856; Bettersworth 297; Street 60)

322:23 **looking at me with that expression** 'that expression' = an expression of triumph—as we learn in the next sentence

322:24 **I was just twelve then** Twelve is now generally taken to be the "age of responsibility . . . under twelve a child is still a young child," but both boys and girls mature (physically, at least) earlier now than they did in the nineteenth century. Our image of Bayard and Ringo would probably be more accurate if we imagined them as about ten. (Peterkin 179; Buck 133, 134)

322:24 **I didn't know triumph; I didn't even know the word** A good bit of *The Unvanquished* has to do with words that someone (Bayard, Ringo, Loosh, Granny, the Union Army) does not understand. Here we have 'triumph.' There will shortly be others ('Gap,' 'Run,' 'fell,' 'sweep the earth,' 'free,' 'horrified astonishment,' 'watch Loosh,' 'Old Hundred and Tinney,' 'lack'.) The Whorf Hypothesis argues that the world can be conceived only in terms permitted by our language and that we cannot experience what our language has no words to designate. Faulkner seems here to concur: he tells us Bayard does not understand Loosh's expression of triumph because he does not have a word for it. (Stephens 152)

322:26 **nother un you aint know** Loosh doesn't mean another word Bayard doesn't know, but another Southern city overrun by the Union Army that you don't know about.

322:27 **Corinth** a city in northeastern Mississippi just south of the Tennessee state line. This time Loosh's report is not premature. Corinth was taken on 29–30 May 1862, about a week after the first unsuccessful river assault on Vicksburg. Corinth is 60–70 miles northeast of Faulkner's fictional Yoknapatawpha County. Memphis was in Union hands by 6 June 1862 and the Tallahatchie Bridge (at the northern border of Yoknapatawpha) by 18 June. The only reason the Union Army had not penetrated into Mississippi earlier and farther is that, since the 9 April 1862 Union victory at Shiloh, twenty miles north of Corinth, Union General Halleck was unexplainably creeping along in what has been called the "slowest uncontested advance ever recorded of any army," less than a mile a day. The fact that Loosh reports the fall of Corinth should make it certain that *The Unvanquished* begins in 1862 and not 1863, since there is no way Loosh could have reported as recent news in 1863 the taking of Corinth if that had occurred a full year before, only a short distance from the Sartoris plantation. Also, we can have some confidence that Bayard would remember when the Yankees first reached his home, since he shot at the first one he saw. By summer of 1863 he would necessarily have been seeing Yankee soldiers for a year. As for which month in 1862 the book begins, we aren't ever told. Given such evidence as we have (the real Vicksburg and Corinth and Tallahatchie dates) sometime in June seems to fit the facts. (Fiske 135, 140; Lee 25–30; Horn 148)

322:29 **in Mississippi too** 'too' is the difficult word here. There would be no point in Bayard's saying what Ringo already knows—that Corinth, like Vicksburg, is in Mississippi. He must mean, then, that in addition to the fact that Loosh for some reason and with obvious emotion has just mentioned Corinth, another thing to be said about Corinth is that it is closer to the Sartoris plantation than any other place the boys have so far heard anyone say the Yankees might be.

322:30 **I've been there** Loosh had said Corinth is 'nother un' Bayard does not know. Whether Bayard really does not understand what Loosh means or whether he is trying to pretend he does not, he responds by taking Loosh's words literally and saying that he does know Corinth and has even been there. Maybe he is trying to regain control of the conversation by doing a bit of bragging, since in the South before the Civil War most people had never traveled more than ten miles from the place they were born, ten miles being as far as a mule-drawn wagon could go and still return in one day. (South Carolinian 682)

322:31 **as if he were about to chant, to sing** as if he were under some almost-religious spell

322:34 **as if his redcornered eyes had reversed in his skull and it was the blank flat obverses of the balls which we saw** as if Loosh were so taken with his own thoughts that he is not really seeing the boys in front of him, as if he were facing them not with the seeing part of his eyes but with the blank non-seeing reverse-side of his inward-looking eyeballs. According to the dictionary, 'obverse' does not mean 'the reverse side,' although that is what Faulkner seems to use it to mean not only here but in other books as well.

322:36 **Far dont matter. Case hit's on the way** 'case' = because; 'hit's' = it is, the 'it' being not just the Northern Army but the better future for slaves which Loosh believes the Northern Army will bring with it; 'on the way' = is coming; 'far dont matter' = it doesn't really make any difference how near or far the Northern Army or the better future may be at the moment, because both are coming and nothing can stop them.

322:38 **On the way to what?** This time Bayard does not understand at all what Loosh has just said. He doesn't ask *what* is on the way; he asks what Corinth is on the way *to*. He thinks Loosh means that Corinth is on the road that leads to some destination beyond it—Nashville, for example, which from Sartoris would be about 200 miles past Corinth.

322:39 **Marse John** Col. John Sartoris, Bayard's father. 'Marse' is short for 'Master'. In Southern speech the 'r' would not be pronounced: MAHSS. 'Marse' (or 'Massa' or 'Master'

• 11 •

or 'Marster' or 'Moster') is used either by itself or followed by a first name or first and last name but never by just a last name. (Doyle 2; Gwynn "Dialect" 10)

322:40 **Tennessee** the state immediately north of Mississippi. For the first year of the war in the west (until summer of 1862) the Union Army had been advancing south toward Mississippi, most of the fighting taking place in Kentucky (north of Tennessee) and then Tennessee.

323:1 **Aint no need for him at Tennessee now** Loosh is saying that the Northern Army has broken through Confederate defenses near the Tennessee border and the fighting is now in Mississippi—which is to say not very far at all from the Sartoris plantation.

323:3 **nigger** the usual word for a black person during time of slavery. When spoken by a white it was no doubt unfeeling but it was not deliberately insulting—as it obviously and always would be today. When used by a black person (as by Philadelphy here) it conveyed mainly exasperation, suggesting that the person being called a 'nigger' was behaving in some "mule-headed, contrary, willfully different, cantankerous, ornery," or irresponsible manner. In the present case Louvinia is concerned over Loosh's telling Bayard something Loosh knows he should not be telling. (Murray 140, 141; Dollard 344)

323:9 **I stooped and set Vicksburg up again** Bayard is trying to persuade Ringo that Loosh must be wrong, that Vicksburg could not have fallen, because 'There it is,' the woodchips representing Vicksburg now standing as before.

323:11 **Ringo didn't move** He is not impressed with Bayard's 'proof.'

323:12 **He laughed at Corinth too** 'too' = Loosh laughed when he said Corinth as he had laughed when he said Vicksburg

323:15 **Father** A boy brought up in an aristocratic Southern household could call his grandmother 'Granny' and his mother 'Mama' (although not 'Mommy'), but his father was always and only 'Father' (never 'Dad' or 'Daddy'). (Wyatt-Brown ix)

323:18 **Yankees** In the South a 'Yankee' is any Northerner—not necessarily a New Englander. Southerners use 'Yankee' in much the same way the Greeks did 'barbarian.' A 'damnyankee' is a Yankee who doesn't have sense enough to stay home. Here 'Yankees' means the Northern soldiers or the Northern Army, also called the Union or Federal Army. (Dohan 217; Stewart 544; Weaver 41; Botkin 5)

323:19 **General Van Dorn and General Pemberton** Confederate Generals Earl Van Dorn and John Pemberton, the two commanders of the Confederate Army in Mississippi during the year before the surrender of Vicksburg. Actually Pemberton did not arrive from Carolina until October 1862, but Van Dorn and Pemberton are the names Bayard now remembers as Mississippi's defenders, and so he tells us their names were the ones he and Ringo used in their behind-the-smokehouse battles. See entry 329:19//15:19 for evidence that Bayard could not expect us to believe that all details of his many-years-later story are necessarily accurate. Bayard is a story-teller, not a historian. (Greene 21, 53)

323:20 **I was just talking too** There are at least three (and perhaps more) different possible explanations for the 'too' in this sentence: 1) I was just talking as Loosh had been just talking, for he hadn't been at Vicksburg or Corinth and so couldn't really know what was happening there; 2) I was just talking as Ringo was just talking, since he has no more real information than I do about whether what Loosh said is true or where Father is fighting now and what Father might or might not know; 3) as I couldn't really have expected Ringo to be persuaded by my setting up the chips again to prove that Vicksburg had not fallen, so I can't really expect him to be persuaded now simply by my words denying that the Yankees are in Corinth.

323:21 **because niggers know, they know things** The folk-wisdom was that black people are closer to nature than whites and therefore have an intuitive access to knowledge which civilization had bred out of whites. Bayard is afraid Loosh's reports about Vicksburg and Corinth may be true and that Ringo, because he is also black, may somehow almost-know they are true. (Cohn 92)

323:21 **it would have to be something louder, much louder, than words to do any good** Whatever I was going to have to do to get Ringo's (and my own) mind off Loosh's disquieting 'news' would have to be something more effective than just talking.

323:23 **So I stooped and caught both hands full of dust** 'So' means 'for that reason,' and to follow Bayard's train of thought we have to understand what 'that reason' is in this particular context: for *what* reason? Because whatever Bayard is going to do next would have to be something 'much louder than words to do any good,' and because (as the saying has it) *actions* speak 'louder than words,' Bayard resorts to an action: '*So* I stooped and caught both hands full of dust' and prepared to throw—so he and Ringo can do their part in defending Vicksburg by acting out a Confederate victory there. Believing will make it so. See 325:29//10:1 and 341:1//32:25 for the opposite side of this way of thinking: 'you didn't believe it and so it wasn't.'

323:25 **flung the dust** threw it at the ground at the upright woodchips like artillery fire, stirring up clouds of dust which resemble the black gunpowder smoke that was such a conspicuous feature of Civil War battlefields. The boys are not throwing dust *at* each other. In the hot Mississippi summer that would have been too uncomfortable. In fact it is probable that the way the boys usually played war did not involve throwing dust at all (Louvinia, who had to wash their clothes, would not have permitted it) and Bayard resorts to dust-throwing on this day only because (as the text says a few lines later) 'it was that urgent' that he and Ringo disprove to themselves what Loosh had reported.

323:26 **Yaaay! Yaay!** Civil War soldiers customarily went

into battle shouting. The Southern battle-cry was a distinctive, high-pitched, quavering war-whoop known as the 'Rebel Yell.'

323:27 **All right** This is a standard expression which means something like: 'since you appear not completely satisfied with what I just said or did, I will say or do something more or different.' In this case Bayard means: 'All right, I will offer you (Ringo) a special deal: this time *you* can be the Southern General.'

323:28 **Grant** commander of the Northern forces in Mississippi. This is the same Ulysses S. Grant who later became commanding General of the entire Union Army.

323:29 **Because it was that urgent** Bayard had earlier said there was something curious in Philadelphy's voice—'I didn't know which, urgency or fright' (322:18//5:5). Maybe what he calls 'that urgent' here is really his *fear* that Loosh's news might be right.

323:29 **negroes knew** Earlier in the paragraph it was 'niggers know,' later it will be 'Ringo was a nigger,' but here it is 'negroes knew.' How explain the switch in terminology? 'Nigger' is what Bayard would have said at age twelve, 'negro' is what he has now learned to say as an adult (for times have changed). The paragraph is switching back and forth between what Bayard was experiencing then and what he knows now as he remembers that earlier time. As we read on, we will discover that for the rest of the book Bayard continues to mix 'negro' and 'nigger' seemingly at random. The point would seem to be to suggest how intensely he still remembers and identifies with his childhood self. (Ross 96–97)

323:34 **even though Ringo was a nigger too** The 'too' here apparently means not that Ringo as well as Loosh was black, but that Ringo was my playmate and friend as well as black. If this were not the meaning, the 'because' which immediately follows ('because Ringo and I had been born in the same month') would make no sense.

323:35 **both fed at the same breast** Ringo's mother's, since

Bayard's mother died when Bayard was born (329:30//16:1)
and Ringo was born in the same month. Ringo's father is Simon, Loosh's brother, presently at the war with Col. Sartoris.

323:36 **had slept together and eaten together** "Squeamishness or fussiness about contact with Negroes was . . . a lower-
class white attitude, while the opposite attitude was . . . associated with 'the quality' " (Woodward 50).

323:37 **Granny** Rosa Millard, Bayard's grandmother, his
mother's mother

323:37 **Ringo called Granny 'Granny' just like I did** This
says a good bit about how young the boys are, since a black
boy would be permitted to call a white woman 'Granny' only
as long as he had youth to excuse him.

323:38 **until maybe he wasn't a nigger anymore or maybe I
wasn't a white boy anymore, the two of us neither, not even
people any longer: the two supreme undefeated** Bayard
and Ringo have been playmates for so long and the distinction between black boy and white boy means so little to them
that maybe it misrepresents reality even to think of them as
black boy and white boy, or even as boys, or even as people.
Maybe it would be more accurate to think of them as twin
personifications of the *quality* of *being unvanquished*, 'the two
supreme undefeated'—not just because in their war game
the South always wins but because their innocence prevents
anything from undermining their certainty that all is and always will be for the best in this their world, the best of all
possible worlds.

323:40 **like two moths, two feathers riding above a hurricane** unaffected in any real sense by the violence about to
overtake them—like any light object which, caught up by a
hurricane and carried above it, can float there unharmed on
the wind's current—in much the same way as Jingus's hat
would ride above the wind rush caused by a passing train in
"Raid" (378:32//88:9). The 'hurricane' in the sentence is no
doubt partly the Civil War but, given the concerns of the
sentence as a whole, it is probably more the longer-lasting

and equally-emotionally-charged struggle between the races (especially in the South) which the Civil War brought to a head.

324:3 **to the other each invisible** hidden by the clouds of dust

324:4 **furious slow jerking of the flung dust** 'furious' because thrown with force, 'slow' because the clouds rise slowly from the ground, 'jerking' because each act of throwing provides the impetus for a new cloud to rise

324:5 **Kill the bastuds** Ringo and Bayard have no idea what 'bastards' means. They must have heard someone call the Yankees that. Also they have no idea, really, what it means to kill someone.

324:8 **dust-colored ourselves to the eyes** Perhaps the boys are wearing Tom Sawyer-like straw hats which keep the dust from above their eyes. Or maybe 'to the eyes' refers to what they see when they see each other—covered with dust. In either case the words complete an idea introduced earlier in the paragraph: Bayard and Ringo are not white boy and black boy; they are both dust-colored.

324:10 **Bayard** His name is pronounced BAIRD (Bay-erd compressed to almost one syllable). His last name is SAR-tor-iss. Sometimes Faulkner said the last name with just two syllables—SAR-tris. He never said sar-TOR-iss. (Faulkner tapes at University of Virginia)

324:11 **she did not now have on the old hat of Father's** Hats have always been symbols of status—crowns, for example, or the headpieces of the Catholic hierarchy. Military officers' hats are different from enlisted men's. Louvinia, even though she is a slave, is the person Col. Sartoris assumes will be the responsible one on the plantation while he is off to war, since he has every reason to believe Granny and Joby are too old, Bayard and Ringo too young, and Loosh perhaps not loyal. So Louvinia wears Col. Sartoris's hat as the mark of her authority. But when Col. Sartoris is present, as now, she does not wear the hat. After the war newly-freed black men took to wearing hats indoors and out as the symbol of their changed status. (Doyle 114).

324:13 **head rag** the bandanna a black woman (field hand or house servant) customarily wore on her head

324:14 **What was that word?** Louvinia's objection is to their cursing (saying 'bastud'), not to their bloodthirstiness (saying 'Kill them').

324:16 **the big road** "big" = main; actually only a dirt lane. In the country anything wider than one-lane roads did not exist before the coming of automobiles.

324:18 **out of frozen immobility** Louvinia's voice arrests their throwing, thus creating a kind of 'tableau vivant' on their 'living map.' See first entry for 321:2//3:2.

324:22 **In the spring, when Father came home that time** earlier in the present year

324:26 **But this time we didn't** The last time they knew they were welcoming home a victorious warrior, but this time, after Loosh's 'news,' they are not so sure.

324:28 **gallery** In Mississippi a 'gallery' is any porch (front, back, or side) big enough to hold a bench or two or a half dozen-or-so chairs.

324:29 **claybank** a word for the horse's color, yellow. Stark Young in *So Red the Rose* tells about the wife of a Spanish Governor in Natchez who was known as the Yellow Duchess because "in her house the gold mirrors, the brass fireplace, the brocade of the curtains and furniture had been in that color, and her coach was lined with yellow silk and painted in gold and buff and drawn by claybank horses" (81). Obviously no horse is truly yellow, so Faulkner tries to be more exact. A few lines later he says the horse is 'almost the color of smoke.' On 370:11//75:21 we read that 'the smoke boiled up, yellow and slow.' On 427:30//160:17 Faulkner describes another claybank stallion as 'like a yellow cloud in the twilight.' On 484:27//242:22 Jupiter is described as 'pale bronze.' So Jupiter must be a smoky-yellowish-bronze, and 'claybank' is the conventional but inexact single word for that color.

324:29 **the gate which was never closed now** no slaves now to open and close it

324:34 **at a steady gait which was not a walk and not a run** a running walk. We have a name now for horses with such a gait—Tennessee Walkers. Their practical and comfortable but not very pretty gait is described as "a simple four-beat cross between amble and walk." The rider does not have to post (use his legs to rise upward and forward in rhythm with the horse's steps in order to avoid being bounced in the saddle). It is said of a Tennessee Walker that "you can set a full cup of coffee on his back and never spill a drop as he tick-tocks along all day." Fifty miles would be a good day's ride but a hundred or more, if pressed, is possible. (Follmer 52, 53; Dunbar 91; Savory 104)

324:36 **a need to encompass earth** a need to overcome distance, to get from Point A to Point B. Perhaps, because 'encompass' literally means an encircling, he had to travel by a roundabout route to avoid running into the enemy.

324:36 **abrogated sleep or rest** canceled or annulled the normal need for sleep or rest

324:37 **relegated to some insulated bourne of perennial and pointless holiday** 'relegated' = banished; 'to some insulated bourne' = to some realm out of touch with everything outside it; 'of perennial and pointless holiday' = where the days' activities consist of games and frivolity

324:38 **so trivial a thing as galloping** so minor and petty a consideration as whether a horse is using one of the gaits show-horses were trained to use: a canter, rack, single-foot, or gallop; "To ride at the trot was to confess that the mount had no schooling" (Phillips 362).

Beginning with 'because there was a need to encompass earth': this part of the sentence essentially says that the concerns of holiday tournaments so popular before the war—

the displays of fine horses and fancy horsemanship—are, for the duration of the war, pointless and obsolete. Now it is important only that a horse get his rider quickly and reliably to where he is going, not how horse and rider look while getting there. (Kerr 4)

324:40 **skirts** that part of a coat which reaches below the hips, that part which had gotten wet when Col. Sartoris forded the creek

325:2 **field officer** major, lieutenant colonel, or colonel, i.e. ranking above captain, below general

325:8 **Well** a standard greeting—like 'hello' but with something of anticipation

325:8 **Miss Rosa** Her name is really Mrs. Rosa Millard, but it is part of Southern manners for a married (or widowed) woman of good social position (especially if she is older) to be called 'Miss' followed by her first name. The polite implication is that, even though she may have children, she is taintless as a virgin.

325:12 **Curry him** brush him with a curry-comb (a brush with bristles made of very stiff wires). The purpose is partly to smarten his appearance but also to remove lather and sweat and so safeguard his health.

325:12 **dont turn him into the pasture** where he might be difficult to catch in a hurry

325:13 **lot** the barn lot, a small fenced area near the barn where animals which may be wanted can easily be recovered

325:17 **in Virginia and Tennessee** The Civil War was fought on two fronts, the eastern and the western. The eastern front centered in and around Virginia. That was the war of Robert E. Lee, Stonewall Jackson, Bull Run (Manassas), and Gettysburg. The war in the west (the one *The Unvanquished* is concerned with) moved south from Kentucky and Tennessee to Mississippi and then east through Alabama to Georgia and finally to the coast. That was the war of Forrest and Sherman, Shiloh and Vicksburg. Col. Sartoris at the beginning of the war had fought in the east but now his troop of irregular cavalry is facing the Federal advance near the Tennessee-Mississippi border.

325:20 **maybe it was because** maybe the reason we looked up to him so much (saw him as big) was . . .

325:25 **when you thought of Father you thought of him as being big** Confederate cavalry General Nathan Bedford Forrest was north Mississippi's real war hero; Col. Sartoris is in some ways his fictional Yoknapatawpha counterpart. Forrest's biographer spells out the Southern image of Forrest on his horse: "standing in his stirrups, his sabre in the air, he seemed to be a foot taller than any other man in the world" (Hergesheimer 211). Bayard apparently is trying to square this idea of a cavalry hero being 'tall in the saddle' with the truth about his father on his horse, for Col. Sartoris (like Napoleon in this respect instead of Forrest) was a short man. Thus Bayard's circular rationalization: Col. Sartoris *couldn't* be as big as his actions make him seem, because that would make him *too* big and you wouldn't believe it, and so he *has* to be short in order for it to be believable that, on Jupiter, he is as big as we know him to be. Faulkner uses a similar idea in a story, "The Tall Men" (1941), where the brothers and father in the McCallum family *seem* tall—in fact *are* tall—although as measured by feet and inches they are not.

325:29 **So you didn't believe it and so it wasn't** This is, of course, the reverse of Bayard and Ringo's acting out their Southern victories behind the smokehouse: there they believed it, and so it was; here they don't believe it (that Father is too big to be believable), and so he isn't (too big to be believable). This is a version of the idea that perception alters reality, an idea for which there is good precedent. According to psychologist W.I. Thomas, "If men define situations as real, they are real in their consequences" (Roebuck 22). However, note that the boys' fighting and winning the Battle of Vicksburg behind the smokehouse each day did not prevent an eventual Confederate defeat there. Also note that the rest of the first half of this page is about something Bayard then believed to be true but later learns was not true at all.

325:33 **that odor in his clothes and beard and flesh** Even the highest officers on both sides of the Civil War must have smelled—not just horse-bad, for most men smelled like horses most of the time, but in need of a bath. (Wicker 63; Green 57–58)

325:34 **powder and glory** Bayard's variation on the words of the Lord's Prayer applied to his father: "for thine is the kingdom and the power and the glory"

325:35 **the elected victorious** 'the elect' is a term from Puritan theology. It refers to those favored by God—those chosen by Him to be saved. Those not among 'the elect' are 'the damned.' Bayard takes it for granted that the South will win the war (will be 'the elected victorious') because a just God *must* have ordained it so; thus Father and other Confederate soldiers are merely acting out God's script whose final act is already determined. As the President of the College of South Carolina saw the situation at the time: "The parties in this conflict are not merely abolitionists and slaveholders— they are atheists, socialists, communists . . . on the one side, and the friends of order and regulated freedom on the other. In one word, the world is the battleground, Christianity and atheism the combatants—and the progress of humanity the stake." When Bayard says he 'know[s] better now' he is referring to the smell which he associated with his father's clothes and beard and flesh; but surely by extension he is also commenting upon the loss of that innocence which had allowed him to assume, since it seemed so clear to him that Southerners were good people acting in a just cause, that God must necessarily be on their side. (Green 10; Myrdal 443)

325:36 **a sardonic and even humorous declining of self-delusion** a good-humored but disdainful refusal to deceive himself

325:37   **which is not even kin to**   which is so different from
that no relationship can be shown

325:38   **that optimism which believes that that which is about
to happen to us can possibly be the worst which we can
suffer**   'Optimism' is the key word here: imagine the worst
you can imagine; assume that is what you will be faced with
next; that, Bayard is saying, is 'optimism,' because what is
going to happen will be much worse than anything you can
now imagine, and what you can and will learn to bear far
exceeds the limits you now believe you could not go beyond.
Edgar, in *King Lear*: "The worst is not / So long as we can
say, 'This is the worst' " (4.1.27–28).

326:11   **I've been expecting you**   Granny must have heard
(and believed) Loosh's report about Corinth. Since Col. Sartoris must now be fighting not far from home, she has been
expecting him to stop by to help them prepare for the coming of the Yankees.

326:15   **You rode hard from Tennessee**   Bayard is trying to
ask a question in an indirect way: Are you still fighting in
Tennessee or have you (as Loosh says) been pushed back to
Mississippi?

326:17   **gaunted you**   made you thinner, emaciated

326:18   **Marse John**   Ringo, like Bayard, calls Granny
'Granny,' and at least as long as Ringo is young that is relatively safe: no one would *believe* she actually is his grandmother. But Ringo does not call Col. Sartoris 'Father.' That
would not be safe, because miscegenation between plantation owners and their female slaves occurred often enough
that someone *could* suspect Col. Sartoris of being Ringo's father, and that possibility cannot be suggested even playfully.

326:19   **folks**   Mississippians like us—black as well as white.
Ringo is not sure people in Tennessee are of the same species as Mississippi 'folks.'

326:20   **Then I said it**   He says what he has been wanting to
ask his father: 'Loosh says you haven't been in Tennessee.'

326:22 **Loosh?** Loosh told you that? He shouldn't have. He must have a touch of 'Yankee fever.' We had better watch him. (Roark 81)

326:23 **dinner** the noon meal. The day's three meals in the rural South were (and are) breakfast, dinner, and supper.

SECTION TWO

326:25 **we built the stock pen** to hide their animals from the soon-to-arrive Yankees

326:28 **rails** the four-to-six trunks of saplings about three inches in diameter, cut to twelve-to-fifteen foot lengths, which, placed horizontally one above another about a foot apart, make up each section of the fence

326:29 **woven through and into** The fence is a 'snake fence'— one whose sections do not attach to posts but are woven together by criss-crossing the ends in a zig-zag fashion. See drawing on page 344//37 of *The Unvanquished*.

326:29 **jungle** Because low land beside a creek is likely to flood each spring, it has never been cleared for cultivation; thus its plant growth is dense and tangled.

326:32 **were not Confederate ones but were Yankee ones** Although the South grew the cotton, the mills were in the North, and so Confederate uniforms became increasingly difficult to obtain as the war went on. Many Southern soldiers eventually wore uniforms (or parts of uniforms) taken from the Yankees. By the end of the war the pants of perhaps most Confederate soldiers were captured Yankee ones. (Wiley *Plain* 9)

326:34 **troop** the Civil War term (Northern and Southern) for a company of cavalry

326:35 **the willow and pin oak, the swamp maple and chinkapin** kinds of scrub trees they are mixing at random in their rush-order fence

327:1 **mules** the standard work-animals of the South. A

mule is the sterile offspring of a jackass (a male donkey) and
a mare (a female horse). Mules are faster than oxen, slower
and smaller than horses. Southerners preferred them to
horses for farm tasks because they are more intelligent, can
work harder and longer, and require considerably less care.

327:2 **where Father waited** to put the rails in place, to do
the actual assembling of the fence

327:2 **And that was it too** There are several meanings here,
all based on Father's working 'faster and harder than anyone
else': 1) another thing Father does on this day that surprises
Bayard, because well-to-do Southern whites before the war
did no manual labor. "Work was what slaves did" and "it was
considered bad form to do what Negroes should do." Even
on a casual trip to town a white slaveowner would have a
slave accompany him in case he bought something which,
however small, would have to be carried. For slave-owning
whites life was pretty much a matter of "graceful lotus-eating
in a land where the abundance of nature had made hard
work seem almost an act of ingratitude." John C. Calhoun
once claimed that "no Southern man, not even the poorest
or the lowest, will, under any circumstances, submit to perform menial labor. . . . He has too much pride for that."
Since this is how Bayard remembers his father from before
the war, he is surprised by what he sees his father doing now:
first he takes off his coat, revealing second-hand and not-
even-Confederate pants, and then he works 'faster and
harder than anyone else'; 2) another instance of Father 'doing bigger things than he was'—not simply what he did but
(as it says several lines later) 'the way he did it'—'going
through the brush and briers almost faster than the mules';
3) another proof of the urgency of the situation—as Philadelphy's voice had been 'urgent, perhaps frightened,' as Bayard had intensified their mock battle behind the smokehouse
by throwing dust 'because it was that urgent'; 4) another indication that there might be some new and threatening development in the war (beyond Loosh's 'news' about Vicks-

burg and Corinth) which Bayard and Ringo have not heard about yet. (Ownby 337; Odum 82; Wecter 23; McWhiney 5–6)

327:4   **racking**   positioning, one on top of another

327:5   **while Joby and Loosh were still arguing about which end of the rail went where**   Joby and Loosh are not willing workers—Joby because he is a house servant and considers any kind of outdoor manual labor beneath his station, Loosh because he senses his impending freedom and does not want to cooperate.

327:12   **side meat**   salt pork, bacon which is almost all fat—not a choice cut but the best the Sartorises now have

327:12   **greens**   usually boiled turnip or collard leaves and stems, but it could be the cooked leafy part of any edible plant—even dandelions

327:12   **milk**   buttermilk—what is left after cream has been churned to make butter. Fresh milk would be called 'sweet milk.' Buttermilk was the usual (and preferred) milk for drinking in the 19th century South. In the years before Pasteur, fresh milk was considered to be unhealthful—as indeed it often was, especially for slaves, since "approximately 70 percent of American [black persons] exhibit an intolerance to lactose—a sugar—which is present in whole milk but not in buttermilk." (Campbell 202; Taylor 87; David 264; Dolan 189; Randolph *Superstitions* 46; Wasson 137)

327:13   **Ringo and I probably had the same vision**   For the next page Bayard tells us not the role Col. Sartoris actually plays in building the fence but what Bayard and Ringo imagine his role will be when he announces they are going to build a fence.

327:20   **partaking not of any lusting and sweating for assault**   not tense or excited as if anticipating a battle

327:21   **that passive yet dynamic affirmation**   a near-oxymoronic combination: having such complete, passive, unquestioning faith in their leader and in whatever he might direct them to do that their faith becomes itself a dynamic force

327:22 **which Napoleon's troops must have felt** The ability
to inspire the confidence and loyalty of his men was one of
Napoleon's most impressive qualities. Faulkner appears to be
suggesting here a kind of Napoleon-Forrest-Sartoris equa-
tion. Consider this passage from one of Forrest's biog-
raphers: "We had that confidence in him which I imagine
the Old Guard had in Napoleon. On one occasion, while we
were supposed to be in a very dangerous position, with the
enemy all about us, we were ordered to go into camp for the
night. There were some new recruits with us, who, seeing
the older members of the command preparing to lie down
and go to sleep, said: 'You don't expect to lie down and go to
sleep with the enemy all around, do you?' The answer was:
'Of course we do; General Forrest told us to do it'." Or consider another anecdote from another of Forrest's biog-
raphers: After the war a troop of Federal cavalry rode out to
Forrest's farm to see him. Forrest's "war horse King Philip
was grazing in the front lot. As the blue-clad cavalry filed
into the lot on the way up to the house, King Philip's training
in many a melee reasserted itself, and he rushed at the blue-
coats, teeth bared and front feet flailing. When some of the
soldiers, astonished at his onslaught, struck at him, Forrest's
wartime body servant . . . rushed to defend the horse. After
Forrest himself had come out and the horse was back in his
stable and things had quieted down, the Federal captain observed, 'General, now I can account for your success. Your
negroes fight for you, and your horses fight for you'." (Cash
Mind 112; Beeching 29; Wyeth 576; Henry 441)

327:24 **boles** the trunks of the saplings

327:25 **dead rails** The saplings, cut and therefore no longer
alive, are now something else—dead rails.

327:25 **He was on Jupiter now** Jupiter is the name of
Col. Sartoris's horse. Bayard and Ringo imagine that Father
will be on Jupiter, giving orders for building the fence as if
he were directing a military attack.

327:26 **frogged** with the ornamental braiding which once
was part of a field officer's uniform

327:28 **pivoting Jupiter** turning Jupiter around so he is facing in the direction he will be charging

327:29 **snaffle** a metal bit placed in a horse's mouth which,
when the rider manipulates the reins attached to either end,
lets the horse know which way the rider wants him to go

327:29 **cocked hat** a hat with turned-up brim on one or
both sides. In theory, officers and cavalry turned up the brim
on the right side, the infantry on the left, but this distinction
was not consistently observed. (Yarwood 92; Schick 180)

327:30 **not loud yet stentorian** 'stentorian' means *very* loud—
from Stentor, the herald in *The Iliad* whose voice was as loud
as fifty men together and could be heard throughout the
entire Grecian camp. Here Bayard must be using it to mean
a voice with great carrying power and authority.

327:30 **Trot! Canter!** *Charge!* the military commands, given
at intervals, for a cavalry charge

327:31 **we could both watch and follow him** Since the scene
is taking place only in Bayard's and Ringo's minds, there is
no reason they could not do both.

327:36 **smoke-colored diminishing thunderbolt** the Colonel's horse exploding into motion: 'smoke-colored' = his claybank color; 'diminishing' = growing progressively smaller as
he moves away from them (and remember that, as the horse
can be seen as smaller, Father can be seen as bigger, without
the two of them together being too big to be believed); 'thunderbolt' fits with the horse's name, Jupiter, for Jupiter was
the Roman god of lightning and thunder, conventionally
pictured holding jagged thunderbolts in his fist. As Bayard
and Ringo imagine it, Father is like a God and his horse is
like a God, too.

327:37 **arcy and myriad glitter** 'arcy' (pronounced ARK-ee)
= Father swinging his sabre in an arc, the sabre glittering in
the sun like an incandescent arc; 'myriad' = very many—
literally 'ten thousand'; 'arcy and myriad glitter' taken together = like flashing lightning—to go with Jupiter's thunder

327:38 **sheared trimmed and lopped** 'sheared' = cut down;

'trimmed' = the side branches cut off; 'lopped' = the excess length at the top cut off so the rails are all more or less the same length

327:39 **sprang into neat and waiting windrows** A 'windrow' is a term from farming which means an orderly stack or row of anything placed where it will be needed next. As Bayard and Ringo imagine the scene, even the saplings seem to cooperate with Father's will—almost as if he were causing the fence to come into being with a few swipes of his sabre and the God-like command: 'Let there be fence!' (Hunsberger 434)

328:11 **sow** a female hog which has farrowed (given birth)

328:12 **moving slower than the cow** a folk expression: any person or animal or process that moves slowly is said to be 'as slow as an old cow' (Randolph *Holler* 173)

328:12 **even while the cow was stopped** an apparent exaggeration, yet a moving sow is unquestionably *moving* slower than a cow that isn't moving at all

328:15 **gap** the space between the fence panels, the space where the fence has not yet been assembled.

328:15 **we never had worried about that** Because they know Joby and Loosh who have been left to finish the job. Bayard is implying that he could have returned a whole day later and Joby and Loosh would still have not finished the fence.

328:16 **full dark** night itself—as dark as it is going to get—distinct from first dark (twilight) when they stopped working. The times of the day in the South: first light, then morning (from when you get up until after dinner, around two), then evening (everything from then on until dark), then night. (Dollard 6)

328:25 **Hawkhurst** the plantation belonging to Sartoris relatives (the Hawks) in Alabama. Dennison Hawk, the father, died shortly before the war began.

328:32 **that was part of the need and urgency too** one more of the unusual urgency-suggesting things that had occurred that day

328:33   **carried the trunk down from the attic too**   'too' = in addition to doing most of the work in building the fence

328:36   **sideboard**   that large piece of diningroom furniture which, outside the South, is usually called a 'buffet'

328:36   **silver service**   the silver tea set

328:38   **each Tuesday afternoon**   In a well-run house weekly tasks were done on their appointed day—the washing on Monday, polishing the silver on Tuesday, the ironing on Wednesday, oiling and polishing the furniture and floors on Thursday, etc. (Haardt 39)

328:39   **why, nobody except Granny maybe knew, since it was never used**   The point of having a silver tea service is not to use it but to have it. That it is almost never used is part of the point in having it. It is the tangible sign of a family's wealth and standing in society. The older the family silver the longer the family has had the social position that goes with money. Silver polished weekly for generation after generation takes on a kind of sheen (called a 'patina') that new silver cannot duplicate. A burned house can be rebuilt and even improved, but old silver cannot be replaced in kind. Thus Granny's concern to protect it and Father's willingness to help. (Martin 120, 121)

329:4   **In the spring when he came home that time**   This would have to be earlier in the same year, 1862. If Father had come home in spring of the previous year, 1861, it would have been almost immediately after his regiment arrived in Virginia and before the fighting had started. The first big battle in the east was First Manassas and that did not take place until July 1861.

329:6   **hickory logs popping and snapping on the hearth**   Hickory logs do make sounds like sudden shots as they burn. Small pieces shoot out on the hearth—like popcorn popping.

329:8   **musket**   a long smooth-bore gun, the standard military gun for both North and South until part-way through the war, when it was superseded and quickly replaced by the rifle, a much more accurate weapon with a much greater effective range. At one of the first engagements of the war, on June 10, 1861 at Bethel Church in Virginia, for well over an hour 2,500 Union troops kept up continual firing at 1,200 of the enemy, both sides armed with muskets, killing only a single Confederate and losing fewer than 20 of their own. At First Manassas it has been estimated that "between 8,000 and 10,000 bullets were fired for every man killed or wounded." A musket can hit a man "at 80 yards; it *may* even at 100 yards. But a soldier must be very unfortunate indeed who shall be wounded by a common musket at 150 yards, provided his antagonist aims at him; and as to firing at a man at 200 yards, you may just as well fire at the moon and have the same hopes of hitting your object." A rifle is accurate at 400 yards or even more.

A smooth-bore musket fires round bullets which float erratically in the air like a knuckle-ball, while a rifle has spiral scorings inside the barrel which impart a spinning motion to elongated bullets which drill through the air like a football pass. One of the chief reasons for the enormous casualties in the latter part of the Civil War was that military tactics were slow to adjust to the unfamiliar deadliness of rifles. Infantry and cavalry charges which might have had a reasonable chance of success if opposed by muskets were suicidal when met by rifles. Similar slaughters for a similar reason followed the introduction of machine-guns in World War I. (Hopley I 358; Price 12; Held 114; McPherson 475; Ripley 15)

329:9 **which he had brought home from Virginia two years ago** This is not possible. The War itself did not start until April 1861 (the firing on Fort Sumter) and there was no serious fighting in Virginia before the battle of First Manassas in July 1861. Thus Father could not have brought home a musket from Virginia 'two years ago.' This is one of the chronological discrepancies which Faulkner failed to correct when he was revising the magazine stories to make them into a novel. What he must have intended is that Col. Sartoris formed his first regiment early in 1861, took it to Virginia, fought for about a year, came back (with a souvenir Yankee musket), formed a new regiment, and is now fighting in Tennessee (or Mississippi). All of that could logically and reasonably have happened by the second year of the war, the summer of "Ambuscade."

329:10 **loaded and oiled for service** It was not unusual, even during peacetime, to keep a loaded gun or pair of pistols over the mantel, although this was more a matter of symbolism and tradition than a realistic defense against possible intruders. (Rose 297)

329:11 **Forrest** Confederate General Nathan Bedford Forrest, a Tennessee slave trader with no military training who started the war as a Private and rose to become a Lieutenant General and the most celebrated cavalry leader of the Civil War (if not of all wars), partly because of his personal bravery (he had twenty-nine horses shot from under him) but mainly because he revolutionized cavalry tactics: instead of attempting dramatic but generally ineffective cavalry charges, he used his horses ('race horses,' an opposing General said they must be) to transport his men quickly to wherever, dismounted, they could do the most good—or damage. Robert E. Lee unhesitatingly named Forrest the greatest military genius of the war, the one "who, with the least means, accomplished more than any other general." Northern General Sherman called him "the most remarkable man our civil war produced on either side. . . . He always seemed to know what I was doing or intended to do, while . . . I could never tell or form any satisfactory idea of what he was trying to accomplish." Sherman sent out five unsuccessful expeditions to kill or capture Forrest: "It must be done, if it costs ten thousand lives and bankrupts the Federal treasury." Forrest survived the war and was the last Confederate General in Mississippi to surrender. (Donald 401; Lytle 105; McCain 218; Tucker 36; Wyeth xix, 342)

329:11 **Morgan** Confederate General John Hunt Morgan, a

cavalry leader from Kentucky. His sometimes waggish exploits did not ultimately have as much impact on the war as Forrest's, but at the time they seemed no less dramatic and daring. He carried with him a telegrapher, a wire-tap expert, who repeatedly caused confusion by sending false instructions to Union armies. Once he even sent a wire directly to Washington complaining about "the inferior grade of mules" being furnished the Union Army—i.e., the mules Morgan's regiment was capturing. (Randall 412; Foote I 570)

329:12 **Barksdale** Confederate General William Barksdale, commander of Barksdale's Mississippi Brigade, killed at Gettysburg leading what has been called "the most magnificent charge of the war" and "the grandest charge that was ever made by mortal man." In General Longstreet's words: "They did the best three hours' fighting ever done by any men on any field." Before the war Barksdale was perhaps the most vehement of influential Mississippi secessionists. (McNeily 231, 232; Foote II 508; McKee 42)

329:12 **Van Dorn** Confederate General Earl Van Dorn, leader of the Confederate cavalry in north Mississippi after Pemberton took over command at Vicksburg. Van Dorn's raid on a Union supply depot at Holly Springs was one of the most spectacular Confederate triumphs of the war. (Angle 377)

329:12 **Gap** a pass in a mountain range—the Cumberland Gap, for example

329:12 **Run** a fast-running stream—as in Bull Run

329:12 **which we didn't have in Mississippi** Mississippi has no mountains and thus no mountain passes or fast-running streams. (Brown, *Glossary* 88)

329:13 **we did own Barksdale** Barksdale was from Mississippi—unlike Forrest and Morgan and Van Dorn

329:14 **Van Dorn until somebody's husband killed him** General Van Dorn was shot by a jealous Southern husband who suspected (apparently with adequate reason) that Van Dorn was having an affair with his wife. In *Absalom, Absalom!*

(1936) Faulkner underscores the irony: ". . . who on one night and with a handful of men would gallantly set fire to and destroy a million dollar garrison of enemy supplies and on the next night be discovered by a neighbor in bed with his wife" (432). Actually there was a five month interval between the raid and the shooting. Van Dorn was shot on 8 May 1863, too late for Father to have known about it and to have told about it when he was home 'last spring.' (Hartje 317, McAlexander 358)

329:16 **a young girl who scratched her name on it with a diamond ring: Celia Cook** This refers to a bit of Oxford, Mississippi, part-history, part-legend which Faulkner tells in detail in *Requiem for a Nun* (1951; pp. 234–237). Briefly: Celia Cook (or Taylor Cook or Cecilia Farmer) was the jailer's daughter. Once when the Confederate cavalry was retreating through Oxford she made it clear by her jeering that she did not approve of their flight. With her ring she scratched her name on the jailhouse window. One of the cavalrymen, General Forrest's son, saw and heard her and was impressed by her spirit. After the surrender in 1865 and before going home he detoured to Oxford to marry her. Because it was already late in planting season he could devote only one morning to introduction, courtship, and wedding. As they rode off on his mule in the afternoon, married, they were still learning each other's full name. Obviously there is a problem with the chronology here, since the point of the story, the marriage (as well as the killing of Van Dorn and Barksdale's famous charge) had not yet occurred at the time of "Ambuscade." What we must be supposed to understand is that Bayard is mentioning stories which he remembers Father telling but not necessarily ones which he told during his previous spring visit—although Bayard may now remember them as stories he told at that time. (Hawkins 248–251)

329:19 **we were just twelve; we didn't listen to that** At twelve we weren't interested in mushy love stories about a jealous husband or a love-at-first-sight marriage.

329:19 **What Ringo and I heard was the cannon and flags and the anonymous yelling** What we wanted to hear was about the fighting and bravery and general excitement 'which all war-telling was full of' (383:37//95:23).

329:24 **Office** an outdoor-man's indoor retreat—what we would call today a 'den'

329:25 **seed cotton and corn** seeds from especially good plants which have been put aside to be used for the following year's planting

329:34 **Patroller** member of a local civilian law enforcement group whose responsibility was to see that slaves were on their own plantations after dark—a responsibility usually given to those whites who had nothing better to do with their time and who got satisfaction from exercising authority over slaves they could not afford to own (Sydnor *Slavery* 78; Meier 62)

329:36 **with his hat off** As a patroller the man is the representative of white authority and has to be accorded some respect (sitting in Father's presence, smoking one of his cigars), but that doesn't eliminate all the customary signs of deference required by differences in social position, and so he has his hat off.

329:37 **could not possibly have been either who or where** could not possibly be the ones the Patroller says he saw or have been where the Patroller says he saw them

329:40 **Coke upon Littleton** a book (1628) by Sir Edward Coke (pronounced COOK) on the Common Law of England. It was the first text which Americans in the 18th and 19th centuries (before the time of law schools) read to learn the law. (Eaton 54; Bledsoe 26)

329:40 **Josephus** a first-century Jewish historian, Flavius Josephus (pronounced Jo-SEE-fuss). The volume in Col. Sartoris's library was probably the same edition Faulkner inherited from his grandfather, *Antiquities of the Jews*, 1811. As for why this book would be in a room where slaves were brought to be questioned, consider this passage: "Let not the testimony of servants be admitted, on account of the ignobility of their soul, since it is probable that they may not speak the truth, either out of hope for gain or fear of punishment." (Thornton 371, 372; Brasch 193; Stroud 46)

329:40 **Koran** the sacred text of Islam, containing the eternal truth as it was revealed to Mohammed by Allah

330:1 **[Mis]sissippi Reports** biannual volumes reporting Mississippi legal cases whose decisions establish new precedents [The "Mis" lost typographically from LOA.]

330:1 **dated 1848** This volume reports a case ("John Bradley v. The State of Mississippi") which ruled that a white man with a knife pursuing a slave, shouting that he would "catch him and have his blood," cannot be charged with intent to commit murder or even with intent to commit manslaughter, but only with assault and battery, and he cannot be convicted of even that lesser charge, though the slave subsequently be found dead of knife wounds, unless a white witness observed the actual stabbing.

330:1 **Jeremy Taylor** a 17th century English clergyman whose books, *Holy Living* and *Holy Dying*, were considered in the early 1800s to belong "alongside Shakespeare and Milton" (Bledsoe 28)

330:1 **Napoleon's Maxims** the standard 19th century source of military knowledge for men who had little or no formal military training

330:3 **History of Werewolf Men in England** No such work exists. Faulkner made up the title, although book peddlers did carry similar items. One real one: *The Book of Knowledge, a Manual of Astrology, Palmistry, and Physiognomy by Ezra Pater, a Jew Doctor in Astronomy and Physic, Born in Bethany Near Mount Olivet in Judea, and Made English by W. Lily, Astrologer.* (Wright 51)

330:4 **the Reverend Ptolemy Thorndyke** Faulkner made up this name too. The name 'Thorndyke' seems to have appealed to him, for when he was trying to enlist in the RAF in World War I he forged a letter of reference from a fictitious

English vicar by the name of the Reverend Twimberly-Thorndyke. (Blotner 206)

330:5 **F.R.S.S.** Actually this is the abbreviation for 'Fellow of the Royal Statistical Society,' but it seems likely that Faulkner was making up an abbreviation which could be understood as 'Fellow of the Royal Scientific Society.'

330:5 **Walter Scott** Sir Walter Scott, the most popular early 19th century British (Scott was from Scotland) writer of adventure novels—e.g., *Waverley, Ivanhoe.* Faulkner: "Every household that at all pretended to be literate had Scott" (Gwynn *University* 135).

330:6 **Fenimore Cooper** James Fenimore Cooper, the most popular early 19th century American writer of adventure novels—e.g., *The Last of the Mohicans, The Deerslayer*

330:6 **Dumas** Alexandre Dumas, the most popular early 19th century French writer of adventure novels—e.g., *The Three Musketeers, The Count of Monte Cristo*

330:8 **Manassas** the Southern name for two major battles approximately a year apart in Virginia which Northerners (and therefore most history books, since it is the victor's whose report history usually adopts) call Bull Run. Here the reference is to the First Battle of Bull Run (First Manassas), July 1861.

330:8 **retreating, he said** Since both battles at Manassas were Confederate victories, Col. Sartoris is being modest about his own role in the outcome. Or maybe we are to understand him to be suggesting that, in losing the volume of Dumas, he lost that romantic view of fighting which so permeates Dumas—that such a view is appropriate only to some pre-war 'insulated bourne of perennial and pointless holiday' (324:37//8:28).

330:11 **boots crossed and lifted into the old heel-marks beside the fireplace** This may seem an awkward posture to us now but it was a common way of sitting by American men in the 18th and 19th centuries. With legs extended in front of him, feet higher than hips and head, a man would rock back on the two rear legs of his chair and rest his heels on something solid—a wall, a stove-pipe, a fireplace. (McDermott 104)

330:14 **too old to have been caught short of tobacco just by a war** too experienced with things that can go wrong to be caught unprepared by so predictable a situation as a wartime tobacco shortage. Tobacco was not a commercial crop in Mississippi, but it was grown for home use. (Phillips 137; Vance 205)

330:16 **Carolina** South Carolina and North Carolina were originally one colony. Following their split in 1729, 'Carolina' by itself was for many years understood to mean South Carolina.

330:16 **body servant** personal servant—called a 'valet' in England and France. To be the master's body servant was the highest position a slave could attain. (Killion xiv)

330:17 **he was still in Tennessee with the army** A Southern officer frequently took his body servant with him to the war—to wash his clothes, shine his boots, prepare meals, run errands, tend his horse. Such servants later were considered 'veterans' of the war and received Confederate pensions. (Wiley *Negroes* 17, 135, 145)

330:21 **waited for Father to begin** to begin telling war stories

330:26 **that's what he was waiting for, though not in the way Ringo and I thought** Father is waiting for Louvinia to finish packing the silver in the trunk in the kitchen, since the agenda for the evening is to bury the silver, but Bayard at first thinks that Father is only waiting for her to finish in the kitchen so that she will also be able to listen to the stories.

331:3 **where we might not be** Louvinia is not thinking of the boys at all. Her mind is completely on what Col. Sartoris had been saying.

331:11 **Vicksburg *fell*? Do he mean hit fell off in the River?** Ringo knows only the 'fall down' sense of 'fell.' Since Father had been fighting at the Tennessee-Mississippi border, he would have no first-hand knowledge about what was happening at Vicksburg, which was several hundred miles south and west. He could only repeat the news (rumors) which he, like Loosh, had heard.

331:15 **Perhaps it was the dark** the first of three possible reasons Bayard gives in this sentence to account for why he and Ringo went to sleep

331:15 **perhaps we were the two moths, the two feathers again** Maybe, by going to sleep, they were retreating to their world of dream-like fantasy again, putting a protective shield between themselves and reality again, above (for they are near the top of the stairs) and not really understanding (or really wanting to understand) the rush of activity below. As for 'two feathers *again*,' see 323:40//7:16 for the first mention of 'two moths, two feathers riding above a hurricane.'

331:16 **perhaps there is a point at which credulity firmly and calmly and irrevocably declines** Perhaps there is a point at which one's mind simply refuses to accept (let alone believe) that which is being presented to it.

331:24 **to what we thought we heard** the sound of digging in the orchard. See 346:18//40:8: 'that night last summer while Father was home, while Louvinia stood in the door of the bedroom without even lighting the lamp while Ringo and I went to bed and later I either looked out or dreamed I looked out the window and saw (or dreamed I saw) the lantern.'

331:24 **though I knew better** though I knew we had been asleep for some time and it was too late now for Louvinia still to be listening to the sound of digging—even if we had actually heard digging and not just imagined or dreamed it. Louvinia is preoccupied by something else. The text doesn't tell us what that is, but it seems reasonable that she would be thinking about what she will have to do (will be able to do) once the Yankees do arrive.

331:30 **the lantern** Since both whale oil and coal oil (kerosene) would be unavailable because of the war, the lantern probably consists of a candle inside a glass wind-shield.

SECTION THREE

331:35 **we wouldn't have to leave the house at all** Apparently it is Granny's rule that the boys play outside except when it rains.

331:36 **Get the cook book** With all the exciting adventure stories in the library which boys would enjoy (Scott, Dumas, Cooper), why would she assume they would want her to read from the cookbook? While wartime shortages have not yet brought on a near-starvation diet, it has been a year since they have been able to eat anything more exciting than basic, home-grown foods. Sugar, imported before the war from Louisiana, is no longer available; certainly nothing as exotic as coconut could be had. Since the last dish at dinner would be a dessert, and since sweets are unobtainable, Granny provides a substitute dessert by reading about cake from the cookbook. The idea comes from Mary Chesnut's Civil War diary: "We keep a cookery book on the mantelpiece, and when our dinner is deficient we just read a pudding or a creme. It does not entirely satisfy the appetite, but perhaps it is as good for the digestion" (778). (Massey 67; Taylor 96)

331:37 **Marengo** Ringo's given name, after a village in Italy which was the scene of Napoleon's victory over the Austrians. According to Napoleon: "My nobility dates from the day of Marengo." Marengo also is the name of a county in the 'Black Belt' in Alabama, the name of the white stallion Napoleon rode at Waterloo, and the name of the South's most celebrated pre-war jackass, Marengo Mammoth. All of these suggest interesting possibilities if Col. Sartoris was the one who supplied Ringo's name (as he probably was, since it was customary for slave-owners to name their slaves). (Payton 424; Fuller 349; Wiener 140; Brewer 547; Lamb 11)

332:7 **Cokynut cake** Desserts made with coconut were traditional for pre-war Southern special-occasion dinners. (Clark *Petticoats* 134; Fabia Smith 17; Frank Smith 200)

332:10 **before it started** 'it' = the war

332:11 **had any of it in the kitchen** House servants and their families ate the same food in the kitchen that they served the white family in the dining room, but the servants did not eat until the white family had finished, and sometimes for a particularly good dish there might not be any left for the servants. (Sydnor *Slavery* 4; Killion 50)

332:20 **I reckon a little more wont hurt us** A little more dessert, even (or perhaps especially) of an imaginary kind, 'wont hurt.' This is the familiar grandmotherly reply to a request for another piece of pie or cake: 'I suppose a little more won't hurt you.'

332:22 **with Ringo already saying, "Where are we going?" behind me** Bayard and Ringo may both believe that all that matters to them is 'what one of us had done or seen that the other had not' (373:36//81:6), but they are not really equals. It is Bayard who determines what they are going to do and when and how they are going to do it. He gets to be the Confederate General twice to Ringo's once. He sleeps in a bed while Ringo has a pallet on the floor.

332:25 **the cabins** the one-or-two-room houses where the slaves lived—sometimes called 'the quarters' (short for 'slave quarters')

332:28 **ghy** going to

332:31 **his eyeballs white and quiet like last night** as they were at 331:11//18:11

332:34 **"Bayard, did you dream hit?"**
"Yes. Last night. It was Father and Louvinia." No, Bayard didn't dream this. He *heard* Father talking to Louvinia. For why he tells Ringo he dreamed it, see 333:11//21:8.

332:35 **Father said to watch Loosh** Again Bayard takes words literally and so does not understand their import. He thinks by 'watch Loosh' Father meant that someone should

follow Loosh around and keep him in sight all the time—
why, Bayard doesn't know.

332:36 **because he knows** Because he knows what? When
the Yankees will arrive? What Yankees look like? Where the
silver is buried? Because he is a 'nigger' and 'niggers know'?
We learn a few lines later (333:4//20:30 and 333:7//21:3)
which of these Father apparently intended.

333:4 **he would know before we did** he would know when
the Northern army was getting close, and if we pay attention
to his behavior, we should be able to tell when to expect the
first soldiers

333:6 **she would have to be white a little longer** Since Louvinia is black, Father has to mean that he is counting on her
to continue to be loyal to his (and her) white family—even
though the arrival of the Yankees will mean freedom for the
slaves. Faulkner has been criticized by some readers for presenting Louvinia as an unrealistic stereotype of a 'contented
darky.' The historical record provides considerable evidence
supporting Faulkner's picture. Loyalty like Louvinia's to a
white family appears to have been at least as common as re-
belliousness like Loosh's. More ex-slaves stayed at home after
being freed than ran off to join the Yankees. Post-war accounts repeatedly mention "the confidence with which masters left their homes and families in the care of slaves during
the Civil War and the almost universal justification of this
confidence." The whites left at home were outnumbered by
slaves and "were wholly at their mercy, and the whites knew
it. All that the slaves needed to gain their freedom was to rise
and assert it, and they knew it." Yet there were virtually no
cases where slaves committed violence against their masters
(or former masters). No doubt this was largely due to civilized restraint on the part of black people, but perhaps it
lends at least some credence to the insistent claim of Southerners that a reciprocal human decency did "in general char-
acterize the relationship" between most whites and slaves
during time of slavery. (Gray 522; Higgins 166; Thompson
102; Gorn 555; Claiborne 145; Doyle 107)

333:8 **when it was getting ready to happen** when the Yankees are about to arrive

333:10 **"I dont know." Ringo breathed deep once** The form of this one-line paragraph is momentarily misleading. It is Bayard who says he doesn't know, Ringo who breathes.

333:11 **If somebody tole you, hit could be a lie. But if you dremp hit, hit cant be a lie case aint nobody there to tole hit to you** Since Bayard knows Ringo believes dreams can't be false, this explains why he told Ringo he had *dreamed* that Father had said to 'watch Loosh.' It saved Bayard from having to try to convince Ringo to help carry out Father's instructions. Why would Bayard use such a heavy dialect in telling us what Ringo says but not for his own words, for at twelve both must have spoken very much the same? It is an adult, educated Bayard who is telling the story. He can still remember how Ringo sounded, but he can no longer imagine himself having once talked like that.

333:39 **watched the road by turns, to get Louvinia calmed down in case it would be late before he got back** so Louvinia would not be too upset to go to sleep at night, so the boys would be able to sneak out without her hearing them

334:2 **Joby's cabin** It is surprising that Bayard would have called the cabin Joby's, since the cabin of a slave family was normally thought of as the wife's. A small house occupied by black people was called a 'cabin'; the same building if occupied by whites would be called a 'house.' To call the house of any white a 'cabin' was provocation for a fight. This was still true a hundred years later and to a certain degree even true today. (Johnson 535; Brown *Voice* 77)

334:12 **that look on his face again which resembled drunkenness but was not** 'again' because at 322:5//4:20 Bayard, looking at Loosh, had commented on the way black persons' eyes get 'when they had been drinking.' Loosh had not been drinking then either, as Bayard now realizes as an adult.

334:16 **the same look on her face** the same as Loosh's

334:19 **again she didn't have on Father's old hat** 'again' because at 324:12//7:30 when Father rode up the drive Bayard had noticed she was not wearing the hat she almost always wore. This time she is not wearing it for a different reason; in this instance she is functioning only as the head of her own family, not as surrogate for Col. Sartoris.

334:25 **Ginral Sherman** Northern General William Tecumseh Sherman, second in command to Grant in Mississippi and afterwards in the east.

334:25 **gonter** going to. Why Faulkner would write this as 'ghy' when Ringo says it (332:28//20:12), 'gwinter' when Philadelphy says it (334:21//23:3), and 'gonter' when Loosh says it here, I don't know, unless for linguistic characterization. The meaning is the same in all cases.

334:25 **sweep the earth** sweep from the face of the earth *everything* in his Army's path—bringing about destruction so severe that "a crow flying over would have to carry its own provisions." (These words were actually said a year later about Union General Sheridan's Army, but they convey the extent of the ruin which 'sweep the earth' became the catchphrase for and which Sherman in 1863 in Mississippi was the first to inflict on civilian property.) Sherman's Mississippi and Alabama campaigns amounted to a dress rehearsal for his later more famous march from Georgia to the sea when his army devastated a corridor sixty miles wide. (McPherson 778; Wolk 98)

334:26 **the race** Loosh means the black race but, as we shortly see, this is not what Bayard understands him to mean.

334:30 **the white folks** Louvinia means the Southern whites. She too apparently believes Yankees are somehow different from Mississippi 'white folks.'

334:35 **They're coming to set us free** Bayard had heard Loosh's words but again he misunderstands their meaning. He takes 'they're coming' to mean the Yankees are just down the road. He takes 'free' to be something *terrible* the Yankees are going to do to them, by 'us' he thinks Loosh means *all* Southerners, not just slaves, and by 'the race' he thinks Loosh means the *human* race as distinct from whatever species Yankees might be. No wonder, in telling his story years later, Bayard tells us five times that he was only twelve. There is, incidentally, a backhanded kind of truth in the idea that the Yankees will set *all* of them free—the slaves from their owners, and the whites from the responsibilities that go with controlling and providing for the slaves. (Wittenberg 161)

335:2 **because he had seen them and would know what to shoot at** Bayard understands Yankees to be some unfamiliar breed, what one person imagined as "a mutation somewhere between the devil and a machine," certainly not just 'folks' in blue uniforms. (Eby 15)

335:5 **Aint** In the mid-nineteenth century 'ain't' was not considered poor usage. Melville, for example, often used it.

335:7 **you have my permission and my insistence, too, to whip them both** Since Bayard later tells us that 'Granny had never whipped us for anything in our lives except lying' (338:13//28:23), Bayard must believe that Granny did not believe them when they told her General Sherman will soon be there 'to set us free.'

335:12 **Ringo was afraid to come up in the bed with me** because Granny had told Louvinia to punish them if they made another sound, and Louvinia is sleeping in the hall outside their door. And because Ringo is more afraid of this than Bayard, no doubt we are to understand that Louvinia disciplines Ringo more rigorously than she does Bayard.

335:15 **Look like hit haf to be us** Since Father had said to 'watch Loosh,' and since no one else is carrying out his instructions, I guess it is up to us.

335:27 **flat and empty as the sideboard** as bare as the buffet with the silver tea service no longer on it. The book began with Bayard and Ringo's creating a 'living map' behind the smokehouse; now Bayard is dreaming of a different map, a surrealistically empty, dead one. Bayard would dream that *this* (specifically) would be the result of the Yankees' coming because he had heard Loosh say that General Sherman was going to 'sweep the earth.' Southern plantation yards were not broad grassy expanses—what we think of as lawns today. In cotton-producing country grass was the enemy, something to be exterminated, certainly not deliberately cultivated. There was one case of a planter who sowed a grass yard and was sued because of it by a cotton-growing neighbor. A well-kept plantation yard consisted of bare, packed dirt, religiously hoed clean of grass, then swept several times a week with a dogwood broom—making attractive, swirling patterns like those in a Japanese sand garden. Bayard had seen Louvinia 'sweeping the earth' hundreds of times, and this is how he imagines General Sherman will sweep (i.e., make bare) their entire plantation, buildings and all—much as Loosh had flattened their Vicksburg. (Vance 158, 159; Faulkner *Intruder* 8; Rhodes 104; Brown *Glossary* 195; Smith *Words* n.p.)

335:28 **all of a sudden I wasn't looking at it; I was there** In his dream he is no longer somewhere *outside* the dream, observing; he is now one of the tiny figures *in* the dream, moving about on the now-desolate landscape.

335:29 **drove** group—a word usually applied to animals but here used for people

335:37 **bright bay horse** 'Bay' is a color of a horse—reddish-brown. A 'bright bay' is shiny reddish-brown.

335:37 **looking at the house through a field glass** If the illustration at the beginning of the story is meant to depict this moment—when the boys first see the Union soldier—then it is inaccurate: they do not have the gun at that time. If it is supposed to be after they do have the gun, the drawing is still not right: it shows the road between them and the house; the soldier could not have failed to see them when they ran to the house and came back with the gun. The artist, Edward Shenton, appears to have felt no obligation to make his 'interpretation' coincide exactly with what Faulkner wrote. Faulkner seems not to have minded; he withdrew a couple of suggestions when Shenton was doing the drawings for a later book, saying, "Mr. Shenton is doing so well . . . I am extremely timid about getting in the way" (Blotner 1528).

335:37 **I dont know what we had expected to see, but we knew what he was at once. I remember thinking, "He looks just like a man."** Southern propaganda led gullible slaves and children to believe that the war was a war between species, humans vs. non-humans, that Yankees had "long horns on their heads and tushes in their mouths and eyes sticking out like a cow." Some slaves when they saw their first Yankees reportedly expressed surprise that "Yankees stand"—on two feet—"just like folks." Perhaps Bayard exaggerates a bit in telling us how much of this he once believed. If he does, he is not the only one to have offered similar exaggerations. (Thompson 151; Wiley *Southern* 13–14)

336:3 **we were running across the pasture toward the house** From a contemporary editorial in the Cincinnati *Gazette*: "To arms! The time for playing war has passed. The enemy is now approaching our doors!" An English visitor in the South reported seeing young ladies practicing firing pistols, "vowing to shoot the first Yankee who comes within sight of their homes." Bayard's and Ringo's attempt to do their part in defending their home may not have been very smart, but again they were simply taking literally the words they had heard. (Foote I 654; Simkins 6; Hopley I 285)

336:10 **his eyes looked like door knobs** Before the 20th century nearly all door knobs in American houses fancy enough to have door knobs at all were a bright glossy white porcelain or glass. Ringo's eyeballs seem as big and white as these door knobs. (Wicker 492)

336:11 **to lift down the musket** Faulkner is playing here with one of the most famous bits of instruction ever given to writers. Anton Chekhov, Russian playwright and short-story writer, arguing that everything in a work of art should be there for some purpose beyond simply adding to the atmosphere, laid down a rule: "If in the first act you hang a gun on the wall, by the third act you must use it." On 329:8//

15:6 Faulkner told us about the gun over the mantel. Now he is using it.

336:13 **though it was not the weight so much as the length** why Bayard had trouble getting it down by himself

336:21 **Do you want to be free?** This is Bayard's convincing argument to get Ringo to help at a time when Ringo seems almost too frightened to move. It is convincing because they both understand 'free' to mean some kind of atrocity. There were stories, for example, that Yankees killed all children, or drowned them, or ate them ("Gal babies mostly, fried"), or ate black children, "roasted." (Gentry 16; Drago 362; Wiley *Southern* 13; Gordon 234; Litwack 120)

336:23 **We carried it that way, like a log, one at each end** At 321:14//4:3 Bayard and Ringo had joined forces to carry a leaking bucket from wellhouse to battlefield for their play war ('we ran, panting and interminable . . . the two of us needing first to join forces and spend ourselves against a common enemy, time, before we could . . .'); now they join forces to carry a musket, aim it and shoot it, this time at a real Yankee. They will later work as one in killing Grumby, but by the time of "An Odor of Verbena" they are no longer two bodies responding to a shared impulse. By then the 'common enemy' will have overtaken them.

336:29 **cocking the musket. We had practiced before** drawing the hammer back until it catches, so a pull of the trigger will release it and fire the gun. The hammer of an old-time musket had to be drawn back against a strong spring—a spring too strong for Bayard's and Ringo's fingers. Two sentences later we learn how they compensated for the strength they lacked. It is a maneuver that would require some practice. (Brown *Glossary* 55)

336:31 **change the cap on the nipple** The cap (which was the actual detonating device) deteriorated with time and had to be replaced periodically with a fresh one. (Brown *Glossary* 45, 140)

336:33 **slid down over the hammer until it clicked** Bayard slid down the barrel of the gun like sliding down a flagpole, hitting the hammer with his crotch. Force = mass times acceleration.

336:35 **riding up across Ringo's back as he stooped** This is how Bayard and Ringo aim the gun. Ringo bends forward, supporting the barrel of the gun on his back; Bayard then tells him to raise or lower his back in order to bring the sights level with the target.

336:36 **Shoot the bastud!** the same thing they had yelled in their behind-the-smokehouse battles: "Kill the bastuds!" (324:5//7:22)

336:37 **I shut my eyes** the first of a series of times when, at the instant of violence, Bayard's senses (or his memory of them) go blank. Hemingway offers one possible explanation: "he had physically or mentally shut his eyes, as one might do if he saw a child he could not possibly reach or aid, about to be struck by a train . . . the actual striking would be an anti-climax, so that the moment before striking might be as far as he could represent." (Hemingway 2–3)

336:38 **vanish in smoke** When a Civil War gun was fired the black gunpowder gave off a cloud of dense smoke. It might be ten seconds before the smoke would lift enough for the shooter to see if he had hit his target. (Brown *Glossary* 155; Clark *Musket* 36; Watkins *Hills* 58)

336:39 **It sounded like thunder** the sound, finally, that is 'louder, much louder, than words' (323:22//6:26)

336:40 **heard the horse scream** 'Scream' is an accurate word for the cry a horse gives when it is suddenly hurt.

337:1 **Hit's the whole army!** exaggerated: not the whole Army, certainly, but a lot more soldiers than they had anticipated

SECTION FOUR

337:10 **the righted chair** Granny's chair which Bayard had used to stand on to get the musket

337:11   **We shot the bastud**   'Bastard' is not a word Bayard or
Ringo would have used in front of Granny if the situation
had not been so desperate as to cause them to forget their
manners. "No gentleman used profanity in the presence of
ladies or suffered others to do so." A tongue-in-cheek (but
nevertheless accurate) explanation for this stuffily-worded
rule: "According to the chivalrous notions of the time . . . [a
lady's] purity of mind and soul . . . could be easily sullied or
'soiled' (which was the current expression) by contact with
any form of coarseness. Even a single obscene word, heard
by chance, could soil a woman. Duels were fought now and
then because some careless gentleman . . . had, in the presence of a lady, used a vulgar expression. When a woman was
once soiled there seemed to be no known way of unsoiling
her. She bore the speck of stain as long as she lived. None of
this applied to the women of the poor, to the wives and
daughters of laborers and small farmers. They were apparently immune, or better say, it did not make any difference
if they were soiled." (Kendrick 37; Woodward *Lived* 170)

337:12   **her face the same color as her hair almost**   white,
drained of color

337:14   **what did you say?**   Like Louvinia earlier (324:14//
8:2), Granny's first and automatic reaction is to Bayard's saying 'bastud.'

337:22   **like somebody had thrown ashes at her**   Her face
was ashen, more gray than black. Whether such a change in
color can actually be noticed on a black person's face, I don't
know, but Faulkner apparently thought it could, for he used
the same idea in his manuscript for "Never Done No Weeping When you Wanted to Laugh": "[Nancy's face] lost its
smooth and shining blackness and became a shallow dry
gray, as though dusted evenly over with woodashes" (*Mississippi Quarterly* 462).

337:22   **Only it didn't need her face**   We didn't need to see
Louvinia's face to know that the situation was serious.

337:26   **blue coats**   Union Army uniforms were blue, Confederate ones gray.

337:32 **What are they trying to tell me** This time it is
Granny who is 'just talking,' because she knows very well that
Bayard and Ringo believe they are telling the truth when
they say they shot a Union soldier. She knows this before she
sees the Yankees ride past the window and before she hears
them shouting. We know that Granny knows the boys are
telling what they believe to be true for she *had* to have heard
the shot ('It sounded like thunder'). She was awake when the
boys got the musket (she called down to them from upstairs)
and she is now downstairs and has already righted the chair
which Bayard had dragged from its regular place to get
down the musket. She can see that the musket is no longer
above the mantel. While Granny can't know what, if anything, the boys actually hit, she has to know they did fire
a shot.

337:33 **when once the musket decided to go off** Bayard hu-
morously shifts responsibility as he advances his recollection

338:2 **on either side of her against her legs, the hard points
of the chair rockers jammed into our backs and her skirts
spread over us like a tent** The boys are crouched in front
of Granny's rocking chair on either side of her knees, her
full skirts spread (as women's skirts were supposed to be
when they sat) and wrapped over the boys, covering them in
front and at the sides. They are not *under* her skirt. This has
to be so because only young women at the time of the Civil
War had begun to wear underclothes, and surely we are not
to imagine Bayard's and Ringo's faces pressed against Granny's bare legs. She is wearing very full skirts but not a hoop-
skirt (a high-fashion item which made movement difficult
and would not have been worn at home by a rural grandmother). To hide behind a woman's skirts was, of course, the
cliché-example of a cowardly action by a man, but Bayard
and Ringo are still boys, young enough to be excused for
allowing a woman to protect them. (Street 80; Cunnington
13, 70, 73, 124; Ewing 40, 85, 120–121; Walkley 45; Knapp
248; McClellan 481)

338:4 **Louvinia told us afterward** Louvinia is the family

story-teller. We are told this again at 339:15//30:11, 339:27/ /30:25, 339:40//31:10, 340:21//32:3, 341:33//33:30, and especially at the end of the following chapter, 368:25// 73:10.

338:11 **Ringo's eyes looking like two plates of chocolate pudding** It is dark behind Granny's skirts. Ringo's eyes still look big to Bayard but they are like plates of chocolate pudding now, not like white door knobs (336:10//25:19).

338:13 **Granny had never whipped us for anything in our lives except lying** Not to lie is a learned behavior, contrary to natural human instincts. Granny has been taking seriously her responsibility to train the boys to grow up to become honorable men.

338:14 **even when it wasn't even a told lie, but just keeping quiet** and so permitting a misapprehension (or someone else's lie) to go unchallenged. The standard of honesty Granny has been teaching the boys is a high one.

338:16 **ask the Lord to forgive us** to forgive the boys for lying, to forgive herself for whipping them for lying

338:20 **the people** the slaves

338:20 **in the quarters** in the slave cabins behind the main house

338:22 **It was that quiet** like 'it was that urgent' (323:29// 7:9); 'that quiet' = resoundingly quiet, the aftershock of their having heard Granny tell two lies—Granny who 'had never whipped us for anything in our lives except lying'

Gentlemen, Lying, and the Southern Honor Code

The word of an honorable man was assumed to be truthful. To question his word—in effect to call him a liar—was an insult he would not tolerate. Boys were trained from their earliest years always to tell the truth. It would seem, then, that to tell a lie under *any* circumstances would necessarily be wrong. That is what twelve-year-old Bayard and Ringo understand and that is why they are so shocked when they hear Granny lie. Yet honorable men did sometimes lie. They were sometimes expected to lie, and the code approved of their lying. Otherwise we would not have the expression 'lied like a gentleman,' nor would Boss Priest in *The Reivers* (1962) have instructed his grandson that "a gentleman always sticks to his lie whether he told it or not." There has never been a society where honorable men were supposed always to tell the truth under all circumstances. As Disraeli put it: "A gentleman is one who knows when to tell the truth and when not to." (Mencken 327; *Reivers* 304; Bok 298)

Among the times when a lie would be preferable to the truth:

1. It is better to lie if harm to the innocent would be likely to result from the truth: the classical example is of the theater manager who discovers an already-spreading fire backstage; wouldn't it be better to give calmly a false excuse for canceling the performance than to announce the fire and risk bringing about injuries and possible deaths from the crowd rushing for exits? "Where peace demands it a lie may be told." "Avoidance of harm . . . overrides the principle of veracity. Just as force would be justifiable as a means to prevent murder, so it would be right to achieve the same objective through a lie." (Bok 74, 109)

2. Extraordinary circumstances sometimes "make the common rules for life insufficient." Moral rules are "a shorthand for all that a good Christian should consider in deciding his conduct . . . sensitive moral judgement might not coincide with the simple conclusions drawn from ordinary interpretations of the rules." One's concern should be "to preserve the moral understanding rather than the rules." If one's only options are two wrongs, sometimes to lie could be the lesser wrong. (Letwin 228)

3. One's word given under duress is not binding. A statement or promise extracted at the point of a bayonet can be expected to be honored only "under bayonet constraint." (Pearson 328–329)

4. "Those who ask questions which they have no right to ask [should expect] to have lies told to them." (Bok 146)

5. "It is permissible to say what is false when the conversation is directed to him who wishes to be deceived"—when the liar and the one lied to "consent to a mutually deceptive relationship." (Bok 266, 129)

6. "If one could give pleasure by telling a harmless lie, tell it." (The Jello, marshmallow, and peanut butter salad you brought to the picnic was wonderful.) (Raven 55)

7. If both parties knowingly and voluntarily consent to the rules of a game, and the rules include permitting misleading or exaggerated statements or actions, then one is not obligated to be truthful. "In a bazaar, for instance, false claims are a convention; to proclaim from the outset one's honest intention would be madness." (Bok 131)

An honorable man does not lie for selfish ends—to perpetrate a fraud or to gain a benefit for himself—but it may sometimes be right for him to lie "when it would be of great value to another." A gentleman insists on his right to make such private evaluations according to his own understanding of the situation. Thus "a good many of those boys didn't mind much *telling* a lie, but they did mind a whole heap if anyone *accused* them of it." (Bok 273; Blotner 99; Bryson 59; E.A. Smith "Oxford" 4)

Women, Lying, and the Southern Honor Code

The Southern honor code applied to adult males only. Women and children were deemed outside it—both for the same reason: their incapacity. "Since they are not bound by the obligation imposed by reason, they cannot properly be said to have either honor or dishonor." Lucas Beauchamp in *Go Down, Moses* (1942) characterized a woman as "a critter not responsible like men are responsible, not to be held like men are held." A Civil War military pass obtained by a woman to travel behind the lines began: "Miss Sarah Jones has permission to visit . . . promising on her honor as a man not to communicate. . . ." The pass was worded that way because there was no such concept as 'her honor as a woman.' Samuel Johnson: "The great principle which every woman is taught is to keep her legs together. When she has given up that, she has given up every notion of female honor and virtue." To remain innocent before marriage and to deny access to her person to all except her husband after marriage was as much in the way of honor that society thought it could expect or demand from a woman. Therefore, a woman could lie if she wished—and not be held responsible for her lies. "A Southern lady could lie about a gentleman but a Southern gentleman could not lie about a lady or, worse still, call the lady a liar." He must "show perfect courtesy and always defer to their opinions. The gentleman's deference, however, was protected from too great strain because the ladies were expected to avoid expressing opinions on all subjects, such as politics, that lay [outside their proper realm and capabilities]." Obviously not all women allowed themselves to be limited to such a demeaning role (Granny and Drusilla, for example), but it was all that nineteenth century Southern society required of them, and some (Aunt Louisa, for example) learned to maneuver effectively within society's expectations. The whole business of women's diminished capacity was probably understood at least partly as a supposedly polite fiction. If this were not so, we would not find occasional modern statements like "Southern women are Mack trucks disguised as powder puffs." (Bryson 24, 32; Moses 52; Hopley I 399; Johnson in Norah Smith 64; Stevens 78; Mitchell 663; Sydnor "Laws" 16; Kendrick 34–35; McKern 3)

A good argument could be made that, since the Civil War, the real status of women in the U.S. has changed even more than the status of American black persons, despite their shift from slavery to citizenship.

338:22 **sitting bolt upright and right on the edge of the chair** This is not just so she can keep her skirts over the boys. It is the way a woman was expected to sit—never allowing her back to touch the back of the chair. (Kane 79)

338:29 **You wont find any locked doors** It is part of civilized Southern manners not to lock doors inside a house. The idea is that a locked door is unnecessary, since no properly brought up person of any age or sex would enter a room with a closed door without first knocking and then waiting to be asked to come in. From *The Reivers* (1962): "Father had taught me that no door required a lock: the closed door itself was sufficient until you were invited to enter it" (301). The Northern sergeant knows nothing of a tradition of manners like this.

338:35 **like she was behind it with a switch** She is having a hard time making her voice ask what she wants to ask.

338:36 **Is he . . . . it . . . . the one who—** Was whoever was shot killed—or maybe just wounded?

338:38 **Broke his back and we had to shoot him** Bayard and Ringo (and maybe Granny for a moment) do not realize that the sergeant is referring to the humanitarian act of putting a hopelessly-injured animal out of its pain by shooting it, giving rise to their 'horrified astonishment' that maybe Yankees ('He looks just like a man') really *are* part of some sub-human species, capable of killing an injured fellow being.

338:40 **I didn't know horrified astonishment either** Why 'either'? At 322:24//5:12 Bayard told us 'I didn't know triumph; I didn't even know the word.' Now, sixteen pages later, he is telling us 'I didn't know horrified astonishment *either*,' but he and Ringo and Granny were all three it—i.e., horrifiedly astonished.

339:4 **regiment** four or five companies—about 1000 men when at full strength, usually about half of that in practice

339:4 **betting on him for next Sunday** Horse races were a frequent form of entertainment when the armies of either side were in bivouac. As a public sport horseracing was largely discontinued during the war, but since most former racehorses were now with their owners in the cavalry, sometimes army races involved very fast (and occasionally famous) horses. (Calkin 36; Chafetz 263)

339:9 **thank God!** The boys already realize they made a serious mistake in shooting at the Yankee—not just because they might be discovered and punished but because they might have killed someone. They are growing up fast on this summer afternoon.

339:16 **bright short beard** 'bright' = of one pure color (as with the 'bright bay' horse at 335:37//25:4). Here it means unmixed with white or gray.

339:18 **took off his hat** The Colonel, realizing he is in the presence of a lady (a word which used to mean something more than 'any adult female'), makes his manners (a Southern expression for performing the courteous actions or speaking the courteous words which civilized social custom calls for).

339:23 **"Ah," the colonel said** Because *The Unvanquished* is fiction presented to us in words, sometimes we are able to make inferences from the text's words which we might not have been able to make had we actually been present at the scene. Here we are told three times that the Northern colonel says 'Ah.' 'Ah' is also what Col. Sartoris said twice when he arrived home (326:12//10:29 and 326:16//11:4). Since both are cavalry colonels and since we already know Col. Sartoris is a good man, aren't we being led (perhaps subliminally) to expect that the Northern colonel will be a good man too?

339:24 **By whose authority?** Official U.S. Army policy at this relatively early stage of the war was that occupying armies "must respect the persons and property of civilians . . . but the civilians themselves must abide by the rules: that is, armies which did not make war on civilians must not themselves be warred on by civilians." If civilians violated this, it was proper for the occupying army to inflict punishment on the violators. To this Grant added: "Cripple the rebellion in every way without insulting women and children." Sherman added: "Protect houses and families as much as possible." But in the Shenandoah Valley, Union General Pope had ordered that "if a Federal soldier were fired upon from any house, it should be razed." What to do, then, in Mississippi when two boys killed a Union horse was still a question for which there was not yet an agreed-upon Army precedent. (Catton 291; Lewis 296; Long 238)

339:31 **if he had enough horses, he wouldn't always care**

whether there was anybody to ride them The sergeant is paraphrasing Lincoln, who had said he could "make a General in five minutes but horses cost a hundred and twenty-five dollars a piece." In terms of military reality, the sergeant's argument might very well be sound. "The unpleasant military truth is that often men are more easily replaced than equipment." (Zall 35; Blair 101)

339:33 **not bothering nobody yet** The effect here is crude for Faulkner, but the 'yet' colors considerably what the sergeant is saying.

340:1 **his eyes going from Granny's face down to where her skirt was spread, and looking at her skirt for a whole minute and then going back to her face** Certainly we are to understand from this that the colonel knows Granny is hiding the boys behind her skirts.

340:4 **Granny gave him look for look** Granny understands that the colonel knows she is hiding the boys. The question is: what is he going to do about it?

340:5 **Do I understand, madam** He addresses Granny as a lady—and pretends to believe what she would have him believe. Since he is a Northerner, he says 'Madam'; a Southerner would have said 'Ma'am.' (Stoneback 19)

340:5 **there are no children in or about this house?** Consider the colonel's only other options: should he accuse her of lying and ask her to raise her skirt so he might search beneath it? This no gentleman would do. And if he did apprehend the boys, what would he do then? Shoot them? "Rule Number One [of the warrior] was: You don't deliberately harm the helpless. It was bad enough when that happened by accident. To do so on purpose was cowardly, beneath contempt." Sometimes the best (the most civilized) way to behave is to pretend not to notice what is clearly before one's eyes, "to decline to acknowledge destructive truths." (Young "Pioneering" 37–38; Cooke 174; Clancy 398; Perry 296)

340:7 **There are none, sir** So Granny lies, trusting that the colonel, as a gentleman, will not challenge her lie. He has addressed her as 'Madam,' she addresses him as 'Sir'—the title of a gentleman, which he is proving himself to be, even though a Northerner.

340:10   **call the men in**   call off the search

340:10   **mount them**   order them to mount their horses and to ride on

340:14   **Where are your ears, sergeant?**   You heard what she said; do *you* want to call this lady a liar?

340:14   **do you really want the artillery to overtake us, with a creek bottom not five miles away to be got over?**   This is the colonel's argument to persuade the sergeant to tell the men to move on. To understand the colonel's point we first have to consider what was the probable function of his cavalry troop on this day (to serve as advance scouts for their following army), then whose artillery (Northern or Southern) might be likely to overtake them if they waste much more time looking for two boys (it would be their own artillery), and then what role the sergeant and his men would be called upon to play at the creek bottom if the artillery should overtake them there. It helps to know that Mississippi has almost no rock, that Mississippi creek bottoms are therefore necessarily mud, and that Mississippi mud (called gumbo) is famous for its adhesiveness. Today Mississippi mud is even bottled and sold as a souvenir for tourists. The colonel is, in short, reminding the sergeant of that 'passive recalcitrance of topography which outweighs artillery' (321:6//3:6). It sometimes took as many as eighteen horses and mules plus fifty men waist-deep in the mud with their shoulders against the wheels to get a single 1,250 pound artillery piece across a muddy stream. (Brown *Glossary* 22; Foote I 405; Gates 45; Catton *Grant* 418; Lytle 130; Fuller 130; Zogbaum 132–133)

340:18   **Then, doubtless, I should be Sergeant Harrison. In which case**   There are only two men present—the colonel and the sergeant. If the sergeant were the colonel (as Harrison has just suggested) then the colonel would have to be the sergeant, in which case (as sergeant) he would . . .

340:20   **a grandchildless old lady . . . alone in a house which**

**in all probability (and for her pleasure and satisfaction I
am ashamed to say I hope) I shall never see again** What
goes with what in this sentence is not easy to understand
without some thought. The next four entries break down the
parts.

340:22 **a house which in all probability** These words go
with 'I shall never see again'—the words which come after
the three-part interruption set off in parentheses: a house
which in all probability he shall never see again.

340:23 **and for her pleasure and satisfaction** He assumes
that Granny would take pleasure and satisfaction from
knowing that he will probably never be in her house again.

340:24 **I am ashamed to say I hope** Thus, because he is a
gentleman being received with at least a show of hospitality,
he is embarrassed to have to say that he hopes never to return again, if that is what it takes to give her pleasure and
satisfaction.

340:33 **sports** running, swimming, riding, hunting, etc.—
outdoor sports that two boys would enjoy

340:34 **game to shoot at** animals and birds—rabbits, squir-
rels, quail, etc.

340:34 **the most exciting game of all** In some contexts 'war'
would be the most exciting game of all, but that is not what
the colonel means here. 'Game' is a word which has two quite
different meanings: 1) a contest (baseball, poker, war) and
2) an animal which is the object of a hunt (a bear, a tiger, a
deer). The text sentence is about 'game' in this second sense
('game to shoot at'), and *man* is the most exciting animal to
hunt, the 'most exciting game of all,' for a man is as intelligent as his hunter, and a man is capable of shooting back.
Hunting is considered enjoyable "in proportion to its chal-
lenges and dangers." (Bruce 44; Connell 80)

340:35 **none the less so for being, possibly, a little rare this
near the house** Most Southern males are off to the war,
and Northern males are usually not found this far south—at
least not before now. The colonel is continuing his hunting
metaphor.

340:36 **a very dependable weapon, I see** This is the colonel's mild joke. He knows it is a dependable weapon because he is familiar with it: it is a captured Union musket (329:8// 15:7). It is dependable also in that it is apparently loyal, since it did not hit a Northern soldier. As to the likelihood that the boys might have hit the soldier, see the extended description of **musket** (329:8//15:7).

340:39 **though I understand that this weapon does not belong to you** In a sense it doesn't. As a Yankee musket it doesn't really belong on a Mississippi plantation, but the colonel is merely following the implicitly agreed-upon script.

341:1 **if it were your weapon—which it is not** if it were your weapon—which we both know it is but are pretending to believe it is not

341:1 **and you had two grandsons, or say a grandson and a Negro playfellow—which you have not** we both know you have them but we are pretending to believe you do not

341:3 **and if this were the first time—which it is not** This part of the sentence appears to be (and is) parallel to the two parts preceding it, but the colonel is not suggesting (as it would at first seem) that he and Granny are pretending to believe that this is not the first time Bayard and Ringo have fired at Yankees, that they have done this before. Instead the colonel is staying even more strictly with the logic of what they are pretending: if this is not your gun, and if you have no grandson and black playmate, then obviously there could not have been *any* incident involving gun, grandson, and playmate. According to the logic of his sentence, this was not the *first* time they had shot at a Yankee; that supposed occurrence was a *non-event*, an event which did not happen, could not have happened. Earlier (about the South winning at Vicksburg) the idea was to make something so by believing it so; here it is to make something, clearly so, not so by asserting 'it is not.'

341:4 **someone next time might be seriously hurt** We were all lucky today: no one was hurt. So we can let this whole matter pass as a boyish prank. But consider what my (and your) position would have been if someone *had* been seriously hurt.

341:6   **homily**   a sermon with instructive moral

341:11   **There is little of refreshment I can offer you, sir. But if a glass of cool milk after your ride—**   She is offering him (enemy but gentleman) something that is very real in the South—Southern hospitality.

341:17   **sheer bravado**   an unnecessary display of daring

341:18   **conduct the gentleman to the dining room**   Our Northern guest deserves the courtesy of being served in the dining room. As one Southern woman later remarked: "it seemed to be the policy of the Yankee government to send one gentleman or two with every regiment to let it be known that there were some gentlemen in the north." According to an Oxford, Mississippi, woman old enough to remember the Civil War, the commander of the first Union garrison to occupy Oxford, a Major Chaffie, "was a man of big heart and kindly disposition and though known to us as a 'Damn Yankee,' he had a fine sense of right, and always held his men in check. The citizens showed their appreciation of his fairness by presenting him with a silver cup on his departure." (Rainwater 178; Minnie Holt Smith, n.p.)

341:30   **Since, doubtless, you wish to live in peace. I have three boys myself, you see**   These two sentences should be read together, for the second explains the first: I understand from experience that, with young boys around, peace is likely to be in short supply.

341:31   **I have not even had time to become a grandparent**   But I am telling you what you know better than I, since I am just a father, not a grandfather.

341:36   **fools cry out at wind or fire**   There is no point in our getting upset over or apologizing for things which are not our fault and which we could not have prevented. Unfortunate incidents are bound to occur during a war; we both understand this. The colonel's words paraphrase what General Sherman later said to the mayor of Atlanta: "You might as well appeal against thunderstorms as against the terrible hardships of war. They are inevitable." Sherman in turn was adapting a rather famous comment made in England by the Rev. Sydney Smith in 1831: "I do not mean to be disrespectful, but the attempt of the Lords to stop the progress of Reform reminds me very forcibly of the great storm at Sidmouth, and of the conduct of the excellent Mrs. Partington on that occasion." No one knew who Mrs. Partington was, but everyone could imagine what her conduct must have been. (Wheeler 422; Cohen 369)

341:37 **permit me to say and hope that you will never have anything worse than this to remember us by** But soon their house is burned, their silver stolen, their servants run off, and Granny joins Bayard and Ringo in shouting 'The bastuds!' (370:17//75:27).

342:3 **all of a sudden I began to holler** Bayard thinks Granny has fainted, but she is relaxing in relief, collecting herself before going on.

342:4 **she opened her eyes then and looked at me; they were looking at me when they opened** "How better might one pinpoint Granny's unrelenting eternal vigilance?" (Hunter 214)

342:7 **what was that word you used?** The boys made a big mistake this day: they extended their playing at war to actually shooting at a Yankee soldier. It turned out they did not kill anyone, and the Northern officer-in-charge proved to be understanding. Still, they did a stupid thing and, if they should try it again, next time they might not be so lucky. It is Granny's responsibility to teach them proper behavior. So she goes about disciplining them for what they have done: 'What was that word you used?' In view of all that has happened, why is it that she decides to punish them only for swearing? The easy answer would be that she is going along with the colonel's pretense: the shooting had not occurred. A better answer is that, while Bayard and Ringo may be young and naive, they are not stupid. They must realize that they have made a serious mistake, one that they are not likely to repeat. If they can't figure this out for themselves, there is no hope for them. Thus there is no point in Granny telling them that shooting at the Yankee was wrong. But this is also clearly a deflection from the far more problematic error of attempted murder. Even in the context of war, this is a gray area for Granny, one that she can avoid by choosing to discipline the boys for a lapse in behavior that she is morally certain is wrong.

342:13 **I could see Ringo's feet** Bayard is looking at the ground, not wanting to face Granny.

342:15 **you told a lie** as Granny very well knows, and in front of the boys, too. Children can be cruel.

342:23 **get a pan of water and the soap** to wash out their mouths with soap as punishment for swearing

342:24 **Get the new soap** Get the strong stuff: homemade soap gradually loses strength after being exposed to the air. (McGinnis 135)

SECTION FIVE

342:25 **as if time had slipped up on us while we . . . were too busy to notice it** Yes, it is getting late on a long and busy afternoon, but that is not all this sentence is saying. Time *has* slipped up on the boys while they were too busy to notice it. They began the day believing that Yankees were less-than-human and that it was up to them to protect their home from these invaders. Now they understand that at least some Yankees are decent human beings, like Mississippi folks, that shooting is not something to be undertaken lightly, and that the morality involved in truth-telling and lying is not as simple as they had imagined. That amounts to quite a bit of growing up for just one day.

342:30 **gourd dipper** A gourd is a long, hard-shelled, ornamental, zucchini-like vegetable. It can be hollowed-out on the bulbous end to make a drinking dipper. Water from a gourd dipper tastes different and better than from a metal one—a fact which people born since about World War II are not likely ever to experience the proof of.

342:37   **he pointed out the cloud bank to tell us what mountains looked like**   Col. Sartoris's explanation parallels the development of our language: in Old English 'cloud' was spelled *clud* and meant a 'hill.' (Funk 339)

343:4   **Looking mighty far**   in time as well as distance

343:4   **Too far to go just to fight Yankees**   Bayard's attempt at bravado: we can fight Yankees without even having to leave home.

343:6   **But it was gone now**   Again there is more being said than just the literal statement. The suds, bubbles, and taste of the soap, 'the sound of the musket' by which they had been caught and 'were too busy to notice it,' are gone, yes, but so is their childish and unquestioning certainty that right and wrong can always and easily be distinguished. How can Yankees be the enemy if the Northern colonel is a Yankee? How can Granny insist that they not swear or lie when she has lied herself (and at the end of the next chapter will say 'bastuds')? The suggestion is not that Granny is not a reliable moral guide; it is rather that moral issues are more complex than easy rules can accommodate. It is hard sometimes to know how one *ought* to behave.

343:7   **iridescent**   a rainbow-like play of colors—as on the surface of a soap bubble

Title, revisited: **Ambuscade**   If an ambuscade is an attack by surprise from a concealed position, what then does the title of the story refer to? The boys shooting at the Yankee soldier from the cedar copse is of course a right answer, but it is not the only right answer. Bayard and Ringo also were taken by surprise on this day. Their fall from innocence, a necessary part of growing up, was, with the help of Granny and one understanding Northern colonel and at the cost of one Northern horse, accomplished gently and so far without serious scarring. No wonder it is a day that Bayard remembers and now tells us about.

CHAPTER II

Retreat

"Retreat" takes place during ten days in the summer of 1863, a year after "Ambuscade." Bayard is thirteen.

344:2 **took the mules out** unhitched the mules from the wagon

344:10 **it's been three years now since I have started anywhere** since before the war began

344:18 **Memphis** a large city just across the state border of Tennessee, about 80 miles northwest of the Sartoris plantation. The war had passed through Memphis at about the time of "Ambuscade" and Memphis has been occupied by the Union Army ever since.

344:19 **hit been hid safe since last summer** 'last summer' = the summer of the previous year, not earlier in the present year

344:21 **I am following Colonel Sartoris' instructions as I believe he meant them** Why would Granny want to go to Memphis if Memphis is now occupied by the Northern Army? If Col. Sartoris had instructed Granny to go to Memphis if the situation got too dangerous at home, Granny would not now say she is following his instructions *as I believe he meant them.* Apparently his instructions require interpretation. We already know from "Ambuscade" what these instructions were ('Watch Loosh, because he knows') and we know what Bayard and Ringo understood those words to mean. Now Granny, having watched Loosh for a year since the Yankees arrived, must have concluded that Loosh is no longer reliable, that he is about to go off with the Yankees, perhaps to betray the secret of where the silver is hidden. From *Flags in the Dust* (1973) we know that Granny has relatives and friends in Memphis (that is where she lived until her husband died) and in Memphis she and the boys and the silver will at least be safe. Union law and order is preferable to the present *no* law and order in Yoknapatawpha. So Granny decides to go to Memphis before Loosh asserts his 'freedom.'

345:3 **called the reward on** The Union Army has offered a reward for the capture (or killing) of Col. Sartoris. To offer a reward for an enemy officer was hardly common military practice, but it was not unheard of: Gen. Forrest, for example, had a price on his head. That there is a reward for Col. Sartoris says a good deal about how troublesome his activities must have been to the Union Army.

345:7 **how come you wanter dig hit up tonight** so Loosh won't be able to make off with the trunk while they are sleeping—his last chance now that he knows they will be leaving

345:17 **fiddlesticks** a kind of genteel swearing—meaning 'something that doesn't amount to anything' since the 18th century (Funk 56)

345:35 **your pappy** She means Joby, who is actually Ringo's grandfather. It is not unusual that Ringo would call his grandfather 'Pappy,' because that is what he had heard his parents call him.

345:38 **sitting behind the stove** sitting *beside* the stove. This is a standard Southern expression.

346:6 **chimney** the sleeve-shaped glass wind-shield of the lantern. Unless the soot inside the glass is scrubbed away the lantern will not give off much light.

346:15 **if he knowed hit** if he knows what is good for him

346:39   **Which?**   another way of asking 'what did you say'?

347:7   **bolster case**   a pillowcase for a long, narrow, tube-shaped pillow

347:23   **I dont believe it lacked much of weighing a thousand pounds**   This is Bayard's exaggeration. The chest is indeed heavy (it no doubt contains other valuables besides the silver) but it could not really weigh anything like half a ton. Joby and Loosh would not have been able to carry it up the stairs.

347:29   **Nummine**   nevermind

348:1   **ere a**   any

348:6   **drawing the quilt up over her face and head**   Black people were believed to sleep with their heads covered with a blanket, especially during times of crisis. As for whether they actually did this or it was just a picturesque story (like an ostrich burying its head in the sand) which whites wanted to believe, there is considerable testimony but no firm evidence.

SECTION TWO

348:17   **We put on our Sunday clothes**   They are going visiting so they wear their Sunday clothes—even though they don't expect to arrive for four or five days. We are accustomed to traveling now and take it more casually, but in the nineteenth century a trip was a big occasion, calling for what used to be called one's 'best bib and tucker.'

348:24   **frock coat**   a man's formal coat that comes down to about the knees

348:24   **napless beaver hat**   a top-hat—napless because over time the nap (composed of fuzzy surface fibers) has worn off

348:35   **Nome**   No, ma'am

348:37   **I speck Marse John got the Yankees pretty well cleant out between here and Memphis**   'speck' = suspect; 'cleant' = cleaned. In the Civil War there was no such thing as a line marking the battle-front, with one Army holding

everything on one side of the line and the other Army everything on the other. Armies did take cities and afterward
occupied some of them (Memphis, for example) but most
cities they did not garrison with troops nor did they seriously
try to control the land between the cities they had taken.
Thus the territory between the Sartoris plantation and Memphis, even though it had been overrun by the Union Army,
is not effectively under Union control. It is in that area
where Col. Sartoris's troop is now fighting—harassing Union
forces wherever he encounters them.

349:7 **Aint I tole you** that we were going to have to bring
the trunk back down this morning after we had carried it
upstairs last night

349:11 **Bring that boy** Ringo

349:15 **they were like a man and a mare** Joby is the man,
Granny the mare in the comparison which follows.

349:16 **a blooded mare** a thoroughbred (and hence high-
strung) female horse

349:19 **Then it does happen: the mare kicks him, not vi-
ciously but just enough** In the man-mare parallel, this
non-vicious kick is when Granny says 'If anything ever came
into your mind that you didn't tell somebody inside of ten
minutes, I dont remember it.'

349:22 **he thinks it is over, so he lies or sits on the ground
and cusses the mare a little** In the man-mare parallel, this
is when Joby says 'I done tole um. And I reckin even you
cant dispute hit.'

349:24 **then the mare turns her head and nips him** In the
man-mare parallel, this is when Granny adds the final touch:
'And put the bed back against the wall.' 'Nips him' works in
Faulkner's sentence, since Granny says this 'without moving
anything but her lips.'

350:8 **Then I stopped looking back** Yes, but only in an im-
mediate, literal sense. Isn't the entire book about Bayard
compulsively 'looking back'?

350:15 **Jefferson** the county seat of Yoknapatawpha County, about four miles from Sartoris, according to a map Faulkner drew for *Absalom, Absalom!* (1936)

350:18 **color of dead leaves** light brown, butternut, the natural color of homespun cloth. By this time in the war most Confederate uniforms were either home-made from whatever was available or were captured Yankee uniforms.

350:23 **Mrs Compson** wife of General Compson. The Sartorises and Compsons are the two 'first families' of Yoknapatawpha County. Twentieth-century Compsons are the subject of another Faulkner novel, *The Sound and the Fury* (1929).

350:26 **sack of salt** Salt was regarded as an absolute necessity for humans and animals. It was the one item the Confederacy undertook to supply to civilians. Bayard and Ringo are going after the family's monthly ration, for they will need it for the mules on their trip and they do not want to descend on their Memphis relatives (even in Union territory) without bringing their own supply of salt.

350:27 **Uncle Buck McCaslin** Buck is not Bayard's uncle. 'Uncle' is a courtesy title accorded to respected elderly males (black or white).

350:27 **Uncle Buck McCaslin came hobbling across the square, waving his stick and hollering** This begins a six-page self-contained set-piece, added when Faulkner revised "Retreat" from his original magazine story. The passage ends at 353:32//51:10 with 'Uncle Buck was hobbling across the square, shaking his stick at me and hollering.' About halfway through the passage, at 351:40//48:20, we read 'this was the reason Uncle Buck came hobbling across the square, shaking his stick at me and hollering, or at least why it was Uncle Buck who was hobbling and hollering and shaking the stick.' It would seem Faulkner is making the same statement four times, but that is not right. See entries for 351:40// 48:20, 352:2//48:22, and 353:32//51:10.

350:30 **two McCaslins, Amodeus and Theophilus** Faulkner pronounced these amo-DE-us and theo-FILE-us Muh-CAZ-lin. Amodeus means 'lover of God' in Latin, Theophilus the

same in Greek. The McCaslins are important characters in
another Faulkner novel, *Go Down, Moses* (1942).

350:33 **bottom-land plantation** Bottom-land is the most fertile land if it can be efficiently drained. The McCaslin plantation borders the Tallahatchie River at the northern edge
of Yoknapatawpha County.

351:4 **horse pistol** a large, heavy pistol

351:6 **that Uncle Buck and Uncle Buddy knew this and that
the niggers knew they knew it** like the Northern colonel in
"Ambuscade" knowing the boys were behind Granny's skirt
and Granny knowing he knew it, or like Col. Sartoris later in
"Retreat" knowing the captured Yankees were escaping at
night, or like the Yankees knowing in "Raid" that Granny
was not really asking to get back 110 slaves and mules and
ten chests of silver. There are times when the best available
course of action is simply not to acknowledge something
which is obviously so.

351:14 **interdict** prohibited—in this case, prohibited from
leaving

351:23 **with both of them even He would have lost His
shirt** "Was," the first story in *Go Down, Moses* (1942), is
where we learn in detail about the McCaslins' skill—especially Buddy's—at poker.

351:37 **their niggers were to be freed, not given freedom,
but earning it** Allowing slaves to earn money to buy their
freedom was certainly not a standard practice but it is not
Faulkner's invention either. There were quite a few slave
owners throughout the South who tried plans something
like that—"a thousand others," Faulkner says in *Go Down,
Moses* (1942)—including a well-known experiment very near
to where Faulkner locates the McCaslin plantation on the
map he drew for *Absalom, Absalom!* (1936).

351:39 **there were others besides niggers** who lived on the
McCaslin land, white people whom the slaves called 'white
trash,' poor farmers who 'owned no slaves and some of
whom lived even worse than the slaves'

351:40 **this was the reason** Because these poor whites loyal to the McCaslins made up most of the men Col. Sartoris recruited to form his regiment, and because Col. Sartoris would need their votes if he intended to be colonel of the regiment, he was more or less blackmailed by Buck and Buddy into allowing at least one of them (in spite of their being 'past seventy') to go with the regiment to Virginia.

352:2 **why it was Uncle Buck who was hobbling and hollering and shaking the stick** The point of this sentence (and of the entire scene) is to explain why it was Uncle Buck and not Uncle Buddy who was left behind in Yoknapatawpha and who could therefore be in Jefferson on this day 'hobbling and hollering and shaking the stick.'

352:9 **dirt farmers** a sarcastic term for one-horse small-scale non-slave-owning farmers existing at or below the poverty level. They stir up the dirt but don't manage to raise much except dust.

352:10 **'white trash'** another contemptuous term. It means not simply poor white people but those who were stereotypically shiftless, lazy, irresponsible.

352:15 **poor hill land** not very fertile land—in contrast to the McCaslins' own rich bottom-land

352:22 **raise** create and equip

352:22 **take to Virginia** In the beginning of the war most of the fighting was in and around Virginia. Col. Sartoris's regiment got there in time to take part in the first big battle, First Manassas, July 21, 1861 (known in the North as the First Battle of Bull Run), an impressive Confederate victory.

352:24 **they were past seventy** Obviously 70 is old to be a soldier, but there were more than just a few active soldiers in both armies who were this old and even older.

353:6 **Second Manassas** Second Battle of Bull Run, also a Confederate victory

353:6 **the men did demote Father** Officers in the Confederate Army below the rank of General were voted on (to be retained or replaced) by their men in yearly elections. The election demoting Col. Sartoris was held 'the following summer after Second Manassas' (353:5//50:10), a battle that took place Aug 29-Sept 1, 1862. Perhaps a partial explanation for the reason he was demoted may be found at 330:7//16:20, where Father explains that the missing volume from the complete set of Dumas was 'lost from his pocket at Manassas (retreating, he said).' If the Col. Sartoris we see in action elsewhere *did* retreat, doubtless it was done in order to avoid unnecessary losses, but that would not have prevented his regiment from regarding it as less than heroic, especially in view of the fact that the battle was a major victory for the Confederacy. Still, if Father were not demoted until after Second Manassas, he could not have been leading his new unit in Tennessee-Mississippi earlier that summer of 1862 (as he was in "Ambuscade"). The contradiction here cannot be reconciled if we insist on the real date for Second Manassas. If we could take Father's demotion to have occurred sometime after *First* Manassas (July 1861)—even as much as eight months after—there would be no problem.

353:9 **his irregular cavalry** a cavalry force of any size not officially attached to some larger military unit. The functions of such troops were to harass the enemy in whatever ways its leader could improvise and to conduct raids to obtain materials in short supply.

353:31 **so that now Uncle Buddy was a sergeant in Tennant's brigade in Virginia and Uncle Buck was hobbling across the square** Faulkner nodded here. If the McCaslin contingent resigned and came home when Father did, then presumably Uncle Buddy would have come back too and would not still be in Virginia. The point of Faulkner's sentence (and the insertion from 350:23//46:21 through 353:35//51:12) is to explain why it was Buck and not Buddy who was in Jefferson to hobble across the square, but he apparently forgot that Buddy would have come back to Mississippi with the others.

353:32 **Tennant's brigade** Northern Army units were generally known by number and State of origin, the Eleventh

Illinois Cavalry, for example. Southern Army units were generally known by their commander's name, as with Barksdale's Brigade. Tennant's brigade thus is a perfectly possible name for an outfit Uncle Buddy might have served with, but there was no real brigade (or regiment or company) commanded by a Tennant (or by any name similar to it).

353:35 **By Godfrey** a euphemism for 'By God'

353:38 **people had begun to stop along the walk and listen to him, like they always did, not smiling so he could see it** Uncle Buck is an eccentric but not a fool, and no one thinks he is a fool. Fortunately for him, he lived at a time and place where eccentrics were not simply tolerated but were appreciated. Today, unless he toned down his way of speaking (i.e., unless he talked more like the way other people do), his opinions would be unlikely to be taken seriously. As Faulkner often stressed in interviews: change is not always progress.

354:3 **out of his own pocket** Col. Sartoris paid for equipping the regiment he organized.

354:6 **a congress of politicians and fools** a group stupid enough to meddle with matters they didn't understand, and so voted Col. Sartoris out of command

354:12 **thinking about Louvinia standing there on the porch with Father's old hat on** We don't learn why Bayard would think this at this moment until 372:33//79:16.

354:17 **Stonewall Jackson** Confederate General Thomas J. Jackson, second only to Robert E. Lee in rank, ability, and loyalty of his men; earned the sobriquet "Stonewall" at First Manassas as a dying tribute from General B.E. Bee as he rallied his troops (Pratt 31).

354:17 **spitting distance of Washington** Most of the first battles of the war were fought in the hundred-or-so miles between the capital of the Confederacy (Richmond, Virginia) and the capital of the United States (Washington, D.C.). Shortly before First Manassas some Confederate forces actually reached the Potomac River at a point just across from

Washington—so close to the capital that the pontoon bridge over the river had to be taken in each night in order to protect against a raid on the city.

354:19   **voted him down to major**   This is the same election Buck mentions at 354:34//52:27 when the men 'voted him out of his own private regiment in kindness, so he could come home.' Apparently Col. Sartoris, if he could no longer be the commander, preferred to come home and form another outfit where he *could* be commander.

354:26   **all you got to say is 'I'm John Sartoris' boy ...'**   See entry for 487:29//247:4 where the implications of Buck's statement are spelled out.

354:27   **rabbits, hunt the canebrake**   cowards, find a place to hide. A rabbit is a notoriously timid animal, a canebrake is a dense jungle of reeds growing too close together for a horse or man to continue the chase.

354:28   **bluebellied sons of bitches**   'bluebellied' by analogy with 'yellowbellied' (cowardly); 'blue' rather than 'yellow' because Union Army uniforms were blue

354:33   **Hell's skillet**   American profanity is now reduced to about four all-purpose words. There was a time (up to about 1900) in America when swearing was not so standardized. People made up their own expressions to fit the occasion and their own personalities. 'Hell's skillet' obviously is a version of 'hell.' It seems to zero in on that part of hell which actually does the frying.

354:34   **John Sartoris is a damn fool**   and

354:38   **John Sartoris is a damned confounded selfish coward**   Buck is speaking ironically. He does not believe Col. Sartoris is a fool or selfish or a coward. He admires Col. Sartoris's abilities as a fighter very much. We know this because Buck's words make no sense if they are taken literally. It is true that Col. Sartoris does not stay at home when he comes back from Virginia, but his reason is not because he is afraid the Yankees might get him there; it is because he has raised still another batch of men to go out and fight the Yankees.

These men are not to protect him; they are 'scouring all up and down the country, finding Yankees.' They are not locating Yankees in order to 'dodge' them when they get 'within a hundred foot' of them; they are on search and destroy missions. And Col. Sartoris has been so successful in his efforts that the Yankees have offered a reward for his capture.

355:18 **It's not a regiment, sir** A regiment on paper and at full strength had 1,000 men. In practice at any given moment most regiments had about 500. Col. Sartoris has only about 50.

355:20 **We had a prisoner last week who said he had more than a thousand** If the enemy could believe that Col. Sartoris, with 50 men, had more than a thousand, clearly Col. Sartoris's troop must have severely disrupted Union Army operations.

355:22 **Colonel Sartoris didn't fight, he just stole horses** There is probably considerable truth in this, for sometimes the most valuable service an irregular cavalry troop could perform was to obtain horses by capturing them from the enemy.

355:29 **"... How old are you, boy?"**
"Fourteen," I said.
"We aint fourteen yit," Ringo said. "But we will be in September ... " This is one of the most important pieces of information for establishing a timetable for the novel—if we know or remember something about nineteenth and early twentieth century American speech, something which Faulkner obviously knew: Today a boy would not fudge in stating his age. He is thirteen until his birthday, then he is fourteen, and that's all there is to it. Not so a hundred years ago. A boy could say he was 'thirteen, going on fourteen.' Technically that meant he was past the halfway point between birthdays. If he wanted to emphasize how young he was, he could say he was 'just thirteen'—even if it was the day before his fourteenth birthday. If he wanted to suggest

how grown up he was, he could say 'almost fourteen'—even if he had just turned thirteen. Sometimes, as here, he might not include the 'almost.' Bayard overstates his age again in "Raid" (377:28//86:20). Since "Retreat" and "Raid" both take place during the same summer, and since we learn in "Raid" that the date is August 1863 (395:10//112:9), and since we know from the present passage that Bayard's birthday is in September, we have most of the information necessary to arrive at a solid chronology for the action of the novel. We also can figure out that Bayard and Ringo were born in September 1849.

355:32 **if we live and nothing happens** a conventional Southern "knock-on-wood" formula

356:4 **another basket with a napkin over it** This basket is from the Compsons and it is not another food basket. It contains rose cuttings for Granny to take to Memphis. The napkin is to protect the cuttings from the sun. Pre-twentieth-century Southern roses were not grafted and could be started by planting a branch (called a 'cutting') clipped from an existing bush. The resulting bush produced more but smaller blooms than our present patented roses. The usual color was yellow. Since most rose gardens were limited to local varieties, a gift in Alabama of an unusual Mississippi rose would be very much appreciated.

356:9 **Suppose they dont never get done fighting** an indirect way of saying 'suppose we don't ever come back here'

356:31 **snuff box** a small, round, cardboard box with a tin lid. Until about World War II and the introduction of plastic packaging, the containers almost everyone used for saving small items were wooden cigar boxes, flask-shaped pipe-tobacco tins, and round snuff boxes.

357:2 **Granny would not come inside to sleep** She was guarding the trunk with the silver.

357:9 **somebody got down** a soldier got off his horse

357:10 **a pine knot** a resinous knot from a pine branch used as a torch. It will burn fiercely for maybe half an hour.

357:10 **we saw the gray** we realized they were Confederate and not enemy soldiers

357:12 **Cockrum** a real town south of Memphis, on the road between 'Jefferson' and Memphis

357:24 **they could almost force him to come in and surrender** To hold a soldier's mother-in-law or son hostage would be a dishonorable thing to do according to rules of civilized warfare. That such a possibility could even occur to the Confederate officer suggests that he must have experienced Union Army behavior which *was* outside the accepted limits of civilized war.

357:27 **My experience with Yankees has evidently been different from yours** She is thinking of the gentlemanly Union colonel in "Ambuscade."

358:11 **I saw six men running in the next field** It becomes clear in a few lines that these running men are Confederates who are being chased by a larger number of Union soldiers.

358:12 **a dustcloud coming fast** One person walking even slowly along a dusty road would stir up a small dust cloud. Many people (or animals) going fast along the road would stir up a big cloud.

358:13 **Them folks look like they trying to make the Yankees take they stock, running hit up and down the big road in broad daylight like that** Joby assumes the dust is caused by Southerners driving farm animals along the road. Actually (as we learn almost immediately) it is from mounted and dismounted Union soldiers chasing the six Confederates.

358:17 **jumped the ditch with pistols in their hands like when you run with a stick of stove wood balanced on your palm** awkwardly holding their pistols in front of them, pointed upward to limit the danger to one another in the event of an accidental discharge

358:21 **holding the mules** pulling back on the reins to keep the mules from moving

358:22 **whiffletrees** small wooden crossbars, usually called 'singletrees,' one behind each mule, between the mule and the front of a wagon. It's a part of an exquisite solution for transforming animal strength into controllable forward motion. As the draft animal moves forward, its energy is gathered by means of a flexible leather harness running back on both sides from a restraining collar to the ends of a whiffletree. The whiffletree is attached by a central swivel to a large doubletree, which extends equally on either side of the wagon's tongue, to which it is attached by a central swivel. The axle of the wagon's front wheels is attached to the wagon by means of a vertical pin through the root of the tongue, which allows the wheels to turn right or left as guided by the tongue. The tongue extends forward between the two animals, who are attached to its forward end, not for the transmittal of energy but for steering. The energy of the animals' forward motion is gathered by the collar and harness, passed through the whiffletrees to the doubletree and thence to the wagon. The swivel arrangement dampens the variable movements of the animals, providing a more-or-less straight and steady movement of the wagon down its path. Steering is managed by moving the animals' heads in the direction desired by tugging the reins attached through halters to bits in their mouths, or by the universal voice command of 'gee' for 'go right' or 'haw' for 'go left.'

358:23 **his eyes like two eggs** like two fried eggs—wide open and with large pupils

358:26 **the five men** five Union soldiers—not the six Confederates who were being chased

358:28 **unfastened the traces** unhooked the chains on both sides of both mules which connect them (by way of the whiffletrees) to the wagon

358:30 **they just took the mules out of the wagon** unhitched the mules from the wagon

358:33 **the mules came out of the dust soaring like hawks** after a short time we saw the mules come back out of the cloud of dust, bucking off their riders with long, soaring leaps

359:17 **rope halter** a part of the harness which slips over the animal's head—used to hold or lead or control it. A good halter is made of leather, but rope will do.

359:18 **a pipe still burning on the ground** someone has just left—obviously in a hurry. We never learn anything more about whoever this was, although it may well have been the Confederate troops we see being chased in 358:11//57:28. Indeed, they may have been members of Col. Sartoris's troop, for the Colonel takes care to return the horse to the stable, where the pipe remains on the ground (361:25// 62:29).

359:25 **we couldn't hear anything either but the old horse's insides** The horse's stomach is growling—not an unusual occurrence, especially with an older horse.

359:29 **Tinney and Old Hundred** the names of the Sartoris mules. See entry for 393:25//109:27 for the meaning of their names. Every other time these two mules are mentioned their names are given the other way around. Here Faulkner is setting up, but not giving away, the joke which makes Granny's raid and subsequent mule-stealing enterprise a success.

359:33 **You reckon I aint followed them mules all my life and cant tell they tracks when I see um** For those of us who live in cities, it might seem impossible that anyone would be able to distinguish one mule's tracks from another's. People can become enormously skilled in all sorts of seemingly impossible activities, and some of these people are farmers.

Also, if Ringo had worked these two mules as often as what he says here implies, what does that tell us about the Sartoris plantation? Was the single family of slaves whose names we know the only slaves on it? If so, it must not have been a cotton plantation. And if it wasn't, what was the source of Col. Sartoris's income—which had to have been considerable. "An Odor of Verbena" notes that Col. Sartoris was not a lawyer (as his prototype, Col. Falkner, William

Faulkner's great-grandfather was). These questions are never answered—in *The Unvanquished* or anyplace else.

360:3 **the slow hollow repercussion of wood** the sound of the horses' feet on the wooden bridge

360:32 **a mesmerised flame** mesmerized = a nineteenth century word for 'hypnotized.' Jupiter (usually the essence of speed and power, a flashing thunderbolt, but now motionless) seems to Bayard's eyes a mesmerized flame, temporarily (but only temporarily) transfixed, ready to burst into power again at his rider's command. 'Mesmerised flame' is an extraordinarily charged, almost lover-like description for a horse standing still.

360:37 **left her sitting there in that wagon in the middle of the road** The report apparently had reached Col. Sartoris that Granny had started for Memphis and did not make it.

361:8 **pone of bread** piece of cornbread

361:10 **After a while** Bayard hesitates before answering because he can't quickly think of a way to say how they got the horse without having to tell his father that they *stole* it.

361:14 **all of a sudden they all began to whoop and holler** They are teasing Col. Sartoris, reminding him that he can't very well discipline the boys for having stolen a horse, because stealing horses is what Col. Sartoris and his men do, too. 'Dont you say a word, Colonel.'

361:27 **sat Jupiter** sat on Jupiter, who was standing still

361:37 **I tole you they wasn't no Yankees gonter stop Granny** Ringo "tells her" this at 346:13//40:13, when they watch the trunk being dug up: 'I bet if she stayed here wouldn't no Yankee nor nothing else bother that trunk nor Marse John neither if he knowed it.' Ringo is here responding to the fact that the Colonel is returning only with horses, Yankee horses, and not Granny. If the Yankees had stopped Granny, she would have been rescued by the Colonel, but since he had obviously gone to where the Yankees were, as evidenced by the horses he was bringing back, and returned without Granny, she must have evaded them and probably had made it all the way to Memphis now. This *could* be wishful thinking, of course, covering Ringo's sense of guilt for having forgotten her, but this explanation fits the elements of characterization of both Ringo and Granny, as we see them team up later.

362:7 **he would whirl completely around until his off side faced Ringo** Horses normally are trained to accept riders only from their left side. The 'off' side is the right side. This horse, because he is blind in his left eye (as we learn shortly) obviously has been trained to be mounted from the 'wrong' side.

362:14 **his near eye** his left eye, the side that custom dictates as the mounting side

362:20 **we stayed there in the trees all day** They are in enemy territory.

362:26 **the nigh side** the near side, the left side

362:33 **shoat** a young pig

363:14 **boring** pulling against the bit, wanting to run faster

363:15 **drive** go faster, drive forcefully with his legs

363:24 *We're holding Jupiter* We're keeping up with Jupiter.

363:26 **he still had Jupiter on the bit** He was still holding Jupiter back, not allowing him to run full speed.

364:5 **in the very time which nourishes the believing of the incredible** It is taking Bayard a moment or so to take in what is happening—since it is something so remarkable as to be called 'incredible.' The time which nourishes the apparently unbelievable is the time during which it takes place, often mere seconds which may be relived often enough to occupy a large part of a lifetime. Compare the consumption of life with that of Gail Hightower's daily formalized recollection in *Light In August* (1932) of a moment that occurred before his birth. There is a limit to what a child can assimilate as it happens because of his or her inexperience; but, given time—and Bayard is recollecting this as an adult—he can believe what others might regard as unbelievable, not only because he witnessed it in its nourishing moment but because he now has enough experience to realize that it *was* remarkable, rare, unusual, incredible.

364:15 **muskets all stacked carefully and neatly and nobody within fifty feet of them** The first thing a soldier learns is never to place his rifle on the ground, because the barrel or firing mechanism might get dirt or dust in it and later fail to fire. Each rifle has a small hook (called a stacking swivel) on the underside of the barrel. Three (or more) rifles can be hooked together to form a tripod which will stand by itself. Forming such a tripod is called 'stacking the rifles' and that is the way rifles not being held are kept off the ground. The drawing for "Retreat" (344//37) shows such stacked rifles. The problem, however, is that none of the rifles can be withdrawn from the tripod unless all are withdrawn at the same time, calmly and without jerking. It simply can't be done in a hurry or without everyone cooperating. Considering that it takes nearly a minute to load and prepare a Civil War rifle to fire once it is in the shooter's hands, if soldiers whose rifles are stacked are caught by surprise, there is not much they can do except surrender—regardless of how small the armed party which surprises them. There were many cases of embarrassing surrenders during the Civil War caused by stacked rifles. Confederate General Jeb Stuart is supposed once to have captured forty-nine of the enemy all by himself, because they stacked their rifles and neglected to post adequate sentries.

365:17 **in their underclothes** Most Confederate soldiers probably did not wear underwear, certainly not the heavy garments issued to Union soldiers as part of their uniforms—long, white underwear, coincidentally called 'union suits' because they were of *one* piece, with shirts and drawers joined together. That Northern soldiers wore underwear seemed treated as a matter of curiosity by Southerners, and Faulkner's scene grows out of that interest.

365:23 **shooting at us for ghosts** Black people and old
women were believed to be superstitious, and at night men
in long white underwear might well look like ghosts to them.

365:36 **I have a better plan than that** The usual practice
with prisoners (at least during the first half of the war) was
to parole them. 'Parole' is a French word that means 'word
of honor.' The prisoner would give his word of honor he
would not fight any more, and then he would be released
and allowed to go home where he would remain until he was
'exchanged' for an enemy prisoner, at which point he was
free to fight again. All of this required considerable book-
keeping and complicated negotiations. Also, not everyone's
word of honor proved trustworthy. By the end of the war
the parole system was no longer operating.

365:36 **One that Joe Johnston will thank us for** General
Joseph Johnston was by then the Confederate military commander in Mississippi. He had said that the most acute military shortages were shoes and blankets. That takes care of
the straightforward meaning, but I suspect Col. Sartoris intended something else, too. Any Union officer incompetent
enough to have his men stack their rifles and then not post
adequate sentries is not an officer the South should want to
hold prisoner. He should be released quickly—so he will
again be in charge of Union troops, for he will surely do
something stupid again.

366:5 **Then he stopped** One of his men told him not to
build up the fire. They planned to escape and wanted complete darkness.

366:14 **moccasins** water moccasins—poisonous snakes which
are sometimes called cotton-mouths

SECTION THREE

367:15 **"I borrowed them"** . . .
   "Who from?" . . .

... "I dont know. There was nobody there ... " This is the way Bayard and Ringo explained how they obtained their horse (361:10//62:12): "We borrowed it." "Who from?" ... "We aint know. The man wasn't there."

367:22 **it was still hot; the rosin was still cooking out of the front steps at six o'clock** If it is that hot, "Retreat" must take place during the summer. 'Rosin' = the sticky sap which oozes from not yet completely dried wood.

367:34 **Dont run, now** The 'now' does not mean 'at this moment'; it is an admonition, as in 'Now don't do anything I wouldn't do.'

368:4 **Father came in running, with his boots in his hand** An Army officer is, by definition, a gentleman. This is a concept that was (and to a certain extent still is) taken seriously. Part of the gentleman-officer code (on both sides, at least at the beginning of the war) was that an officer could lead his men in an orderly retreat but he could not do *anything* that could be construed as running from the enemy *if he were in uniform.* The last part of the uniform to be put on was his boots. Thus an officer in boots was in uniform; an officer not in boots was not in uniform. Col. Sartoris is free to run from the Yankees on this day because he is *carrying* his boots.

368:7 **carbine** a small rifle, preferred by cavalrymen because it is lighter, shorter, and easier to handle on a horse than a conventional long rifle

368:7 **carrying it in one hand like a lamp** raised, in front, slightly off to side, to protect against accidental discharge. Like a lamp because, if directly in front, those behind would get no light, and raised, so the light would spread over the ground for all.

368:21 **threw down with the carbine and shot at us point-blank with one hand like it was a pistol** The wording here is perhaps misleading: 'threw down with the carbine' means that he jumped quickly off his horse, holding the carbine; 'shot at us point blank with one hand like it was a pistol' means that he pretended to shoot at them by pointing his hand, not the carbine, *as if* he were firing a pistol. It cannot mean that he actually did shoot, for at such short range it would have been impossible for him to miss. Also, a soldier—even a Yankee—would not have been likely to shoot two thirteen year-old boys, one black, just because Col. Sartoris had succeeded in getting away.

368:25 **Louvinia kept on trying to tell us about it** Louvinia is the family story-teller. She begins transforming events into stories even while the events are still being acted out.

368:26 **smoke beginning to come out of the downstairs windows** The Yankees in their frustration at not having captured Col. Sartoris have set fire to the house.

368:40 **Boots and pistols** Col. Sartoris is asking Louvinia to hand him his boots and pistols, but he is also making a play on the cavalry command to prepare to ride: 'Boots and saddle.'

369:1 **Take care of Miss Rosa and the chillen** It was traditional to put trusts to slaves *in words*. There is a considerable history of such trusts being faithfully carried out in spite of great difficulties. So Col. Sartoris's words here are more than just an appropriate parting remark to Louvinia.

369:1 **I go to the door but I just a nigger** I tried to cover his escape by lying to them at the door, but they didn't believe me.

369:10 **Granny turned to run back toward the house** Bayard consistently avoids telling us very much about the most dramatic of the actions he witnessed or participated in. It is as if he closes his eyes and ears to (or blocks out his memory of) violence. Consider what he reports (or really what he fails to report) immediately after he and Ringo fire at the Yankee in "Ambuscade," about the actual capture of the Union soldiers in "Retreat," about the blowing up of the bridge and their wagon going into the river in "Raid," about the killing of Granny in "Riposte," about Grumby shooting at him and his shooting Grumby in "Vendée" ('I reckon I heard the sound, and I reckon I must have heard the bullets . . . but I

dont remember it. I just remember the two bright flashes . . .
and now my arm came up . . . and the pistol was level and
steady as a rock'), and when Redmond fired his two shots in
"Verbena" ('I heard no bullet. Maybe I didn't even hear the
explosion'). This refusal (or inability) to look closely at violence is no doubt part of Bayard's character, but perhaps we
shouldn't make too much of it, since it is also a consistent
characteristic of most of Faulkner's writing. He never describes the scene of Temple's rape by corncob in *Sanctuary*
(1931), either, or Joe Christmas's slitting Joanna Burden's
throat in *Light in August* (1932). Faulkner is obviously more
interested in the effects of violence on his characters than in
the violence itself.

369:33 **gonter general me to Jordan** going to lead him to
the 'River Jordan' where on the other side, the Bible has told
him, he will find the 'promised land,' the 'land of milk and
honey'

370:7 **whut they tole him cant be true** Yes, what Loosh understands 'free' will mean for him is ultimately no less naive
than Bayard's and Ringo's innocent understanding of 'free'
before they shot at the Yankee soldier in "Ambuscade."

370:15 **we were all three saying it, Granny and me and
Ringo, saying it together: "The bastuds!"** Clearly there
must have been extreme provocation for Granny to use the
word 'bastards.' She is outraged because the Yankees have
burned the Sartoris house and stolen her silver. War among
civilized nations had traditionally been limited to contests between armies. Civilians were spectators, not principals. It was
Northern Generals Sherman and Grant who, in Mississippi,
changed forever the character of war by introducing the
concept of '*total* war'—destroying private property, punishing civilians. Granny (as did many others) finds this change
in the rules barbaric, unconscionable.

CHAPTER III

Raid

"Raid" takes place from 7 August to 21 or 22 August 1863 when Bayard is thirteen. It is a month-or-so after "Retreat"—just long enough for Granny to learn where the Union Army had gone which carried away the silver. We know "Raid" occurs in August of 1863, because that is the date on the Union Army repossession order (395:10//112:9). We know Bayard and Ringo are still thirteen because their birthdays won't be until September.

371:1 **pokeberry juice** a pinkish lavender substitute for ink, made from the berries of a weed

371:15 **the hat and the parasol and the hand mirror** essential equipment for a Southern lady. Since the Sartoris house has been burned, Granny has to borrow these items from Mrs. Compson. The purpose of the parasol is to shield her face from the sun and thus keep her skin white, for one outward sign that a woman was a lady was her untanned skin, which testified that her husband (or father) was well-to-do and she did not have to perform any chores out of doors. The surprising thing in the passage is that Granny did not also borrow gloves. We have to assume she was outside and therefore wearing her gloves when the Yankees set fire to the house, for white hands were as important to a lady as a white face and neck.

371:18   *Colonel Nathaniel G. Dick*   the name of the gentlemanly Union Colonel in "Ambuscade"

372:1   **nailing them to the barn door like two coon hides**
Raccoon fur has some value. A hunter skins the animal and then stretches the hide by pegging it to a wall and letting it dry. Louvinia's exaggeration here anticipates what Bayard and Ringo will later do with Grumby's body—peg it on the door like a coon's, as Buck explicitly recognizes (445:20// 186:4).

372:4   **Joby's cabin**   Joby's and Louvinia's cabin must have been the best of the slave cabins, since it is the one Granny and Bayard move into when the big house is burned. Joby and Louvinia obviously have moved to a different cabin. Whether there are *many* other cabins (i.e., whether the Sartorises have a cotton plantation with many field hands or just a country home with only the one family of house servants) is never made clear.

372:16   **Then what?**   If the Yankees should think it was a gun, what would we do then? Granny has learned from her experiences. The gun, even when it was capable of shooting, did not stop the Yankees from stealing their mules in "Retreat," but her being a lady did result in her being treated decently by the colonel in "Ambuscade." So this time Granny will rely for protection on what has worked in the past: the symbols of feminine gentility—hat, parasol, and hand mirror.

372:33   **Louvinia began to act just like Uncle Buck McCaslin did the morning we started to Memphis**   This passage explains one in "Retreat" (354:12//52:2) where Bayard thinks about Louvinia while Uncle Buck is talking—a passage that could not be fully understood then because we don't learn the basis for the comparison until now. Not telling what a reader needs to know at the time it would make it easy to understand, perhaps even obvious, is a hallmark of Faulkner's style. He tells you what you need to know when it will do the most good, have the greatest impact, provided you have been paying attention. This suspension, this elliptical style, is one of his greatest gifts, for it is precisely how everyone learns what's worth remembering, through accretion and recollection.

373:4 **the ash pile and the chimneys** all that is now left of the Sartoris house

373:15 **team** a pair of horses or mules (or oxen or goats or any animals that can be hitched together to work as a pair)

373:35 **that didn't count with us, anymore than the difference in the color of our skins counted** Bayard no doubt means this and no doubt believes it, and his words do point in the general direction of truth but, even with Bayard and Ringo, white and black are not fully equal: in their war games behind the smokehouse Bayard got to be the Southern General twice to Ringo's once, and although they slept in the same room Bayard had a bed and Ringo a pallet on the floor.

373:37 **what one of us had done or seen that the other had not** thus Ringo's concern about coconut cake

373:40 **I know now it was more than that with Ringo** 'it' = what counted

373:40 **though neither of us were to see the proof of my belief for some time yet and we were not to recognise it as such even then** Obviously, the reader is being alerted to be on the lookout for this proof of Bayard's belief (that something more than just being one-up is what counted with Ringo), while at the same time being warned that it won't be easy to discover, since neither Bayard nor Ringo recognized it as such when they themselves encountered it. Although no later passage can be found which perfectly fulfills the demands of this proof, it seems clearly to anticipate the final separation of Bayard and Ringo as companions close enough so that competition of this nature might matter. The next passage amplifies this point.

374:3 **as if Ringo felt it too and that the railroad, the rushing locomotive which he hoped to see symbolised it** The rest of the paragraph spells out what 'it' is in this sentence: a blind, reasonless impulse on the part of the slaves to leave their homes, seeking they don't really know what—except that they hope it will be better than what they have known. Faulkner calls this hope a 'delusion' and what they will find a 'doom'—a judgment which the history of black people for the hundred years after the Civil War unfortunately supports. Perhaps the fact that slaves had sometimes been assisted in escaping to the North by an abolitionist network called 'the underground railroad' has something to do with a railroad being an appropriate symbol for their impulse to find a better life.

374:5 **the impulse to move** Slaves were legally free once the Union Army arrived. This was the substance and guarantee of Lincoln's January 1863 Emancipation Proclamation. In some localities the newly-freed slaves left their homes en masse. There were many reasons for their leaving and any reader can readily imagine what most of them were. There is one reason, however, which some readers might not know: one of the differences between a slave and a white had always been that a white, being free, could move about without first having to get permission from anyone; consequently many now-free slaves wanted to test their freedom by proving they actually could take off without permission and without special papers. Eventually at least half returned to the general area they had left—many (like Loosh) to work for their former masters.

374:7 **seeking a delusion** Whatever it was the newly-freed slaves thought they were seeking (the 'promised land' which they understood was on the other side of the River Jordan), they did not find it. For the 'good life' one needs money, land, education, a job, a stable society; but these were not automatically conferred upon black people when slavery was abolished or when Northern armies destroyed their masters' property.

374:7 **a delusion, a dream** These are not synonyms; they

are in this case opposites. When Ringo said 'if you dremp hit, hit cant be a lie' (333:12//21:9), we knew his faith in dreams was naive. So too, it will turn out, is the slaves' faith in their dream.

374:15 **blind to everything but a hope and a doom** like Bayard and Ringo behind the smokehouse acting out their play war as a 'shield between ourselves and reality, between us and fact and doom.' 'Reality' in both cases is 'doom.'

374:21 **even our own dust moving ahead of us** the horses are going so slow they don't even keep up with the dust drifting forward from their hooves

374:26 **here they come again to git these uns** 'these uns' = their borrowed horses. Ringo thinks the Yankees are about to take their present team—as they had in "Retreat."

375:8 **gins** pronounced "jins"; cotton gins, a shortening of 'engines,' practicable machines for separating cotton seeds from cotton fiber. Gins were adopted on a wide-scale in the early 1800s. One gin could do the work of fifty men or women and made cotton for the first time a commercially profitable crop. Before then cotton had been more expensive than silk.

375:16 **I dont see no dust** The marching slaves are resting before starting again to walk in the night when it is cooler.

375:26 **I began to smell them** Those who want to believe Faulkner had his share of racial prejudice point to passages like this one. At one time it was the nearly unanimous testimony of Southern whites, and many Northern ones as well, that black people (and their cabins and blankets) had a distinctive and unpleasant odor. Although this impression persisted well into the middle of this century, it seems to have diminished to insignificance today. Yet it is hard to believe that so many otherwise-honorable whites would have been lying about or imagining something that was not so. Apparently there must once have been some real, physical, non-subjective justification and explanation for this phenomenon. The fact that we can't now identify its causes doesn't mean it was not once real. The whole matter is difficult to explain. Certainly no one has yet done so satisfactorily. Easy explanations don't work, since both the diet and sanitary habits of poor persons of both races were essentially the same. The subject is usually self-consciously ignored—which perhaps avoids offending anyone but does not get us closer to the truth. The following are at least some of the relevant facts: 1) all people have odors—we all have individual odors which dogs, for example, recognize—but most human noses are not capable of identifying most of these smells; 2) a few people do have a distinctive and unpleasant odor which almost everyone notices; 3) certain foods (garlic, for example) produce a distinctive smell on the part of those who prepare and eat them, but poor persons of both races had essentially the same diet; 4) the smell attributed to black people was often specifically distinguished from the smell of sweat; it was described as a kind of musty smell, more insistent in their houses than on their persons; 5) people who sweat in the sun and do not bathe and change to clean clothes will smell of sweat; but this is true of whites as well as black persons, and the washing habits of poor whites were no better than those of slaves or, later, freedmen, although it may well be that the amount and type of labor required of black people may have been a contributing factor.

376:14 **"Who do you belong to?" Granny said. Then she didn't answer** How *can* she answer this question? Granny words it as if she still believes the woman is owned by some white person, but the reason the woman is on the road is that she is demonstrating that she does *not* belong to someone else. Granny is a decent woman trying to be helpful, but she hasn't really understood what the slaves are doing or why they are doing it.

376:26 **hunkered down and swaying on her hams** 'hams' = thighs; 'hunkering' (comes from 'haunches') is a way of squatting, flatfooted, buttocks between the heels and almost but not quite touching the ground. This is still a common way of resting for people (men and women) brought up in rural areas.

376:31 **gum and cypress** two kinds of trees

376:39 **Were the others there in that bottom?** Granny asks Ringo this because black persons were thought to have extraordinary powers of vision—especially at night. Faulkner seems to have believed this, for it comes up in several of his books, *Intruder in the Dust* (1948) in particular.

377:4 **That was the morning of the sixth day** Coming after 'it was like passing through [a country] where everybody had died at the same moment' (375:34//83:30) the wording here has to be an ironic reminder of the final verse of the first chapter of *Genesis*: "And God saw everything that he had made, and behold, it was very good. And the evening and the morning were the sixth day."

SECTION TWO

377:15 **Hawkhurst** the name of the Hawks' plantation. A 'hurst' is a wooded hill.

377:26 **the place where the house should have been and there was no house there** Not long after the Confederate surrender at Vicksburg a considerable part of the Union Army was ordered east and north to anticipated battles at Chickamauga and Chattanooga in eastern Tennessee. Early August 1863 would be about the time this Army would have passed through Hawkhurst in northwestern Alabama. This Union march was notorious for its gratuitous destruction of civilian property—a kind of trial run for Sherman's later march through Georgia to the sea. Since the present time in "Raid" is mid-August 1863, we are apparently to understand that the house at Hawkhurst had been burned only a very short time before Granny and Bayard and Ringo arrived.

377:28 **I was just fourteen then** Bayard may say he is fourteen, but he is anticipating his birthday. He won't really be fourteen until the following month, September. He similarly overstated his age in "Retreat" and will do so (again in August) in "An Odor of Verbena." In "Ambuscade," in the summer of 1862, Bayard was twelve. In "Retreat," the following summer, he was thirteen and Ringo said they would both be fourteen in September. "Raid" takes place in August of the same year as "Retreat."

378:1 **Jingus** Slave-owners sometimes gave their slaves classical names—Caesar, Pompey, Venus, etc. Jingus is short for (and a corruption of) Genghis Khan.

378:25 **stob** a short stake—in this case to mark the place where the shadow must fall in order for it to be time for the train

378:35 **Jingus' old hat bouncing** Jingus stood close beside the track and, when the train went by, extended his arm and let go of his hat. The air displaced by the fast-moving train formed a stream whose up-draft kept the hat floating on top of it (like feathers riding above a hurricane). When the train had passed by, the hat was sucked into the vacuum behind the last car and fell to the middle of the track.

378:37 **piles of black straws** the charred remains of burned railway ties. They had been used to make fires to heat the rails so they could be bent around trees. This effectively took the railroad out of operation permanently, for the South had no rolling mills and thus no way for rails once twisted to be straightened out and re-used.

378:38 **cut** the long, narrow gash in the woods where the trees had been felled to make a path for the railroad tracks

379:2 **had taken each rail and tied it around a tree** This is historically true. Southerners called these rails-around-trees 'Sherman's neckties.'

379:11 **Bobolink** an appropriate bird-name for a horse belonging to a family named Hawk

379:13 **Drusilla riding astride like a man** Women in the 19th century (and before) were expected to ride side-saddle. To ride astride was considered not merely unfeminine but actually obscene. A woman was arrested in New Orleans just a few years before the Civil War for outraging public decency by riding astride.

379:20 **crokersack** a Southern term for a burlap bag

379:24 **She was not tall, it was the way she stood and walked** which made her seem taller than she really was—like Col. Sartoris (325:16//9:28): 'He was not big; it was just the things he did, that we knew he was doing . . . that made him seem big to us.'

379:25 **She had on pants, like a man** Remember that Granny was able to hide and protect Bayard and Ringo in "Ambuscade" *because* she was wearing a skirt. Advantages as well as inconveniences go with traditional women's clothing and roles. Drusilla eventually pays a severe price for her attempt to transform herself into an 'almost-man.' The kind of clothes Drusilla wears will continue to be an issue in the book. The most obvious example is, of course, the trunk of dresses her mother brings to her in "Skirmish at Sartoris," but even more interesting is her yellow ball gown in "An Odor of Verbena" (see entry for 468:24//219:8).

379:25 **She was the best woman rider in the country** Bayard even at fourteen admires and is attracted to Drusilla. Earlier on the page he had said 'They *said* she was the best woman rider in the country' [emphasis added]. Now, after watching her a bit, he removes the qualification.

379:30 **in Alabama or Mississippi either** Hawkhurst is in Alabama—the northwestern part—about 100 miles from the Sartoris plantation in northern Mississippi. We know it is about 100 miles, because it took Granny and the boys six days to get there; a wagon drawn by mules can go slightly less than twenty miles a day.

379:30 **killed at Shiloh** the first really big battle in the west, just north of Corinth, April 6–7, 1862—more than a year earlier, shortly before "Ambuscade"

379:32 **Hello, John Sartoris** Why would Drusilla call him by his father's name, since ten lines later (380:2//90:3) it is clear she knows his name is Bayard? She is complimenting him in a non-gushy way, suggesting how much he has grown since she last saw him before the war started. She is suggesting that he is beginning to look like his father—and to act like him too, for no doubt she has heard about his shooting at the Yankee in "Ambuscade" and about his role in capturing the Union soldiers in "Retreat." (The entry for 487:29// 247:4 will have more to say about the significance of Drusilla's words here.)

379:40 **I'll finish Bobolink for you** finish rubbing him down and cooling him off

380:19 **put the pistol to Bobolink's ear and said I cant shoot you all because I haven't enough bullets . . . but I wont need but one shot for the horse and which shall it be?** Faulkner re-uses a version of this scene in *A Fable* (1954) when a groom shoots a racehorse rather than allow him to be seized and put out to stud.

Why the Yankees Didn't Take Drusilla's Horse

Union soldiers generally stole or destroyed whatever Southern property they wanted to, but it was the near-unanimous testimony that they did not use force against women. "Women were almost as safe from violence . . . as they would have been had the invading regiments been friendly troops visiting the cities and towns of the South for gala occasions" (Simkins 58). Southern women sometimes took advantage of knowing they would not be harmed. A girl of Yazoo County, Mississippi, who was threatened by Union troops with being carried away on a river boat: "'Backing up against a huge cypress tree, I took my little revolver from the pocket of my underskirt and cocked it, and placing the muzzle against my breast, I declared that only my dead body should be taken on that boat.' Consternation struck her captors, according to her account, and she was released" (Simkins 47–48).

380:22   So They burned the house and went away   They settled just for burning the house—which is what they had intended to do in the first place (see 380:8//90:11).

380:24   you could have raked Ringo's eyes off his face with a stick   Ringo is excited and his eyes are popping.

381:17   scabbard   a sheath for a sword

382:1   But we cannot be responsible   Aunt Louisa is not a sympathetic character. This remark is so self-centered as to be chilling: we didn't cause the slaves' problem and so we don't need to do anything about it. Drusilla's reply to her mother is firm but very gentle under the circumstances. Perhaps part of Drusilla's untypical response to the war can be explained by the negative example of her mother.

382:3   Those negroes are not Yankees, Mother   Drusilla and Bayard both consider Southern black people to be Southerners. So do Ringo and Louvinia. The idea that the term "Southerners" refers only to persons who are white has always been more a Northern attitude than a Southern one.

382:8   Brother John   Col. Sartoris is not Aunt Louisa's brother. She is related to the Sartorises on Bayard's mother's side (thus on Granny's side, who is Bayard's mother's mother). 'Brother' as Aunt Louisa uses it means 'brother in the fellowship of the church'—as in 'Brother Fortinbride will now lead us in prayer.'

382:29   listening to Cousin Drusilla   The next several pages give us Drusilla's story of the locomotive chase and the boys' reaction to her story. Key words in this passage—ones important to understanding what Bayard and Ringo are experiencing as they listen—are a series of 'its.' Only by figuring out what 'it' means each time (they are not all the same) can the passage be made to make sense.

382:34   **Because this, to us, was it**   'it' = what we had been waiting for ever since the war began: evidence that war truly can be romantic and uplifting and glorious—as those who have written about war have said it is

383:4   **But that was it**   but that was all we knew, the extent of what we had evidence of

383:7   **petty precisian**   one pedantically concerned with accuracy and literal truth. One might say these annotations are the product of a petty precisian.

383:14   **we had to believe that the name for the sort of life we had led for the last three years was hardship and suffering** This is accurate—if we stretch a bit. The war had been going on for more than two years but not (by eight months) for three. Also, 'hardship and suffering' did not immediately descend on Mississippi or Alabama with the start of the war. Still, the statement is one we can accept: people suffering from war would be likely to exaggerate how long their suffering had been going on.

383:16   **we had no proof of it**   'it' = that war could be glorious, that it could be more and different from the shabby soldiers and prosaic actions which we had actually witnessed

383:18   **obverse of proof**   not simply 'no proof' but evidence that seemed to show the *opposite* of what was true

383:20   **crowbait horses**   skin-and-bones horses, supposedly better suited for serving as dead meat to attract crows than for riding

383:28   **the very necessity for which was the fruit of the absent occupations from which, returning, they bore no proof** the need for their returning from time to time to perform household tasks (for which they were poorly suited, since they had never done them before) was a result of their being occupied elsewhere as soldiers, for which they also were untrained; curiously, even though they brought with them no evidence of their skill as soldiers, their coming home was a direct consequence of their being away engaged in those 'absent occupations'

383:33 **there's more to it than this** that war amounts to more than the unromantic actions and uninspiring events which we had so far seen

383:35 **And then to have it happen** 'it' = *proof* that war can be glorious

383:37 **poste and riposte** terms from fencing: thrust and counterthrust

383:39 **unlimber** disengage a cannon from the horses pulling it and then get it ready to fire

383:39 **lurid grime-glare** the black powder-smoke and the flash of cannon firing

383:40 **demon-served inferno** a hell created and sustained by the diabolical side of human beings

384:1 **shrill-yelling infantry** This refers to the famous Rebel Yell, an unearthly part-cheer part-warwhoop which Southern soldiers shouted as they went into battle.

384:3 **Because this was it** 'it' = an instance of what we had heard was possible but up to now had no evidence of: a moment when war was indeed romantic, noble, glorious

384:4 **toad-squatting guns** Some Civil War cannons had short, very thick barrels, looking not unlike toads crouched before springing.

384:5 **amphitheatric** as if in an amphitheater, with people on all sides in position to watch

384:7 **the sorry business which had dragged on for three years now** 'the sorry business' = the war. There is a problem with 'three years now.' What time is meant by 'now'? Is it the time of Drusilla's telling the story in August 1863 or the time of the chase itself at some unspecified earlier date? 'For three years now' is perhaps barely possible if we understand the 'now' to refer to the moment of Drusilla's telling (for by August 1863 the war had been going on for more than two years) but 'three years now' won't work if we have to figure 'now' from the necessarily earlier-than-August time of the chase itself. *The Unvanquished* doesn't tell us exactly when the chase is supposed to have taken place, but we are told it was long enough ago for the rails twisted around the trees already to be annealing into the bark. That does not suggest an especially recent event. As we read on, we will soon come to other sentences where 'three years ago' is clearly (and certainly) meant to be understood as measuring from the time of the chase, not Drusilla's telling. Thus (even though we have to close our eyes to the timetable of the real war to do it) we have to accept Faulkner's apparent intention: the chase, as Drusilla tells it, occurred some time in the past when the war had been going on for three years—and that is, of course, impossible if Drusilla tells the story in 1863. Atlanta (where the chase started) would not even be in Union hands until 1864. The discrepancy here is not particularly bothersome, but it exists and there is no way to get around it. I can think of two possible explanations. One stems from the fact that, in the original short story text of "Raid," the date on the repossession order (395:10//112:9) was *1864*, not 1863. When, in revising, Faulkner changed this date to make "Raid" fit with the timetable of the rest of the novel, he apparently failed to make corresponding changes to his several three-years-ago sentences in Drusilla's story. The other possible explanation is given in the entry for 386:7//99:1.

384:8 **congealed** come together into one mass—as water freezes (congeals) into a piece of ice

384:9 **gambit** a maneuver which invites a response

384:10 **two batteries** two companies of artillery

384:15 **not for preservation, since hope of that was gone** not for preservation of their pre-war society which Southerners had been fighting to be allowed to continue, for the war had already destroyed that pre-war world—see the burned houses, runaway slaves, dead brothers and fathers, etc.

384:22 **annealing** on the way to becoming permanently fixed

384:25 **pristine** pure, untouched, intact

384:25 **straight and narrow as the path to glory itself** a variation on a Christian set-phrase: 'straight and narrow is the path to salvation'—as opposed to 'smooth and easy is the road to hell and destruction'

384:27 **Drusilla told about that too** 'that' = the people who were there to watch as the two locomotives rushed by

384:28 **'Atlanta' and 'Chattanooga'** Atlanta is in Georgia, Chattanooga in Tennessee—the points of departure and destination for the locomotive chase.

384:33 **warned by grapevine** warned by information relayed (God only knows how) from plantation to plantation

384:35 **impeding** limiting or hindering

384:38 **roundhouse** a repair and storage building for locomotives, so-called because it was circular in order to accommodate a massive turntable used to reverse the direction of the engine upon its exit

385:1 **her or it** a choice of pronouns is provided three times in this clause in support of the dual metaphor established for the locomotive: 'mistress' or 'horse'

385:12 **the gray generals** the Confederate generals

385:15 **that's all it was** The locomotive chase didn't accomplish anything practical; it simply offered one moment of glory, 'a glimpse of that for which you have suffered and been denied.'

385:20 **track which had seen no smoke nor heard no bell in more than a year** The implication is that the track, since it connected a city under Union control (Chattanooga) with a city deep in Confederate territory (Atlanta), had not been used for a year.

385:21 **I dont think it was intended to do that** not intended to change the eventual outcome of the war

385:23 **honor denied with honor, courage denied with courage** Courage is being met (denied) with equal courage, honor with equal honor, as in the old, idealized stories of war where the participants were noble and the struggle fierce but fair, with respect being paid the winner by the loser. Bayard's attempt to re-define for himself the abstractions 'honor' and 'courage' become chief concerns of the last chapter of the book, "An Odor of Verbena."

385:27 **as if Drusilla's voice had transported us to the wandering light-ray in space in which was still held the furious shadow** Such a wondrous moment surely cannot have disappeared forever. Surely some light-ray somewhere in space must still hold at least the shadow of an occasion too glorious to be permitted to fade completely. Drusilla's telling of the story recovered for us that 'wandering light-ray' so that we too were able to see, months afterward, what we had not been present to see when it actually happened. This is an idea first introduced into western literature by Chaucer in "The House of Fame" and reversed in time by Faulkner in Quentin's thoughts in *The Sound and the Fury* (1929): "It was a while before the last stroke ceased vibrating. It stayed in the air, more felt than heard, for a long time. Like all the bells that ever rang still ringing in the long dying light-rays and Jesus and Saint Francis talking about his sister" (97).

385:30 **which existed inside the scope of a single pair of eyes** Obviously, a locomotive chase over many miles would have been witnessed by many pairs of eyes, but the moment here being described was 'arrested in [the] human sight' of Drusilla, who makes it live again in the retelling. In the *Paris Review* interview of 1956, Faulkner said that "The aim of every artist is to arrest motion, which is life, by artificial means and hold it fixed so that a hundred years later, when a stranger looks at it, it moves again since it is life" (Stein 255). This episode demonstrates perfectly how exacting was Faulkner's aim.

385:34 **inviolate** unchanged, intact

385:34 **wailing through its whistle precious steam which could have meant seconds at the instant of passing and miles at the end of its journey** The same steam which drives the locomotive's wheels also blows its whistle. Blowing the whistle therefore reduces the locomotive's speed at the moment of blowing and lessens the distance it will be able to travel before running out of fuel or water. But the satisfaction gained from the defiant gesture makes the loss 'cheap at ten times the price.'

385:37 **the tossing bell** the bell atop the locomotive which tosses back and forth with the rocking of the train

385:38 **the starred Saint Andrew's cross** the Confederate battle-flag

385:38 **nailed to the cab roof** so it could be seen by those watching the locomotive rush by

385:40 **like the golden spurs themselves** Knights of medieval times were supposed to have worn (and in fact apparently sometimes actually did wear) spurs made of gold.

386:7 **they couldn't take back the fact that we had done it. They couldn't take that from us** Understand that Drusilla's story is of a true and famous event in Civil War history, sometimes known as The Great Locomotive Chase and sometimes as Andrews' Raid. It took place on 12 April 1862. Drusilla gets most of the details right: the start from Atlanta, the destination Chattanooga (although she doesn't account for how that route would bring the locomotive past Hawkhurst in western Alabama). But there is one enormous difference between the story as Drusilla tells it and the way history (or Buster Keaton's famous silent film, "The General") records the event: it was not a Confederate band which captured a Union locomotive from a Union roundhouse; it was a *Union* group led by James J. Andrews of Ohio which made off with a *Confederate* engine ("The General") and outran for 90 miles all Confederate attempts to catch or block them. When they were at last captured, Andrews was executed as a spy; he and others in the group were awarded the first Congressional Medals of Honor ever issued. Atlanta was in Confederate hands at the time and would continue to be for another two years. But facts do not inhibit a good storyteller. The differences between Drusilla's story and actual history were not mistakes on Faulkner's part. He was rewriting history. As Faulkner put it in *Absalom, Absalom!* (1936): 'There is a might-have-been which is more true than truth' (Rosa, 118:29) and 'There are some things that just have to be whether they are or not' (Shreve, 266:3). Or, perhaps better put in his draft introduction to *Sartoris* (1929): 'And so I improved on God, who, dramatic though He may be, has no sense, no feeling for theatre' (Putzel 375).

386:11 **Missy Lena** a corruption of the classical Roman name Messalina

386:21 **the house** Aunt Louisa, Drusilla, and Denny are living in a slave cabin but, since their former family house has been burned, where they live now has become 'the house.'

386:29 **that quality which Father and the other men brought back from the front—the power to do without sleep and food both, needing only the opportunity to endure** This is what Bayard told us in "Ambuscade" (325:35//10:11) that he 'know[s] now to have been only the will to endure, a sardonic and even humorous declining of self-delusion.'

387:11 **I'm keeping a dog quiet** Bayard is given a lesson in metaphor and in human behavior here. Since, as Bayard says, he hasn't seen a dog, it must be a figure of speech, but it isn't a simple analogy, as in Shakespeare's "Cry 'Havoc!' and let slip the dogs of war" (*Julius Caesar* 3.1.273). Rather, in an extended ironic comparison of the life they led in peace with the life they are leading in war, Drusilla describes the dog of despair within her kept quiet by the stick of self-discipline.

387:15 **I just have to show it the stick now and then** Literally, all that is needed to control the behavior of a dog is to show it the stick with which it has been physically disciplined; figuratively, all Drusilla has to do to keep from being overwhelmed by her losses is to remind herself of what she once had every reason to expect—a quiet, peaceful life, with marriage, a family, and 'negro slaves to nurse and coddle' (387:20//100:26)—now reduced to a principle worth fighting for.

387:16 **Who wants to sleep now, with so much happening,**

so much to see? Obviously, Drusilla continues to speak with bitter irony, yet it becomes clear in this and subsequent stories that the circumstances of war have uncovered a die-hard soldier within.

387:40 **Thank God for nothing** Drusilla means these words literally: everything she had (or expected to have) has been killed or destroyed, and 'nothing' is what God has left her with. She doesn't even have to sleep alone, because she has learned how to do without sleep.

388:27 **the set** the direction and pull

389:2 **the bed** the wooden body of the wagon

389:18 **It was just a sound at first, like wind** 'It' = the sound made by the mass of slaves, finally reaching the river, moving into the water. 'They made a kind of long wailing sound' (389:26//104:1), then 'we could hear them scream-ing' (389:33//104:10), then 'the singing everywhere up and down the river bank, with the voices of the women coming out of it thin and high: "Glory! Glory! Hallelujah!"' (390:15//104:3). Later, after the wagon is forced into the river, 'they were still marching down the bank and into the river, sing-ing' (392:15//107:29).

389:29 **turned sideways in the traces** the horses turned in their harness at right angles to the front of the wagon

389:38 **Millard** Granny's name is Rosa Millard.

390:12 **like split-cane clothespins being jerked along a clothesline** 'split-cane clothespins' are large home-made clothespins cut from local bamboo. Bayard is looking up at the bridge and into the sun. He sees the line of soldiers in silhouette crossing the bridge. He can't see details—just their shapes and motion. From a distance and with the sky as background they look to him like a row of clothespins bob-bing on a clothesline being playfully tweaked or strummed.

390:37 **by the head-stall** by the bridle

391:7 **then the bridge vanished** the temporary bridge, mined with explosives for destruction after the troops have passed over, has exploded prematurely

391:15 **little toy men and horses and pieces of plank floating along in the air** the men and horses, reduced by distance to the size of the boys' pretend-Vicksburg behind the smoke-house, seem like toys tossed into the air

392:1 **like the earth had fallen out from under** a continuation of the apocalyptic imagery of 389:34//104:10: 'the earth had tilted up'

392:3 **rushed down slow** Faulkner has not frozen this particular moment, but he has slowed it down so that all that happened in a rush to young Bayard can now be recollected in cinematic slow-motion by the adult storyteller.

392:5 **across the river I saw a cliff and a big fire on it running fast sideways** There are two possible explanations for this, both involving relative motion: either the setting sun or a large campfire on the opposite bank, though stationary, appeared to be moving because the wagon Bayard was observing from itself 'was moving fast sideways' (392:7// 107:20). The sun seems most likely: 'It was sunset; now there was a bright rosy glow quiet beyond the trees and shining on the river' (390:2//104:19). This is like 391:2// 106:2 when, with the wagon stopped, 'for a minute I thought we were going backward,' because the whole mob of slaves and soldiers was rolling past them.

392:15 **they were still marching down the bank and into the river** Like lemmings they went into the water, and like lemmings they drowned. Hundreds of them drowned. They had to, because the river is the Tennessee River (which is not quite the Mississippi but is nearly as big) and at least one universally observed restriction placed upon slaves was that they were never allowed the opportunity to learn to swim. This incident of cavalry holding slaves back from a bridge and precipitating a mass slave drowning is something that actually happened several times, on succeeding days in December 1864, between Milledgeville and Savannah, Georgia, and it provoked outrage in both Northern and Southern newspapers when it was reported. Faulkner's version

changed one important fact: the cavalry which was responsible for the drownings was not Union but Confederate cavalry under Gen. Joe Wheeler. But to Faulkner the story-
teller (or to Bayard, the rememberer), that was not the way
it ought to have been, and so that is not how Faulkner tells
it. As he once said: 'A writer is a liar, ma'am. That's why they
call it fiction' (Alderman tape 3).

SECTION THREE

393:7 **Damn this war. Damn it. Damn it** because a decent
old grandmother now has to be rescued from a river 100
miles from her home because she is trying to cope with the
disruptions brought on by the war. The words are Col. Dick's
as told to us by Bayard, but the feeling is perhaps as fully
Faulkner's as any passage in the book.

393:9 **darkies** a polite, even friendly (although patronizing)
word at the time for black people

393:12 **corps** a military unit of at least two divisions—4,000
or more men

393:16 **the sound of the army like wind far away** we are to
hear the murmuring sound made by masses of people as distant wind here and at 389:18//103:23, where the slaves being held back from the river by the cavalry sound 'like wind'

393:29 **I guess the General will be glad to give them twice
the silver and mules just for taking that many niggers**
Since *two* hardly qualifies as 'that many,' the orderly must
have written some larger number of slaves, 'one hundred
ten,' in fact, as we are about to learn.

394:2 **now it began to go fast again** 'again' = as Bayard told
us it had at 389:37//104:13

394:7 **Philadelphia; that's in Mississippi** There is a Philadelphia in Mississippi, located northwest of Meridian. It was
once the state capital.

394:16   **The General said to give you another hundred with his compliments**   If the order calls for '110 negroes' and Granny is getting 'another hundred' with the General's compliments, then she must be getting 210. Understand that the Union general would *like* to get rid of as many slaves as possible. See the extended discussion of this passage in the mini-essay below.

394:25   **set of trees**   a pair of whiffletrees and a doubletree (See 358:22//58:11 for a detailed description.)

394:27   **two span**   two teams. Almost anyone could drive one mule; it takes only a bit more skill to drive a team, but to drive two teams, one in front of the other, is considerably trickier and requires experience.

395:10   **August 14, 1863**   We can have some confidence that Faulkner considered and intended this date, since in revising the magazine story of "Raid" he changed the year from 1864 to 1863.

395:14   **Ten (10) chests**   Granny says 'tin,' the orderly hears and writes 'ten.' See the extended discussion of this passage in the mini-essay below.

395:15   **One hundred ten (110) mules . . . One hundred ten (110) negroes**   Granny names the slaves first, 'Two darkies, Loosh and Philadelphy,' then 'The mules, Old Hundred and Tinney.' The orderly reverses the sequence, converting 'Old Hundred and Tinney' into 'One hundred ten' and 'Loosh and Philadelphy' into 'loose near Philadelphia,' applying the number to mules and negroes alike.

Old Hundred and Tenny are plausible names for mules. Mules which work as a team were often named as a team. Old Hundred was the most-often sung hymn in the *Baptist Harmony*, the metrical version of the hundredth psalm, now usually called the Doxology. It was generally known as "the slow one." While all mules are slow, Old Hundred must have been slower than most. Tenny is short for Tennessee, and "Tennessee" was the title of the hymn on the following page in the hymnbook—the other half of a familiar two-page team (White and King 51–52).

Why the Yankees Gave Granny Ten Chests of Silver

The few Faulkner scholars who have discussed this episode are not happy with it. Joseph Blotner attributes the Union Army's extraordinary requisition to an unexplainable "clerical error" (848). Cleanth Brooks finds the whole incident "wildly improbable" and says it presents "a disturbing problem of tone" (95, 96). Blotner and Brooks are both right, but only if we take what Bayard tells us to be Faulkner's inept attempt at realistic fiction. But it is not. All that a reader is implicitly asked to agree to believe is that Granny and Ringo and Bayard and Col. Dick do (or did once) exist, and the events described (or something like them) did once happen, not that the detailed account of these people and events as told to us years later by Bayard is *intended* as a literally truthful report. If we take the adult Bayard to be a *storyteller*, with vocabulary and imagination equal to Faulkner's, and "Raid" to be his telling a *tale* of the old times, an idealized moment in Sartoris family history, then the episode really poses no problem.

It is axiomatic that "the way it was" seldom makes, unrevised, the best story; even a novice storyteller takes it as a right and responsibility to improve upon both God and previous tellers, so how faithful to literal truth should anyone *expect* the details in Bayard's story to be to whatever happened one day in 1863? How much of his story would Bayard *want* anyone really to believe?

The distance back to exactitude becomes still greater if a reader should finally realize that Granny's spectacular overcompensation in "Raid" is not even simply a *story* but rather a *tall tale*—skillfully and elaborately orchestrated from a base of truth but not intended to be taken as truth itself.

Tall tale telling is an ancient and subtle art, often unappreciated and even unrecognized except by its own practitioners. A first-rate tall tale has three distinguishing qualities:

1. There is no identifiable line where a story ceases to be just a story and becomes a tall tale, but to cross that line between the plausible and the implausible without being caught in passage is what makes a tall tale tall. A story obviously impossible from the start is not a tall tale; Baron Munchausen was a liar, not a teller of tall tales. Neither does a tall tale seriously attempt to con the listener or reader into believing something that isn't true and couldn't be true. That might sometimes happen, but when it does, the listener has proven to be too gullible to be a proper audience for the performance.

2. All details of a tall tale must be *explainable*. This doesn't mean they must be genuinely believable; unlikely misunderstandings are quite within the rules—it is all right, for example, for soldiers to pretend to believe that the initials on the cracker barrels, "B.C.," do not stand for Brigade Commissary but rather for the date of the hardtack's manufacture—but the details must always be such that it would be at least technically possible for a humorless person to believe them literally. Tall tales and facts *go together*—necessarily so. Facts support, not negate, the tale. The more facts that support an absurd conclusion, the taller (and therefore better) the tall tale.

3. A tall tale is offered in the spirit of fun. The thing to be appreciated is the good-humored virtuoso performance of the telling. Sometimes the tale ends by identifying itself as a tall tale and sometimes it maintains to the end its pose of seriousness, but always, after it is over, there is (or should be), explicitly or implicitly, a shared grin. The grin is the performer's bow and the audience's applause. For the teller to continue to pretend beyond story's end that it is true, or for his listeners to think it might be, would defeat the purpose and spirit of the performance.

Bayard as tall tale teller could successfully defend each point of his story in "Raid" should anyone challenge his "facts":

1. The Union Army's burning of the Sartoris house and mak-

ing off with civilian mules and silver takes place precisely at that real moment in historical time, and at that precise location, north Mississippi, when and where, by decision of Northern Generals Grant and Sherman, war ceased forever to be a limited and honorable contest between opposing armies and became instead "total war," waged against civilians as well as soldiers. Granny Millard (as did many others on both sides during the Civil War) found this change in the rules barbaric. Thus she, who had punished Bayard and Ringo earlier for calling the Yankees "bastuds," joins them in shouting "The bastuds! The bastuds! The bastuds!" (370:15//75:26)

2. Granny's raid on the Union Army to recover her property was not, realistically and historically, an exercise in probable futility. In Mississippi and Alabama in 1863 there were *no* uniform official Union Army rules for dealing with southern civilians who made claims for confiscated property. Each commander determined his own policy, and policies varied widely (Roland 76; Sitterson 217; Silver 259). Gen. A.J. Smith, the man responsible for the burning of downtown Oxford, Faulkner's hometown—a gratuitous vandalism of a totally non-military target—seemed to take sadistic pleasure in denying all Southern claims. To a plantation owner who, mounted on a mule, complained that Union soldiers had robbed him of everything he owned, Gen. Smith said the men could not have been part of his command, "because if they were my men they wouldn't even have left you that mule" (Catton *Grant* 438). Not all Union officers, of course, pleasured themselves in the same way. The colonel of the first Union cavalry troop to arrive in Oxford is remembered in local histories for his kindness and generosity, especially to older women, especially those struggling to run plantations in the absence of men. For example, to the Widow Sample, an old lady near Oxford, he returned six mules, a wagon, and provided a wagonload of salt from Union stores—because she had taught all the children of her 100 slaves to read. The name of this real Northern cavalry commander was Col. Dickey (Cadwallader 33–34)—not quite the same as Granny's Yankee benefactor,

Col. Dick, but close enough to explain Faulkner's choice of name and to give Granny's successful mission in "Raid" a Lafayette County precedent.

3. The Union Army would be happy to get rid of as many slaves as possible. By the time Sherman's Army reached Savannah in 1864, he is said to have had 50,000 freed slaves with him, clinging to his horses and men, shouting and praying (Stone 179, Wiley 15). Under such circumstances it was nearly impossible for his Army to fight. The events in "Raid" occur a year earlier, when ex-slaves were just beginning to come to the Northern armies. If 400–500 had by then attached themselves to Col. Dick's corps, for Granny to take away 210 would be an enormous service. As Col. Dick's orderly says, the General would "be glad to give them twice the silver and mules just for taking that many niggers" (393:29//109:30).

4. The situation with the mules is a bit more complicated. An army needs mules—on average one mule or horse to every four men. But Mississippi and Alabama are mule country; confiscated Southern mules are being brought in every day—more than the Army could use (according to Gen. Sherman himself, quoted in Brooks 95). The mules given to Granny could easily be replaced from the nearest Quartermaster pen in two or three days. If the General decided it was time to give his men a few days' rest—and recall that his troops had just suffered a disastrous accident crossing the river—a temporary mule shortage could provide a good excuse.

5. The matter of the chests of silver is complicated in a different way. Obviously silver has real value. Silver tea-sets and spoons could be melted and made into coins. But that would be done at the U.S. Mint, which was in Philadelphia, nearly 1,000 miles away. A fighting army would welcome an excuse to get rid of ten militarily-useless chests whose heavy wagon had to be wrestled across rivers and creek bottoms at every advance.

So, if the tall tale explanation for the inflated numbers in the official order is that they are deliberate distortions of Granny's request—if Col. Dick is *pretending* to misunderstand, as he had pretended not to understand in "Ambuscade" that Bayard and Ringo were hiding behind Granny's skirts—then the Union Army's order can be justified (at least for a tall tale) on all points: the Army would *like* to get rid of the slaves and heavy chests and is willing to be temporarily deprived of some mules to do so. There is, however, another tall-tale possibility, well supported by the text. Maybe Bayard's story asks us to go along with the idea that the Northern soldiers actually *do* misunderstand what Granny says she has lost.

As Granny describes for Col. Dick the chest, slaves, and mules, his orderly makes notes of what he understands her to say, and then Col. Dick passes these notes on to his General, and the General instructs *his* orderly to prepare an official document authorizing the return of Granny's property. Surely Bayard and Faulkner could reasonably have expected their audience to know the parlor game where one person whispers something to another, who in turn whispers to another, and so on, with the result that the message ultimately received resembles only slightly the message originally sent. And in the five-stage transmission of Granny's spoken request to official written order the chances for garbling are especially great: Granny has just been pulled from the river and is in poor condition to talk, and she has a Mississippi accent which to Northerners sometimes produces a language wondrous strange. Note that Bayard awakens after Granny has begun her complaint (393 : 19//109 : 18): Col. Dick asks him to describe their losses, perhaps out of courtesy to an old and exhausted woman, perhaps to ease the communication. But Granny insists on doing it herself. She says:

> "They took the silver and the darkies and the mules. I have come to get them. . . . The chest of silver tied with hemp rope. The rope was new. Two darkies, Loosh and Philadelphy. The mules, Old Hundred and Tinney" (393 : 9//109 : 7).

Once a reader realizes this is a tall tale, part of the confusion that results from the way this is transcribed by the orderly clears up fast: the names of the slaves, Loosh and Philadelphy, already well-established in the reader's mind, account for the words "captured loose near Philadelphia." The names of the mules, Old Hundred and Tinney, become "all hundred and ten each" (Mizener 147; Brooks 96; Ingram 112). We can get around Granny's specifying *two* mules and slaves by changing the "two" to "too"—by hearing what she said as "the rope was new, too."

That much is easy. But how Col. Dick, or his orderly, or the General, or the General's orderly, could go from "*the* chest" to "*ten* chests" is not so easy. "The" does not look like "ten" nor does it sound like "ten." It is almost as if Bayard (or Faulkner) is throwing down a challenge: now that you know the game I am asking you to play, here is a harder one.

The Army necessarily had at least two wagons loaded with chests—one wagon with officers' chests (each officer was entitled to a chest for his dress uniform, spare boots, writing materials, mess gear, etc.) and another wagon with the confiscated Southern chests supposedly containing silver. The soldiers had to have some term by which to refer to these confiscated chests to distinguish them from the officers' chests. What must the chests with silver have been made of? Chests expected to remain buried in the ground for the duration of the war in rainy Mississippi and Alabama where a pine coffin will disintegrate in approximately a year have to be metal—or, more exactly, metal shells over wooden frames, like pirates' treasure chests; Sears and Roebuck catalogs at the turn of the century were still showing more metal-covered trunks than all other kinds. And the standard American word for any kind of thin metal is tin.

So, the wagon with the confiscated Southern chests would be the one with the tin chests—and to go from "tin" to "ten" is no distance at all in the South, for they have identical pronunciations.

Bayard's tale of Granny's successful raid on the U.S. Army combines a series of individually factual or technically possible details and arrives at an outcome which is manifestly absurd. No real army commander is going to give to an enemy civilian his entire supply of mules plus ten chests filled with silver—no matter what anyone thought Granny said or how much they might wish to be unburdened of the chests. And if he *were* stupid enough to have approved such an order, the fact that he might afterward be able to point to specific misunderstandings which could have accounted for each part of the order would not, in real life, constitute an acceptable explanation for his stupidity. Idiots do not remain Commanding Generals, except, perhaps, in tall tales told by the enemy. Such explanations involving unlikely possibilities do satisfy precisely the requirements of a tall tale. And that is what Bayard and Faulkner have given us—a story with an absurd conclusion which is explainable with reference to fact (although not common sense) at every step— which is to say: a tall tale. Our reaction to Bayard's story should be a grin, our applause for his ingenious performance, not an embarrassed complaint that the episode seems less convincing than we would humorlessly like.

395:20 **forage** hay and corn to feed the mules

395:26 **fodder** dried cornstalks and leaves to feed the mules

395:29 **It's the hand of God** providence, a conventional Christian explanation for why things happen the way they do, an explanation which disclaims personal responsibility

396:10 **We like fifty** 'Like' and 'lack' might well be pronounced the same in many Southern accents.

396:27 **Whose hand was that?** Granny may have said it was 'the hand of God' which provided the first 63 mules, but the next 47 are theirs due to the hand of Ringo.

396:32 **All I done was to told him how much the hundred and ten liked** Ringo is playing here—with the pronunciations of 'liked' and 'lacked.'

396:34 **Sides, hit aint no use in praying about hit now** an argument to forestall Granny's usual behavior when someone she is responsible for (including herself) has lied

397:6 **missy** a form of 'Miss' used when the speaker (always a black person) wanted to show respect (and sometimes affection) for the woman concerned

397:9 **I'll see to it** I'll make it my business to see that you get punished

397:12 **we had almost enough mules for everybody to ride** If they now have 110 mules and if about half of the original group of freed slaves have now left, then they really must have had about 210 persons in the group to start with— the extra hundred provided with the General's compliments.

397:13 **Ringo drove now. He didn't ask; he just got in and took the reins** This is the point at which Ringo begins to take over. Bayard for a year or so will be in the background.

397:22 **They aint hardly worth fooling with** since there are only twelve of them and Ringo so far has been dealing with bigger numbers. He is being smart, flippant.

397:32 **Granny say come here** the strongest command Ringo knows to give

398:6 **The extra twelve is horses** This would seem at first rather conspicuously not to add up: if the order calls for 110, and if they already have 100, then it would seem they are 10, not 12, short. But Ringo has not made a mistake. He is, in fact, waiting for the Union officer to object to his arithmetic, because he has a ready answer: the official order says that the bearer is to be 'repossessed' of 110 mules, etc. This means that Granny is to be given 110 mules *in addition* to whatever mules or horses had pulled the wagon from Mississippi. The fact that the two original horses have drowned does not affect the arithmetic. As for how Ringo goes from mules to horses, that part is simply a bluff.

398:9 **mount us with captured stock** provide us with captured horses

398:14 **It's the General's own signature** In the Army one might question (and sometimes even argue with) a Captain or a Major or conceivably a Colonel, but with a General no one argues. You do whatever he (or a paper signed by him) tells you to do, regardless of how stupid you may think the order to be.

398:33 **got shed of** got shut of, got rid of

398:37 **there our chimneys were** Since it took six days to reach Hawkhurst and another day (August 14) to get the silver, mules, and freed slaves, and since the wagon would certainly not go faster with its load of ten trunks of silver than it had before when it was empty, we can reasonably figure that the return trip would take at least another seven days, especially since they would have to go up or down river to find a bridge or a ford to cross back over. So they must have gotten back to Sartoris on about 21 August—or a day or so later.

CHAPTER IV
Riposte in Tertio

"Riposte in Tertio" takes place a few days in October 1864 and then a few days just before Christmas 1864, a year and a half after the events of "Raid."

Title: **Riposte in Tertio** Originally called "The Unvanquished" in its magazine publication. The title is a fencing term meaning, literally, 'a counterthrust to the third position,' or, in effect, 'a counterthrust after parrying an opponent's attack,' which is essentially a description of Granny's mule-swindling operation as a response to the invasion of the Yankees.

SECTION ONE

400:1 **Ab Snopes** pronounced 'ab' (short for Abner), not 'Abe' (short for Abraham); Snopes rhymes with 'mopes.' Ab is the progenitor of Faulkner's extraordinary family of shady rural con-artists, the endlessly-multiplying Snopeses. One of Ab's sons, Flem, is the central character in three later Faulkner novels—*The Hamlet* (1940), *The Town* (1957), and *The Mansion* (1959).

400:24 **he told me and Ringo to look out for Ab** Col. Sartoris's revised-to-fit-new-circumstances version of 'Watch Loosh'

401:2 **while you had him in the traces, you better watch him** While you are hooked up with him, you had better pay attention to what he is doing.

401:7 **has to dodge them durn critters** There is always the chance that patrols of either the Union Army or the Confederate Army might decide to requisition (i.e., confiscate) any mules they see, so Ab has to try to sneak the mules into Memphis by way of fields and woods and back roads.

401:8 **Forrest** Confederate General Nathan Bedford Forrest, by this time commanding the few Confederate forces still fighting in Mississippi

401:9 **Smith** Federal General A.J. Smith, charged with capturing or killing Forrest at whatever the cost. He led three spectacularly unsuccessful campaigns against Forrest.

401:13 **sell them to a e-quipment officer** sell the mules to the Federal Quartermaster officer (Supply officer) in Memphis, as Ab would say in his country dialect

401:24 **his commissary train** Federal Army supply wagons

401:27 **draw for the whole pay wagon** Ab is being sarcastic, suggesting that she save them all a great deal of time and effort by requisitioning the money directly instead of requisitioning mules to sell.

401:29 **The money was in new bills** U.S. banknotes. That Granny would be interested in getting U.S. money tells us that she knows by now that the South will lose the war and only U.S. money will be worth anything.

401:30 **the can** probably a flat, flask-shaped pipe tobacco tin with flip-lid. This would fit smoothly under the front of Granny's dress.

401:36 **She just looked like somebody that has quit sleeping at night** like Drusilla (387:5//100:10)

402:3 **hip patches** scars over the obliterated brands

402:4 **trace galls** chafed spots caused by the rubbing of the traces (that part of the harness which goes along each side of a mule); Ab's point is that it would be highly unlikely anyone would mistake a burned-over brand for a spot rubbed raw by harness

402:10 **relief regiment** replacement regiment

402:16 **So you sold them further back than three days ago** It was only two days ago that Ringo went to Mottstown to check on the mules in the new regiment. The regiment had to travel from Memphis to Mottstown (about 100 miles) and it had to have arrived there before Ringo could know to go there. Thus the regiment could not have mules that Ab had sold to the Quartermaster in Memphis just three days ago—which is what Ab claimed he had done. All of this is a roundabout way of showing that Ab is not trustworthy and that Granny knows it.

402:21 **I may even have a chance to find out what they say they paid you for them** Granny is suggesting that Ab sold the mules to an individual Federal regiment and not to the Quartermaster in Memphis (as he says he did) and that he might have received more than the 50 dollars per mule he told Granny he was paid.

402:35 **For six thou-sand and seven hun-dred and twen-ty-two dollars and six-ty-five cents** Granny and Ab keep different kinds of accounts: Granny knows how many mules they have sold back to the Yankees (105) and Ab knows exactly how much money he has told Granny he got for them ($6722.65). Since that would be an average of 64 dollars per mule, it is no wonder Granny is suspicious of Ab's report of his latest sales at 50 dollars, because the value of mules had consistently gone up as the war dragged on.

402:37 **the dollar and thirty-five cents I spent for whisky that time the snake bit one of the mules** Whisky was a folk remedy for snake-bite. But the whisky was supposed to be drunk, not rubbed on the bite, and it was a remedy for humans, not animals. I have never heard of anyone trying to get a snake-bit mule to drink whisky and Ab is not exactly *saying* that that is what he did. He only says he bought the whisky when the mule got bit, not what he did with it. Hiding behind that technicality in wording would be Ab's defense if Granny challenged this item on his expense account—which Granny very well knows and so says nothing. Coping (or trying to cope) with the Snopeses is a basic survival skill which sooner or later all Yoknapatawphans discover they need to learn.

402:39   **sawn oak wheels**   solid wheels made from slices of a trunk of an oak tree

402:40   **started out a year ago with two**   Old Hundred and Tinney, the team stolen by the Yankees on Granny's unsuccessful attempt to reach Memphis in "Retreat." Since it is October now and since the mule swindling could not have begun until after they got back from Hawkhurst with the sample repossession order in August 1863, and since we know they requisitioned some mules in the months of April, May, and July, the present October must be October of 1864, a year and a half after the time of "Raid."

402:40   **forty-odd**   an indefinite number greater than forty but less than fifty

403:1   **you have sold about fifty-odd more back to the Yankees a hundred and five times**   Therefore each mule sold to the Yankees had been sold to them an average of two times.

403:13   **Kernel**   The spelling indicates the harsh twang of Ab's hillman speech. Most Southerners would say 'Cunnel.'

403:14   **General Grant**   by this time the Commander-in-chief of the entire Union Army

403:16   **Miz**   the standard Southern pronunciation of 'Mrs.'

403:30   **I had been there long enough for them to begin to get warm**   Granny had been praying for a long time.

403:39   **he hitched it to Louvinia's clothesline**   a convenient place for him to hitch the mule but certainly not one Louvinia would have tolerated before Ringo had taken over as leader of Sartoris Enterprises

404:7   **How many**   How many mules does Newberry's regiment at Mottstown have?

404:9   **Four with; fifteen without**   four with U.S. brands, fifteen without brands

404:11   **Twelve**   twelve that we requisitioned before and sold back to the U.S. Quartermaster at Memphis

404:11   **Out of that Oxford batch**   the twelve we sold back that we originally requisitioned at Oxford

404:13 **July the twenty-second** we requisitioned those twelve mules on July 22

404:15 **the saw chunk** a sawed-off section of a tree trunk used to sit on

404:18 **declined even to try to learn to print his name when Loosh was teaching me** This doesn't say that Loosh had taught Bayard to read and write. It simply says Loosh taught him to write his name. At that time there were many people who could write their own name but could not write anything else and could not read at all.

404:27 **12 or 9 or 21 mules** the number of mules they had previously obtained at these locations

404:30 **Complete** All the mules these outfits have are ones we previously requisitioned and sold back. Do you suppose Granny's requisitions were for the exact number of mules each regiment or troop had on hand? For a smaller number? For a larger number? Obviously she could never go back to any unit a second time.

405:1 **It's October now** Granny's and Ringo's mule-swindling operation has been going on for at least six months—at least since April (405:4//126:14), perhaps longer. Thus "Riposte in Tertio" takes place in October 1864, a year after "Raid." Bayard and Ringo were fifteen in September.

405:13 **Mister Snopes** Granny is reminding Ringo of his manners. Ab Snopes is white and an adult; therefore to any boy (black or white) he is *always* 'Mister Snopes,' no matter how undeserving of respect they may hold him as a person.

405:19 **Four to keep and fifteen to sell back to um** They would keep the four branded ones and sell back the fifteen unbranded ones.

405:20 **a even two hundred and forty-eight** this figure contrasts Ringo's accurate record keeping with Ab's approximations: 'forty-*odd*' and 'fifty-*odd*' (402:40//123:12).

405:21 **Confedrit mules** replacement mules for Old Hundred and Tinney. The Southern word for replacement or substitute *anything* during the war was 'Confederate.' Parched corn was 'Confederate coffee,' pokeberry juice was 'Confederate ink,' a farm wagon was a 'Confederate carriage,' reading from the cookbook a 'Confederate dessert,' etc. It is still sometimes said that a debt will be paid in 'Confederate money,' meaning worthless.

405:21   recovered and collected interest on, let alone the money   If 'collected interest on' doesn't refer to the money they received when they sold some of the mules, then Ringo must be considering Old Hundred and Tinney as an 'investment' which has paid a greater than hundred-fold return.

405:32   Get the pen and ink   Ringo gives the orders, Bayard runs the errands. The next line says *'They* kept the paper. . . .' Bayard understands and accepts that Ringo has passed him and that Ringo and Granny are running the business and he is just a part-time helper—as Drusilla says later about her role with Col. Sartoris's troop: 'I was just another man and not much of one at that.'

405:37   *Department of Tennessee*   Union forces still in the West were officially in the Department of Tennessee.

406:5   mules Ringo had examined and approved   Apparently if most of the mules had U.S. brands, Ringo would not approve the batch as targets for requisitioning.

406:16   always remembered to put in rope   The importance of the rope becomes clear at 407:32//130:12 and 407:35// 130:15.

406:23   We was on 'F' last time . . . It's 'H' now   Ringo is going through the alphabet. Doubtless they have used 'G' before, as a part of the General's rank/signature.

406:29   Now we done used up 'P' too   He is trying to avoid repeating capital letters—whether first or last names.

406:30   when we run out of letters, maybe we can start in on numbers. We will have nine hundred and ninety-nine before we have to worry, then   After thirteen names the capital letters would have to start repeating. But numbers, as Ringo understands them, go up to 999, so it would be a long time before they would have to repeat. As for why he doesn't want to repeat capital letters: since he has only recently learned to write and since the only model of male handwriting he has is the original and legitimate requisition and since hand-written capital letters tended to be much more flamboyant and individualistic than small letters (or numbers), he is probably afraid that a distinctive capital letter might be recognized. Maybe with only one model he doesn't really know which flourishes in the letter are really necessary to make a capital P.

407:32 **the lead rope** The mules are in a column, one in back of another, joined together by rope. The front mule has another rope, the lead rope, which Ringo, sitting at the back of the wagon, holds at the other end. When the wagon moves, the string of mules necessarily follows.

408:2 **Damn that Ringo** Earlier, Granny punishes Bayard and Ringo for swearing and would not normally swear in front of them. However, war transforms people dramatically, and the once-fastidious Granny, now a notorious mule thief, seems to have begun to learn to swear when 'the bastuds' burned down the house of her son-in-law (370:17// 75:27).

408:13 **lightwood** wood that gives a quick, good, long-lasting light. A 'lightwood splinter' would be a pine-knot torch, in effect a very large long-burning match.

408:20 **That damn Newberry had his copy in his pocket** Consider what must have been the repercussions the following day at each of the Union camps Granny had raided— when more mules were requested to replace those given away. An order must have been issued long ago to commanders of all U.S. Army units to be on the lookout for an old woman running a scam with forged requisitions. But, as anyone with any experience in an organization knows, it is easier to write and send a memorandum than to get it read and acted upon.

408:35 **Heyo the road** the customary way to call to someone on the road, especially at night

409:13 **And the team too** Since we left behind the team and wagon, we have also lost two more mules.

409:29 **Did I holler loud enough?** Ringo had devised a plan to be put into operation if the Yankees should ever discover they had been swindled shortly after Granny had left their camp. Each time, as soon as they were out of sight of the camp, Ringo would lead the mules off the road to Ab Snopes in a woods. Then Ringo would go to the other side of the road, away from Ab and the mules. If the Yankees should ride up to the wagon, Ringo would shout from his side of the road that one of the mules had broken loose. The Yankees would ride off in Ringo's direction, taking them farther from Ab and the mules and allowing Bayard and Granny to walk away from the wagon. Since it is dark, no one is likely to get caught. It is a good plan and it worked. Where did Ringo get the idea? His experience may be limited but he learns from such experiences as he has had. He is doing here intentionally what he did unintentionally when he and Bayard and Col. Sartoris captured the sixty Union soldiers in "Retreat"—making noise in the bushes and so misleading the enemy.

410:9 **Two hundred and forty-six** Granny is counting here in the same way Ringo did when he added 100 and 12 and got 110 in "Raid" (398:6//116:17). She is taking into consideration the team they brought with them—which now they will neither be able to sell back to the Yankees nor give to people in the hills and which, therefore, they have not really 'handled' as part of their operation.

SECTION TWO

410:29 **dogrun** fenced enclosure where the hounds were kept

410:30 **gallery** here a balcony for slaves

410:31 **balustrade** wood railing in front of the first row of seats in the gallery

410:33 **Sunday calico dress** Calico usually is a cheap, mass-produced, glazed cotton cloth with a bright, gaudy pattern—the typical material for slaves' Sunday dresses. Here, for Granny's Sunday dress, it must mean a different kind of calico, the heavy cloth imported from Calicut, India, where the original (and expensive) calico was made.

410:36 **prayer book** Episcopal services follow the traditional pattern of the Church of England, with set prayers and responses and very little of the improvising customary with other Protestant denominations. Episcopal prayers are spelled out in the prayer book. Even the minister uses a prayer book, because there are special prayers for each Sunday and for other holy days.

410:39 **Last summer when we got back with the first batch of mules from Alabama** not the summer just before the present October but late in the summer of the year before that

411:12 **stole** part of a priest's ceremonial costume—a long, narrow, band worn behind the neck, over the shoulders, and down the front to about the knees

411:15 **the first time they had ever seen anyone kneel in a church** The Episcopal practice of kneeling to pray is not customary for Baptists and Methodists (which is what most Southern non-aristocrats were—and are).

411:17 **Brother Fortinbride wasn't a minister either** 'either' = in addition to the other things at the church which were different now from the way they had been before the war

411:20 **he said that Jesus came to him and told him to rise up and live and Father sent him back home** Like Rev. Goodyhay in *The Mansion* (1959): "According to the reverend, he was already safe and dead . . . when all of a sudden Jesus Himself was standing over him saying Fall in and he did it and Jesus said TenSHUN, about-FACE and assigned him to this new permanent hitch right down here on the edge of Memphis, Tennessee" (268).

412:10 **cotton bagging** burlap—the coarse material used for wrapping cotton bales

412:14 **wishes to bear public witness** to confess her sins publicly

412:30 **about they also serve** from Milton's "Sonnet on His Blindness": "They also serve who only stand and wait."

SECTION THREE

414:25 **last time we would see any uniforms at all except as the walking symbols of defeated men's pride and indomitable unregret** except when the outnumbered and overpowered but still unrepentant Southern soldiers came home after the war wearing their uniforms—at first because they had nothing else to wear, later because of continuing pride

414:37 **Ringo's picture** Since there is no longer a need for the paper for requisitions, Ringo can use some of it to draw pictures. The book begins with a 'living map' of Vicksburg; now we have Ringo drawing what once was Sartoris.

415:14 **I can even ride in that gate on a horse and do that** which is something even you can do

415:19 **you can move into town and keep busy all winter** The Yankees have burned Jefferson, so there is a lot more there that Ringo could draw if he gets satisfaction from drawing buildings as they were before they were destroyed.

415:22 **like the chine knuckle bone in a ham** white like the end of a hambone

415:34 **I would have known him now even if I hadn't before** by his swearing

415:37 **He said that pen is down there in the creek bottom** 'He said' = Ab said

415:38 **If you meet man woman or child and they so much as smile at you, shoot them** Obviously he doesn't mean this as an order to be taken literally. He is frustrated because Ringo has beaten him with words and his men are laughing.

416:6 **Who do you reckon *he* is?** Ringo thinks Ab has told

the Union soldiers where the mules are hidden. He is probably right.

416:11   **already had her sunbonnet on**   ready to go outside

416:37   **left handed trace galls**   raw spots on the left hip
caused by rough places on the harness

416:38   **castoff bandsaw bands**   jagged metal instead of
leather, rope, or chain

417:3   **God help the North if Davis and Lee had ever thought
of the idea of forming a brigade of grandmothers and nigger orphans**   Compare with 403:14//123:28: 'What I wonder is, if somebody hadn't better tell Abe Lincoln to look out
for General Grant against Miz Rosa Millard.'

417:4   **Davis**   Jefferson Davis, President of the Confederacy

417:4   **Lee**   Robert E. Lee, Commander-in-Chief of the Confederate Army

417:10   **evacuation orders**   orders to leave the area. There
was no single time when all Union troops were withdrawn
from Mississippi, but almost all had left by the end of 1864.
The significant fighting was by then hundreds of miles east
of Mississippi and there was no danger of a Confederate
counter-offensive in the west.

417:14   **man to man**   The lieutenant's problem in talking with
Granny is that there is no precedent in civilized warfare (or
in gentlemanly behavior) for dealing with a woman (especially an elderly one) who has acted as enemy. Women were
supposed to remain in the background. Granny hasn't, and
the generally accepted conventions of military behavior
don't fit the present situation.

417:20   **I dont know**   Granny *doesn't* know. The lieutenant
asked the wrong person. Granny knows how many mules
they have handled, Ab knows how much he told her he
sold them for, but Ringo is the one who would have kept
track of how many were sold back more than one time, for
that is what interests him—how *badly* they had beaten the
Yankees.

417:31   **too busy running the reaper to count the——**   The next word would be 'sheaves.' A reaper is a machine that cuts grain in the field and then binds it into bundles called 'sheaves.' The sentence is a Northern set-expression for someone so busy making money he doesn't have time to count it.

417:36 **haze them** literally: harass them—in effect: drive them

418:9 **voucher** an official document promising to pay a certain amount

418:13 **held——** The next word would be 'sacred.' The lieutenant hesitates because he realizes Granny is an honorable woman but, since she is also a mule thief, swindler, and forger, he doesn't have a firm grasp on just what her standards of fair-play are. He doesn't know on what grounds to appeal to her not to tamper with the voucher.

418:15 **I am a poor man; I have no grandmother** The two clauses are meant to be read together. The second explains the first.

418:16 **the auditor should find a warrant in the records for a thousand dollars** That Granny might add extra zeros is what worries him—like transforming 1 chest to 10 chests, or a team of mules into 110. (See mini-essay on WHY THE YANKEES GAVE GRANNY *TEN* CHESTS OF SILVER, page 110.)

418:25 **provided them hill folks dont take a example from them Yankees** and confiscate those mules too

418:35 **chancel** that part of the church immediately in front of the altar, between the altar and the pews

418:40 **I have borne false witness against my neighbor** I lied to the Yankees.

419:15 **lost cause** This has become a catch-phrase for the Southern attitude toward the war as seen in retrospect: it was a noble cause which God inexplicably permitted to go down to defeat, a prayer that went unanswered.

419:30 **until he had sold them last nineteen mules to somebody** like Loosh taking advantage of his last opportunity to tell the Yankees where the silver was buried

419:38 **Go on home and get the soap** A few pages earlier
  Granny herself had said 'Damn' in front of Bayard (408:2//
  130:22). She now punishes Ringo for saying the same thing
  because the scam is now over. She has publicly confessed her
  sin and distributed the profits of that sin; now it is time to
  return to her role as guardian of her young charges' morals.

420:2 **the can of soap** Home-made soap is usually soft, not
  unlike the fat which is its major ingredient. It does not
  harden into cakes and so is stored in a can.

SECTION FOUR

This section marks a distinct and very great shift in the tone of
the book. Up to this point Bayard's story has been mainly of the
adventures of two boys, a father-hero and a resourceful grandmother, and kindly or inept Yankees. Everything has been fun
and games; even the burning of the Sartoris house has not dark-
ened Bayard's vision. But suddenly, with the killing of Granny,
the game itself changes—the rules and the attitude of the
players.

420:22 **It was Christmas** Christmas of 1864, not long before
  the end of the war in late spring of 1865. 'Christmas' here
  has to mean the Christmas season, not the day itself, because
  we learn later (425//157, 429//163, and elsewhere) that
  Granny was killed just *before* Christmas.

420:22 **we had just heard from Aunt Louisa at Hawkhurst
  and found out where Drusilla was** This statement is all
  right here but it will cause difficulty when we get to the next
  chapter. We are led to understand here that Granny knew
  about Aunt Louisa's letter before she was killed, but in
  "Skirmish at Sartoris" we are told (448:4//190:1) she was already dead when the letter arrived. Also the present passage
  says that Bayard and Ringo knew what the letter said at
  Christmas, but in "Skirmish at Sartoris" we are clearly told

(448:4//190:1) that they did not read it until January or February. These contradictions are not especially serious, but they are real and can't be reconciled.

420:23 **she had been missing from home for almost a year** Since this letter was received in December 1864, Drusilla must have left home not many months after she told Bayard in August 1863 that she would like to ride with his father's troop.

420:25 **she was with Father away in Carolina** She no doubt was with Col. Sartoris but they would not at that time have been fighting in Carolina. The fighting did not reach the Carolinas before 1865.

420:26 **like she had told me** like she had told me she wanted to do

420:38 **as soon as the last Yankee regiment was out of the country** In the four-or-so month interval after the Union Army pulled out of Mississippi and before defeated Southern soldiers made their way back home, there was no effective law enforcement in Mississippi. Outlaw bands like Grumby's roamed virtually unopposed, stealing from helpless civilians. It was the last (and least excusable) chapter of the war in Mississippi.

421:4 **raiding commission** Irregular cavalry (called 'Partisan Rangers') like Col. Sartoris's were officially charged with obtaining needed military supplies—by requisitioning them from civilians or by taking them from the enemy. Such authorization, in the hands of unscrupulous men, could be (and too often was) used as an excuse to cover all manner of dishonest and selfish and barbarous behavior.

421:17 **all Granny had to do was to write out one of the orders and sign Forrest's name to it** forge one more requisition, this time a Confederate one. Ab apparently thinks it is Granny who must have done the actual writing of the requisitions. He has a typical poor white's attitude toward black people and their abilities and has no more respect for Ringo than Ringo does for Ab.

421:21 **that expression on her face** 'with that look on her face when she had quit either arguing or listening to you at all' (420:19//149:5).

422:9 **that you might frighten a brave man, but that nobody dared frighten a coward** A brave man's reaction to a surprise will at least be rational and therefore predictable within limits, but God knows how a coward will react, what irrational and inappropriate response he is likely to make.

422:16 **cotton compress** a building containing apparatus for pressing cotton into bales and for storing the bales until they are shipped. Most of the building is simply a cotton warehouse.

422:16 **Tallahatchie River** a real river, relatively small but navigable, which forms the northern boundary of Faulkner's Yoknapatawpha County

423:9 **We tried. I keep on saying that because I know now that I didn't. I could have held her** Yes, Bayard could have held her. Certainly Bayard and Ringo together could have held her. Even Louvinia had been able to hold her to keep her from going back to the house when it was burning. Bayard and Ringo, whom Granny won't let go with her to meet Grumby because at fifteen they already 'look like men,' allow her to walk down the lane, alone. They run after her only when it is too late—and that is something they will always have to live with.

423:17 **when and why they took fright and left, I dont know** Maybe it is because it is too painful for him to remember, but Bayard is not being honest with himself (or us) here and in the next sentence. He *has* to know when and why Grumby's men took fright and left. See the next entry.

423:19 **at last I couldn't bear it any longer. Then Ringo and I were both running** Because 'I couldn't bear it any longer' is an evasion of the truth. Bayard and Ringo suddenly began running, knowing it was already too late, because they heard the sound of Grumby's shot. They *had* to have heard it: gunshots make noise; Bayard and Ringo are not deaf.

423:32 **tallow dip** a candle

CHAPTER V
Vendée

"Vendée" takes place from a very few days before Christmas in 1864 until about February 23 in 1865.

Title: **Vendée** Pronounced 'von-DAY'; 1) The Vendée is a region in western France where, from 1793 to 1795 during the French Revolution, the Vendéans, opposed to the democratic revolution and sympathetic to the aristocracy, conducted a violent (and successful for a time) last stand against their invaders (known as 'the Blues'). This episode in France's civil war is called "The War of the Vendée." The similarity of the Vendée (region and war) to the American South during America's Civil War was frequently noted at the time and was recognized by Faulkner. 2) 'Vendée' also suggests 'vendetta'—a Corsican and Sicilian term for the duty of the nearest male kinsman of a murdered person to kill the murderer. Since Col. Sartoris was not at home, under the old Southern honor code it was up to Bayard (even though he was only fifteen) to avenge Granny's killing.

SECTION ONE

424:1 **we buried Granny** This has to be shortly before Christmas 1864, since we learn (429:38//163:22) that Christmas day itself occurs after her burial and after they start their hunt for Grumby.

424:12 **the sum, the sharp serpent's fang** what the pain adds
up to. Faulkner's wording echoes *King Lear*: "How sharper
than a serpent's tooth it is / To have a thankless child"
(1.4.287).

424:14 **they didn't have to walk in** because there were no
longer Yankees in the area, they no longer had to conceal
their U.S. branded mules

424:17 **long black smears** scars or discolored places where
the U.S. Army brand had been burned off, perhaps smeared
with grease to protect the wound while it healed

425:1 **like a grown person coming in where the children are
getting ready to play a game and telling the children that
the game is all right but that grown folks need the room
and the furniture for a while** This is like what has just happened in the book: Bayard's experiences of the War had
been all fun and games until Granny was killed, but now all
has become serious.

425:13 **dark red dirt beside the red grave** The soil in parts
of Mississippi (and in parts of several other southern states,
especially Georgia) is truly red—red to a degree that one
who has never seen it cannot easily imagine or believe.

425:23 **croker sacks** burlap bags

426:31 **Because he was older than us; it was like it had been
at the old cotton compress that night with Granny** like
that night when Bayard said he couldn't keep Granny from
going to the cotton compress to meet Grumby. Now Buck
says, 'I'm going! You cant stop me!' Bayard is saying that he
and Ringo were not able to override the authority they had
been conditioned to grant to older people.

427:2 **that's all we'll need for Ab Snopes** Ringo looks down
on Ab, despises him. Since he doesn't know Grumby as a
person, he blames Granny's death more on Ab than is probably justified.

427:24 **wet ammonia steam** ammoniac smell of the mules'
urine

427:29 **something that looked like a yellow cloud** the clay-bank stallion seen from a distance on a dark, rainy day

427:34 **we hadn't slept much lately** Like Drusilla and Granny, they are learning to do without sleep.

427:38 **for a minute . . . I believed that Ab Snopes was Grumby** It is never made clear precisely what connection Ab had with Grumby's band. The most likely possibility seems to be that Ab was trying to profit both from Granny's raid on Grumby and from his being a new member of Grumby's band. When he learned that Grumby had four stolen horses which Ab could sell if Granny could obtain them, he encouraged her to try her requisitioning scam on Grumby. When this resulted in Granny's death, Grumby's men forced Ab to stay with them as a kind of hostage. They left the four horses at Ab's house to make it appear, if the horses were discovered, that Ab was the one who would gain by Granny's killing and therefore the one responsible for it. Buck apparently figured it this way, since he guessed right about going to Ab's house first to check for the horses, but he also knew it was Grumby and not Ab they were really after.

428:2 **if it was Ab Snopes that shot your grandmaw, I'd be ashamed to have it known** It would be somehow dishonorable for Granny to have been killed by someone as no-account as Ab. In *The Hamlet* (1940) Faulkner says that the killer and the one he kills are "wedded and twinned forever now by the explosion" (934). Who would want to be twinned with Ab?

428:4 **He aint Grumby: he's better than that** 'better' in the sense that he will be useful in helping us capture Grumby, who might otherwise be skillful enough to evade them

428:7 **He's the one that's going to show us where Grumby is** 'It wont be a house or cabin they will ever pass as long as Ab Snopes is with them, that he wont leave an indelible signature, even if it aint nothing to capture but a chicken or a kitchen clock. By Godfrey, the one thing we dont want is to catch Ab Snopes' (428:13//161:15).

428:8 **They just hid them horses here because they thought this would be the last place you boys would think to look for them** Uncle Buck cannily figures that, since Grumby would have learned from Ab that the boys would know of the connection between them, the best place for them to hide the horses would have been in Snopes's lot, since the boys are smart enough—at least Ringo is—to assume that that would be too obvious.

428:16 **the one thing we dont want is to catch Ab Snopes** because Ab will leave a trail—'his indelible signature'—of outraged, defenseless people he has robbed, which will make him (and thus also Grumby) easy to follow

428:31 **"And then what are you going to do with him?" Uncle Buck said. He was almost whispering now. "Hey? Hey?"** Compare with Drusilla's voice as she gives the duelling pistols to Bayard in "An Odor of Verbena" (480:35// 237:10): 'her voice whispering into that quiet death-filled room with a passionate and dying fall . . . in the same tone in which she had said "Kiss me" last summer . . . speaking in a voice fainting and passionate with promise.' Both Uncle Buck and Drusilla want (and expect) Bayard to seek vengeance, to kill. Both are offering a gun for him to do it. Bayard accepts Uncle Buck's urging but refuses Drusilla's. See entry 482:8//239:8 for a discussion of why Bayard reacts differently and why we, as readers, react differently to his decisions.

428:38 **canted** lying on its side

429:3 **Mister Snopes aint here** Husbands and wives once referred to one another as 'Mister' and 'Missus.' This is still true for some older Southerners.

429:10 **I reckon you had** It is raining. Southern hospitality is a real thing. For Mrs. Snopes not to ask Buck to come in out of the rain is an extreme breach of manners—a way she would not have acted under normal circumstances, and thus an indication that there is something unusual about the present situation.

429:14 **They aint in Alabama, because she told us so** because she told Uncle Buck that Ab *had* gone to Alabama and
because Uncle Buck assumes (correctly, it turns out) that she
had been instructed to lie

429:17 **Grenada** Assuming Faulkner's fictional Yoknapatawpha County to be located in approximately the same spot in
Mississippi as his actual home county of Lafayette (and the
distances he gives us from Yoknapatawpha to Memphis and
New Orleans and its relation to the Mississippi, Tallahatchie,
and Yocona rivers all suggest Yoknapatawpha *is* a fictional-
ized Lafayette), then Grenada (a real town) is about 50 miles
south of Jefferson.

SECTION TWO

429:34 **lasted from that December afternoon until late February** The pursuit of Grumby lasts about two full months.

429:35 **one night we realised we had been hearing geese and
ducks going north** signs that winter is nearing its end

430:21 **a wire snapper** The business-end of a whip—the
part that causes the pain and makes the sharp sound—is
called the 'snapper,' sometimes the 'cracker.' It is made of
leather; the kind and stiffness of the leather determines how
much pain and damage the whip will inflict. In this case the
boy's shirt was so thoroughly shredded that it was as if a
snapper made of wire had been used.

430:27 **It was a long way, but it wasn't far** They had been
chasing Grumby for many days and many miles, but since
Grumby did not flee in a straight line but instead had doubled back several times (as most animals do when they are
being pursued), the chase had never gotten very far from
Jefferson.

431:5 **either three or thirteen** A number somewhere between three and thirteen, too many to count exactly in the
short time available—something like 'umpteen.'

431:8   **one of the others grabbed his arm**   Apparently this is Grumby who stops one of the other men from shooting Ringo. We infer this from 441:19//180:20 where he says that Grumby lost his nerve and 'refused to cover the first mistake'—i.e., refused to kill the boys and Buck who were chasing him.

431:20   **cotton pen**   a small shed, more often called a cotton-house, used for storing the cotton until it can be taken to the gin

431:22   **the man began to holler "Hello! Hello!"**   Calling out was prescribed behavior—good manners, in fact—for anyone approaching a house or campfire, especially at night. The idea was to provide advance notice that someone was coming, to eliminate the suggestion of surreptitiousness and for safety, to keep from getting shot.

431:24   **short coupled**   with front legs and back legs relatively close together, not with the long back of a race-horse

431:32   **lace leather**   a long, narrow leather strip—the kind used for boot laces, for example

431:32   **stuck into his pants like a lady's watch**   No, ladies did not wear their watches stuck into their pants; 'like a lady's watch' is misleadingly placed in the sentence. The pistol is on a leather strip which goes around his neck—a leather strip like one a lady's watch would be attached to.

431:35   **pommel**   a rounded knob at the front of a western saddle

432:36   **Did Grumby steal your hog too**   Legally, slaves were not permitted to own anything of value. No slave could have owned a horse, for example. But masters did sometimes permit slaves to keep chickens or a pig. If Grumby had stolen something from Ringo valuable enough for Ringo to chase after him, the stranger's question assumes it must have been a hog. Or perhaps this explanation takes the stranger's words more literally than he intended them. He may simply have been asking 'Since Rosa Millard obviously was not also *your* grandmother, what did Grumby do to get *you* so mad at him'—i.e., how did he gore *your* ox?

432:39 Save your breath to snore with tonight Keep quiet— you are talking too much.

433:4 Two is correct Ringo deliberately misunderstands the 'too.' Since the stranger had patronized him (with the re- mark about the hog), Ringo is showing off his linguistic sophistication.

433:13 we done got a little Alabama Grumby evidence our- selves. That something or somebody has give Grumby a change of heart about killing women and children You say you met a man who said Grumby was going to Alabama, but just three days ago we ('we' meaning Ringo, when he fell in the window of the house where Grumby's men were) saw Grumby stop one of his men who was about to shoot him (Ringo).

433:34 *I wonder if he knows that her off back shoe is gone* The 'off back shoe' is the right rear one. (The 'nigh back shoe' would be the left rear one). A horse with a shoe missing would be particularly easy to track. Since it is very unlikely that none of the men in Grumby's band would have noticed the missing shoe, we must be meant to understand that, for some reason, they are deliberately making it easier for the boys to follow them. Apparently Grumby's men are fed up with having to keep on running away and want to bring the whole episode to an end—even if it means that the boys kill Grumby. Eventually the men in fact do turn Grumby over to Bayard and Ringo.

434:14 soaked the strip in hot salt water The idea is to clean the wound and to constrict the blood vessels and stop the bleeding. This was at a time when any medication or treatment thought to do any good had to be either painful or taste terrible. Getting salt water would have been no prob- lem, for they would have had salt with them for their mules. See entry for 350:26//46:21.

434:23 the black man a man with black hair and beard—a pronounced brunette. This is one way 'black' used to be used, although it was only *unpleasant* brunettes who were called 'black men,' and dark-haired women were never called 'black women.'

434:34 **Something he was telling us last night . . . Something that we are going to find out today** We learn what this is on the next two pages—that Grumby's men plan to give Ab to Buck and the boys, hoping they will settle for punishing just Ab. The stranger had already told them: 'Take a stranger's advice and stick to him [Ab]' (433:31//169:12).

435:4 **slough** swamp, stagnant water. Pronounced 'sloo.'

435:6 **last night it made ice and now we saw the moccasin** They see a water moccasin (a poisonous snake) frozen across the path, its head fixed in the ice. It is not dead. It had been warming itself in the sun and simply didn't make it back to the water when the temperature fell. When the sun has a chance to shine for a time, the moccasin will thaw out and be all right again.

435:11 **There's the sign** 1) A water moccasin has a distinctly triangular head and a long narrow body. Thus a frozen one looks very much like an arrow—in this case pointing beside the path in the direction of the slough. 2) Hunters of outlaw guerrilla bands at the end of the Civil War were called 'snake hunters.' The arrow points to Ab, tied to a sapling—thus a 'snake in the grass.' Buck later (436:38//173:30) refers to the hide-out for Grumby's men as a 'snake den.' 3) According to Mississippi folk belief, seeing a snake in the road is a sign that one's enemy is near.

435:19 **where the five horses had stood while the men that rode them had watched the road** This sentence recognizes explicitly something that has been true for the entire time Buck and the boys have been chasing Grumby—that Grumby and his men could at any time have pulled off the road, doubled back a hundred yards or so, then hidden and waited, and shot Buck and the boys as they passed. They chose not to do this because Col. Sartoris would soon be home. Grumby is already in enough trouble with Col. Sartoris for having shot his mother-in-law. If he should compound his mistake by shooting the Colonel's only son too, Grumby would not be safe from Col. Sartoris and his men even if he ran all the way to Texas. Grumby's only chance for survival is to persuade Col. Sartoris that he realizes he made a mistake in shooting Granny and is sorry about it and is trying to make up for it by not shooting Bayard even though Bayard has been trying to kill him for nearly two months.

436:17 **to set Ab Snopes up with a moccasin** to compare him with a moccasin

436:22 **the worst thing that could happen to him would be for us not to do anything to him at all** so it would seem that Ab had convinced the boys that he was not responsible in any way for Granny's death, that it was all Grumby's fault. Grumby's men had, after all, left Ab for the boys in the hope that the boys would settle for punishing just Ab.

437:30 **galluses** suspenders

437:33 **That's hit. Whup me** As Ab had said (436:26// 173:16): 'I made a mistake. I admit hit. . . . The question is, what are you fellows going to do about hit?' What they did about it was determined by custom: the status (social and family) of the principals determined the form of the punishment. If one gentleman 'offended' another (whether by calling him a liar or coward, or by merely implying he might be a liar or coward, or by insulting a female member of his family by, for example, killing her) the remedy was the same: the offended man challenged the offender to a duel. If an inferior committed the offense, he was dealt with as befitted his status: he was horsewhipped—the same punishment meted out to slaves. Ab was an inferior; therefore he was whipped—by Ringo, which was in itself an assertion of Ringo's superiority (even though black) to Ab.

438:12 **a passel** a parcel, a bunch, a lot

438:16 **They left us early the next morning** Bayard can be certain Uncle Buck will be safe with Ab and that Ab will do everything possible to look after him, for Ab is already in trouble with Col. Sartoris (once he gets home) and he certainly will not do anything to cause the McCaslins too to want to punish him.

SECTION THREE

438:29 **Ringo and I went on . . . we lost count of time** Since the hunt does not end until late February, Bayard and Ringo must have continued after Grumby by themselves for about three weeks, for it was near the beginning of February when Buck went home (429:39//163:18 and 431:18//165:30). It surprises me that the boys follow Grumby by themselves for this long, but that is what the text tells us.

439:9 **his bare toes pointing down and his head on one side** The black man is dead. Grumby's men have killed him and pinned the note to him. Their point is to get the boys' attention and to show that they are serious when they warn that they will kill the boys if they continue to follow them. A note pinned to a murdered man by the murderer (explaining his action or warning against an attempt at retribution) was not an uncommon practice. Mink Snopes in *The Hamlet* (1940) thinks just after he has killed Houston: "What he would have liked to do would be to leave a printed placard on the breast itself: *This is what happens to the men who impound Mink Snopes' cattle*" (935).

439:27 **one more chance. Take it, and some day become a man. Refuse it, and cease even to be a child** Bayard does make his choice (although to kill Grumby was not one of the options the note offered) and he does become a man at least in the sense that he acts out a man's role. Later, in "An Odor of Verbena," he chooses again from these same options. Then he chooses differently, and he becomes a man in yet a different sense.

440:29 **If you had done what I wanted done that night in**

December, you wouldn't be where you are now 'that night in December' = when Grumby shot Granny; 'done what I wanted' = kill Bayard and Ringo too that night, instead of running off

440:32   maybe for a minute Ringo and I and Grumby, too, all thought the same thing all thought the man was going to stab Grumby with the knife

440:37   Have you got him Do you have him covered with your gun?

441:5   Boys He is talking to the other members of the gang.

441:7   these boys Bayard and Ringo

441:7   since you are so delicate about children, maybe they will be delicate with you Since you didn't kill them when you had the chance, maybe they won't kill you now that they have the chance.

441:19   lost your nerve again and refused to cover the first mistake have not ambushed and killed Bayard and Ringo and, at first, Buck while they have been chasing us

441:21   raising the country outraging everyone enough so that they *all* came hunting for you

441:33   remember that Texas is a wide place, and use that knowledge I strongly advise you to keep far away from us in the future.

441:40   Ringo and I were on the ground off our mules, standing

442:4   heavy as a firedog heavy as an andiron, an ornamental metal device for holding logs in a fireplace

442:11   I could hear my voice; it sounded faint and far away, like the woman's in Alabama that day See 430:21// 164:18: 'a woman with a little thread of blood still running out of her mouth and her voice sounding light and far away . . . saying "Kill them. Kill them."' Bayard's comparison is appropriate, since in a minute or so he will have killed Grumby.

442:13   You shot three times. You have got two more shots in it Revolvers are now standardized as six-shooters, but this was not always the case. At one time there were four, five, six, seven, and nine-shooters. In Mississippi during the Civil War Southern revolvers were as often five-shooters as any other kind.

442:18 **he passed it from his right to his left hand and let it hang again, pointing down** We learn in *The Hamlet* (1940; p. 756) that Grumby called himself 'Major Grumby,' a Confederate officer. An officer was (and to a certain extent still is) by definition a gentleman. Gentlemen settled their disputes by duels. In Europe and in New Orleans and in South Carolina, duels were formal and the rules were spelled out in great detail (the code duello). In rural Mississippi the protocol for duelling was much less formal (seconds, for example, were seldom used) but there were certain generally accepted principles: the opponents faced each other at about 30 feet; each had a pistol and each was entitled to two shots; the shots could be taken in any sequence; moving was not permitted until both had fired two shots or until one man had fallen; the starting position for a duel was with the pistol pointing down, alongside the leg, and held in the opposite hand from the one that will do the shooting. Thus when Grumby, facing Bayard, passed his pistol 'from his right to his left hand and let it hang again, pointing down,' he was assuming the conventional position for a Mississippi duel. The only non-standard feature at the beginning of Grumby's and Bayard's duel is that they seem to be closer to each other than 30 feet, and at less than 30 feet it would be almost impossible for anyone accustomed to using a pistol to miss a target as large as a man.

442:21 **a yellowhammer** a woodpecker

442:26 **Well, she's safe enough now** the gun is harmless now

442:39 **two bright orange splashes** flashes from the muzzle of Grumby's gun as he fires twice

443:3 **I reckon I heard the sound** of Grumby's gun firing

443:3 **I reckon I must have heard the bullets** the sound of

Grumby's bullets going by Bayard's head. A shooter does not hear bullets going away from him—i.e., does not hear bullets he himself has fired.

443:4 **I reckon I felt him when he hit me** when Grumby charged Bayard after he had fired

443:11 *I have got to hold onto it* hang on to his own pistol which Grumby is trying to wrench from him

443:22 **He shouldn't have tried to run from us in boots** This is the sentence which ties up what we have been told on the two preceding pages and offers the rationale for what happens next. Although Grumby followed some of the protocol established for Southern duelling, he clearly did not fire to wound or kill Bayard, but only to try to overwhelm him in order to disarm him and escape his vengeance. After all, from his colleagues' point of view, it was his squeamishness about shooting minors that had gotten the gang into this fix in the first place. But from Bayard's point of view, the duel is off when Grumby, who according to the code must stand and accept his opponent's return fire, having shot first, turns and runs. "Boots" symbolized "officer and gentleman" (see entry for 368:4//72:19); Grumby, in running, demonstrates that he is neither, only the murderer of Granny, whose death must be avenged.

443:26 **the pistol was level and steady as a rock** Bayard shoots Grumby with the steadiness of a skilled hunter. He shoots him in the back and does not feel this to be at all dishonorable. Grumby has demonstrated that he is not honorable (see above entry). He has, in fact, behaved like an animal and has been tracked as a hunter might track game; therefore Bayard shoots him like an animal.

SECTION FOUR

443:31 **the old compress** the compress where Grumby killed Granny

443:33 **what we had to carry now** it took 'the rest of that day and part of the night' to reach the compress because they were carrying Grumby's body back to the scene of his crime; 'now' they are only carrying Grumby's right hand

444:2 **already had the piece of wire** a wire to attach Grumby's hand to Granny's grave marker

444:3 **after two months; it was almost level now** Since they put Grumby's hand on Granny's grave on the night of the same day they killed Grumby, and this occurred two months after Granny is buried, and she was buried before Christmas, then 'late February' (429:34//163:18) when the Grumby episode is finally over must be around February 23.

444:7 **Now she can lay good and quiet** knowing that she has been properly avenged

444:13 **It wasn't him or Ab Snopes either that kilt her . . . It was them mules. That first batch of mules we got for nothing** This statement by Ringo is sometimes taken as Faulkner's summary of Granny's moral downfall: that once she compromised with truth, her decline was swift and her fall inevitable. This is not very convincing; one could as easily argue that had she never discovered the good her actions did for her community, she never would have become an over-reacher, or that had she compromised with what she believed to be right, the relentless pursuit of what was rightfully hers, she would never have died.

444:26 **the surrendering** Southerners referred to the official end of the War as 'the surrender.' This did not occur until April, but almost all fighting in and around Mississippi did in fact stop several months before that.

445:14 **Fotch back** 'fotch' is past tense of 'fetch' (go, get, and bring back)

445:17 **expiation** that which purifies (as by a rite), that which satisfactorily concludes by having done what had to be done

445:20 **all except the right hand** There was no specific Southern tradition for cutting off the hand responsible for a killing, nor were there examples from the original Vendée uprising, other than a few distant beheadings, but there are several related traditions Faulkner may have had in mind. The chief one was biblical—an eye for an eye, etc., but it was also part of Islamic and Hebrew law to cut off the hand of a thief, making the punishment fit the crime. Additionally, it was the paw of a mountain lion which had mauled his mother that young Bedford Forrest brought back to show he had exacted revenge.

445:23 **Aint I told you he is John Sartoris' boy** Didn't he behave as a son of Col. Sartoris *ought* to have behaved? See entry for 487:29//247:4 where the significance of Uncle Buck's words is discussed.

CHAPTER VI

Skirmish at Sartoris

The present action of "Skirmish at Sartoris" (the day of the election and wedding) is in late August 1865, the summer after the war is over. It is sometimes claimed that Faulkner has this 1865 election occurring two years too soon, two years before elections were actually held in Mississippi after the War. That is not exactly right. While the first state-wide election in which black people voted (an election to select representatives to meet to try to arrive at terms for Mississippi to be readmitted to the Union) was not held until 1867, the 1865 "Skirmish at Sartoris" election is a local one (for Town Marshal of Jefferson). County histories testify that there never was an interruption to such local elections during the War or after (a Sheriff or Mayor dies, so they elect a new one). And while it is true that no black people *succeeded* in voting in a Mississippi election before 1867, it is not true that in Mississippi (and elsewhere in the South) black people did not *try* (even if unsuccessfully) to vote before then—which is what happens in "Skirmish at Sartoris."

Title: **Skirmish at Sartoris** 'Skirmish' is a military term for an engagement not involving a large number of troops and resulting in no more than a few casualties. The war which the present skirmish is a part of is the ongoing War Between the Sexes. 'Sartoris' is what the Sartoris plantation is called. Some plantations were given names (like Seven Oaks, for example) but most were known simply by the name of the owner.

SECTION ONE

446:1 **that day**   the day of the election when the ballots were
finally cast at Sartoris. We learn in "An Odor of Verbena"
that the election for the Legislature which Father won eight
or so years later takes place near the end of August, so if late
August is the regular time for elections in Mississippi, that
would make the month of the present action in "Skirmish at
Sartoris" August too. There is no other specific evidence for
what time of the year the election occurs, but there is nothing in the novel or in history which would make August an
unlikely month.

446:8 **I think I know the reason**   Know the reason for what?
There are two answers, both right, although to different un-
derstandings of the question: 1) The reason the men are
lined up in a military-like fashion is that 'they were still soldiers' and they 'dont want to quit that world'; 2) The reason
for the confrontation between the men and the women is
that 'when you have lived in a world ordered completely by
men's doings . . . you dont want to quit that world.' And so
the men and the women were now 'actually enemies.' If this
is not clear, see the next entry for further explanation.

446:17 **now Father's troop and all the other men in Jefferson, and Aunt Louisa and Mrs Habersham and all the
women in Jefferson were actually enemies for the reason
that the men had given in and admitted that they belonged
to the United States but the women had never surrendered**
If we take this simply to mean that the women had never
surrendered to the Union Army and therefore had never
admitted that the South belonged to the United States (as
the men had), I think we would be missing Faulkner's main
meaning. In fact, that reading of the sentence would not
even be right, for consider 465:27//215:1 about Mrs. Wilkins: 'she was a woman and so wiser than any man, else the
men would not have gone on with the War for two years

after they knew they were whipped.' Faulkner's point seems
to be a different one. The men had accepted that they had
lost the war and were prepared to go about building up the
country again within new groundrules imposed by the victorious North—'as though . . . [they] had joined forces with
the men who had been our enemies' (454:3//198:22). They
would try to retain some features of the pre-war South
(white supremacy, for example) but they realized much of the
way of life they had known before the War (especially the
formal institution of slavery) was permanently finished.
The women, however, had not surrendered, and they were
insistent upon retaining certain of the values and customs
they had always known—as if the war had not occurred.
What they are insisting on in this story is that Col. Sartoris
and Drusilla should marry, since they have been living together. In a larger sense, the women are attempting to rees-
tablish the importance of family and morality which a war
over slavery, regardless of its outcome, has no justification
for disrupting.

446:23 **I remember the night we got the letter and found out
at last where Drusilla was. It was just before Christmas
in 1864** This is Aunt Louisa's second letter (she wrote
three). We don't learn about them in the order they were
written or received. Since Granny was dead before Christmas (425//179, 429//187), since Bayard knew what the letter
said before Christmas (420//169), and since he started after
Grumby before Christmas, the letter must have arrived at
Sartoris in the very short interval between Granny's death
and Christmas of 1864. But at 448//218 we are told that Bayard didn't read the letter until the time when he and Ringo
had spent a night at home after their chase of Grumby had
begun and Grumby had doubled back past Jefferson. If they
didn't read it until then (necessarily sometime in January or
February), they could not have known what it said before
Christmas, although the text tells us (here and on 420//169)

that they did. There is no satisfactory way to resolve this discrepancy. Also, on 420//170 we learn that Bayard and Ringo brought the letter back from Jefferson while Granny was still alive; but on 448//218 Mrs. Compson had sent the letter out to Sartoris after Granny was dead. These two contradictions can't be resolved.

"Skirmish at Sartoris" tells about three letters from Louisa, one from Col. Sartoris, and one written by Drusilla. In chronological order (as distinct from the order in which we are told about them in the story) these letters are:

1. a letter from Father in July 1864 (447:6//216:23) from Carolina, six months after the Yankees and his troop left Mississippi (447:24//217:17). He says nothing about Drusilla's having joined his troop.

2. a month after that (thus August 1864) Aunt Louisa's first letter to Granny, saying Drusilla was gone—Aunt Louisa said she didn't know where (447:29//217:23).

3. Aunt Louisa's second letter, addressed to Granny, which arrived before Christmas 1864, just before (after?) Granny died and which Bayard and Ringo read at the time (or did not read until January or February 1865?). The letter said that Drusilla had been gone for almost a year and that after she had been gone for six months she had stopped by Hawkhurst and told her mother she had been with Father's troop for six months (448:13//218:22).

4. Drusilla's letter to her mother, telling her where she now was (at Sartoris), written at Father's insistence after Bayard remembered to show Aunt Louisa's second letter to Father and Drusilla. Drusilla's letter must have been written in early spring 1865 (i.e., some time after Bayard and Ringo and Father and Drusilla were all home but before 'spring' by which time Aunt Louisa had received the letter and had written to Mrs. Compson).

5. Louisa's third letter, addressed to Mrs. Compson, in the spring, after the War was over (449:24//220:26).

447:1 **the Yankees had burned Jefferson and gone away**

The Union Army did burn Oxford, Mississippi, in August 1864—just before leaving the area.

447:2 **we didn't even know for sure if the War was still going on or not** This would likely be true in northern Mississippi in late 1864-early 1865. The fighting in that area had for the most part stopped (although there were exceptions to this, especially some very successful late cavalry raids by Nathan Bedford Forrest), and it was not known in Mississippi whether the war was continuing or winding down in the east.

447:3 **for three years the country had been full of Yankees, and then all of a sudden they were gone** This is essentially historically accurate, although Union forces continued to occupy Memphis at the southwestern tip of Tennessee.

447:5 **We hadn't even heard from Father since July, from Carolina** This won't mesh with the facts of the war. The July when Father wrote would be July of 1864, and the fighting had not reached the Carolinas by then. Atlanta had not been taken by then, Sherman's march through Georgia to the sea had not begun by then. Carolina did not become a battleground until early 1865—by which time Father and Drusilla were about to leave (or had already left) to come home to Sartoris.

447:6 **Carolina** Carolina by itself always means either the two Carolinas considered together or just South Carolina.

447:8 **Ringo and I were fifteen then** 'then' = not (as a first reading of the paragraph might lead one to believe) when they received the letter from Father in July 1864 but when Aunt Louisa's second letter arrived in December 1864

447:12 **it had been opened once and then glued back** maybe by Aunt Louisa, deciding she had more to say after originally sealing it, although there is another possibility: the envelope was worn and dirty but the text says it was still possible to make out that it had been sent from Hawkhurst. Maybe the name of the person it was addressed to (Granny) was not legible, and so the postmaster had to open it to learn whom it should be delivered to. And since Mrs. Compson was Granny's friend, maybe he then gave it to her to be sent out to Sartoris (for this was fifty years before the time of rural free delivery). Thus the information in the letter could have been known (by the Jefferson postmaster and Mrs. Compson) and maybe the main part of its message (that Drusilla was with Father) was relayed to Bayard before Christmas and before he read it—thereby technically (although perhaps not convincingly) satisfying what the text literally says, but Granny did not learn it (because she was dead) and Bayard did not actually read the letter until January or February.

447:16 **cut with scissors from wallpaper** Paper was one of the Confederacy's chief shortages. Any kind of paper (wrapping paper, wallpaper) that happened to be available was used for letters.

447:17 **written on both sides** to save paper. Also, after finishing a page, the paper could be turned sideways and the writing continued—over the previous writing and at right angles to it. This was hard to read, but not impossible.

447:22 **But I didn't tell Father. Maybe I forgot it** 'forgot it'? Bayard is being less than honest with us and with himself here. He didn't tell Father about Drusilla's wanting to join Father's troop because he didn't think that was something Drusilla ought to do.

447:23 **Then the Yankees went away, and Father and his troop went away too** We learn in the next line that Father wrote a letter in July 1864, six months after he had left, so he must have left Mississippi at or near the beginning of 1864.

447:24 **Then, six months later, we had a letter from him about how they were fighting in Carolina** For them to receive a letter six months after Father left Mississippi is all right, but not a letter about the fighting in Carolina. It would be more than half a year after that before the fighting would reach the Carolinas.

447:26 **a month after that we had one from Aunt Louisa that**

Drusilla was gone . . . about how she did not know where Drusilla was This is a month after Father's July letter, which means Aunt Louisa's letter was written in about August 1864. It is interesting that Louisa didn't write to Granny about Drusilla's being gone until she had been gone for more than half a year (Drusilla had left home near the start of 1864—see 420:24//170:3 which says that by December Drusilla had been gone almost a year). Apparently Aunt Louisa had been hoping at first she would not have to tell anyone about Drusilla's absence. Another possibility, of course, is that Aunt Louisa wrote this August letter *after* Drusilla had stopped by and told her mother where she had been. If that is the case, Aunt Louisa's letter to Granny was an indirect way of trying to learn what, if anything, Granny knew about Col. Sartoris and Drusilla's being together.

447:36 **we didn't know where Drusilla was either** Father's letter written in July (his last letter) didn't say anything about Drusilla's being with him, so Bayard and Granny wouldn't know about it, but Drusilla had to have been with his troop for about six months at that time. Obviously Father realizes that having Drusilla with him is something that others are not going to approve of, and so he doesn't mention it.

447:39 **all living men blue and gray and white and black** this covers all male bases—Yankee, Southern, white, and Negro

448:3 **then the next letter came. Only Granny wasn't there to read it because she was dead then** This is Aunt Louisa's second letter—the Christmas one. Again we have the contradiction about when the letter arrived in relation to Granny's death. According to what we were told at 420:27//170:7, Granny was still alive when the letter came.

448:17 **you are only an aunt** an aunt in the loose sense of being an older female relative. Granny is not Aunt Louisa's sister.

448:23 **who had deliberately cast away that for which he died** i.e., honor. While it is true that the South was fighting to preserve honor, Aunt Louisa is substituting a different meaning of 'honor' when she argues that Drusilla's father was fighting to preserve Drusilla's honor.

448:29 **That's how it sounded** exaggerated, overblown, sentimental, scarcely sense-making rhetoric

448:29 **a pineknot** a pine branch used as a torch

448:33 **the highest destiny of a Southern woman—to be the bride-widow of a lost cause** This is Aunt Louisa's romanticized notion of the noblest of all roles for a Southern woman: to have been engaged to a Southern soldier and for him to have been killed before they could marry—killed while fighting for an honorable and glorious cause in which they both believed but which God chose not to smile upon.

448:37 **living in a word that Aunt Louisa would not even repeat** The word is 'sin': 'living in sin.' Or perhaps she means 'adultery.' In either case, it is an exaggerated delicacy which would cause her not even to mention such standard words.

449:4 **how Drusilla had been gone for six months** This is true, but the wording is a bit tricky—if not actually misleading. Aunt Louisa is writing this letter in December. She is not saying Drusilla had by then been gone six months, for at 420:24//170:3 we learn she had gone 'almost a year.' In order not to be lying Aunt Louisa would have to mean that Drusilla had been gone for about six months when she stopped by home to tell her mother she had been with Father's troop for six months. Drusilla had to have told her mother this sometime around July or August—either shortly before or shortly after Aunt Louisa's first letter to Granny (see entry for 447:26//217:19). The fact that Aunt Louisa did not write her next letter to Granny until December tells us that she waited another four or five months after learning where Drusilla had been, apparently trying to decide whether it would be better to try to hush up the whole matter of Drusilla's being with Father or to announce it and try to bring about a marriage. By getting straight just when Drusilla joined Father's troop, when she stopped by home to tell her mother about it, what Louisa said about Drusilla in her first and second letters to Granny, what Father failed to report in his last letter home (July 1864), and when Bayard finally told his father and Drusilla about Aunt Louisa's second letter, we discover that Aunt Louisa and Father and Bayard and Drusilla were all being less than forthright in what they wrote or said or did—Father and Drusilla because they knew others would not approve, Aunt Louisa and Bayard because they did not approve.

449:8 **in the garments not alone of a man but of a common private soldier** Aunt Louisa is objecting here not just to Drusilla's taking on the role of a man but to her dressing as an ordinary soldier instead of as an officer, for the distinction between enlisted man and officer in the Civil War was chiefly based on social class, not military training and certainly not upon military skill or knowledge.

449:14 **actually pretended she did not even know what Aunt Louisa was talking about** If Aunt Louisa were consistent, she should have been pleased if her daughter's innocence kept her from understanding what she meant. But Aunt Louisa doesn't believe at all in the reality of innocence, just in the importance of insisting that the appearance of it be preserved. Drusilla's pretending not to understand her mother is probably Drusilla's way of pointing out the inconsistency—which her mother is too convention-bound to understand.

449:19 **At least dont call him *Cousin* John** There are several possible meanings here: 1) Don't add the appearance of incest to your other transgressions; 2) The term 'Cousin John' was a cliché and joke—a euphemistic name for an older man who was having an affair with a younger woman. The pretense (which no one believed) was that she would be safe with him, because he was her cousin and thus could not

possibly have a romantic interest; 3) 'Cousin John' was one
of several terms for an outhouse. It would be indelicate for
a lady to refer to it when strangers might overhear.

SECTION TWO

449:25 **It was in the spring and the War was over now** the
spring of 1865—shortly after the events in "Vendée." General Forrest formally surrendered in Mississippi on May 8,
but the fighting had been over and the men had started
home several months before that. Bayard is fifteen (going on
sixteen).

449:27 **build the house** rebuild the house that had been
burned—on the same foundation but this time considerably
larger (as we learn in the next story, "An Odor of Verbena").
Where Col. Sartoris got the money for such a project in the
post-war impoverished South we are not told, although we
are also not told what became of the ten chests of silver.

449:34 **the other cabin** If this means that there were only
two slave cabins in the old slave quarters, then Sartoris could
not have been a working cotton plantation—which leaves the
source of Col. Sartoris's income (pre-war as well as post-war)
unexplained.

449:36 **And so one night I remembered Aunt Louisa's
letter** It is hardly likely that Bayard could for several
months have forgotten a letter in which Aunt Louisa had
said she didn't know where Drusilla was. The 'And so' which
begins the sentence reveals Bayard's train of thought. Drusilla had been sleeping in the same cabin with Bayard and
his father. Aunt Louisa's letter had been concerned that Drusilla and Father were together, sleeping together. 'And so,'
Bayard says, he 'remembered' the letter and showed it to
Drusilla and his father. Aunt Louisa may be presented as a
not-very-sympathetic almost-fool, but Bayard seems to realize she has grounds for her suspicions and complaint and a

good measure of justice on her side—even though it takes him some time before he 'remembers' to produce the letter. It is not easy for an admiring son to criticize his hero father's moral behavior.

450:5 **surrey** a carriage with full front and back seats; in automobile terms like a four-door sedan or limousine

450:29 **the quarters** the slave cabins grouped near the main house

450:33 **had not made one of the number** was not one of them

451:9 **buggies** smaller and less pretentious than surreys; like a coupe or two-door sedan

451:26 **You poor child** Bayard is fifteen and he has already killed Grumby and strung up his body. He is not interested in being called a 'poor child' by Mrs. Habersham.

451:26 **So I didn't stop** Bayard understands that Mrs. Habersham is about to gush over him, and he doesn't want to listen to any of her patronizing sympathy.

451:37 **What other reason can you name why she should choose to conceal herself down there in the woods all day long, lifting heavy weights like logs** Mrs. Habersham is implying that Drusilla is pregnant, that she is ashamed and therefore concealing herself from them in the woods, and that she is probably trying to induce a miscarriage by 'lifting heavy weights like logs.'

452:1 **log-yard** the place where the logs were gathered before running them through the sawmill

452:2 **bandsaw** the cutting blade at the sawmill

452:2 **the blindfolded mule going round and round** the mule, walking in a circle and hitched to the end of a large spoke, provided the power for the saw; it was blindfolded to keep it from being stopped by distractions

452:8 **brogans** crude, stiff shoes

452:18 **My condition** Drusilla understands Mrs. Habersham to mean that she assumes Drusilla, an unmarried young woman, is pregnant. Drusilla's apparently genuine surprise and indignation at this is our best evidence that the charge is groundless.

453:10 **a gum twig in her mouth** not like chewing gum but like chewing on a flavored toothpick

453:11 **Father's old hat on top of her headrag** Since Col. Sartoris is back, the hat no longer proclaims the role she filled in his absence. But Granny is dead, and now Louvinia is in charge of that part of the plantation and household which is a woman's responsibility. Thus the hat still is an outward sign of authority, although now of a different kind.

453:16 **Is that what you believe** Do you also believe that John and I have been having a sexual relationship and that I am pregnant?

453:17 **Then Louvinia moved. Her hand came out quicker than Drusilla could jerk back and lay flat on the belly of Drusilla's overalls, then Louvinia was holding Drusilla in her arms like she used to hold me** Louvinia seems to like Drusilla and she ends up holding Drusilla to comfort her, but Louvinia *is* a woman, so she checks for signs of swelling in Drusilla's belly before she says 'I knows you aint.' Louvinia's position is much more sympathetic for the reader than Mrs. Habersham's or Aunt Louisa's, but in the Battle of the Sexes Louvinia pretty clearly lines up on the side of the other women.

453:23 **We went to the War to hurt Yankees, not hunting women** How completely Drusilla has by now taken on a male role and attitude should be clear from the way she words this statement.

453:25 **I knows you aint** She knows Drusilla isn't pregnant—and, since Drusilla is young and healthy and not pregnant, Louvinia is willing to believe that Drusilla and Col. Sartoris must not have been having a sexual affair either, since that is what Drusilla appears to be genuinely claiming.

453:26 **It didn't take them long** It didn't take long after that for the women (including Aunt Louisa) to see to it that a wedding was arranged for Col. Sartoris and Drusilla.

453:33 **For four years we had lived for just one thing . . . to get Yankee troops out of the country . . . and now that had happened** Even though there had been a Union garrison in Memphis since June 1862, additional Union troops to assist in the reconstruction did not begin to arrive in Mississippi until about a year after the end of the war.

453:38 **We were promised Federal troops** The period of disorganization of the last months of the war did not end with the killing of Grumby (and others like him) and the return home of the Confederate soldiers. Many of the newly-freed slaves simply refused to work—not just for their former masters, but refused to work at all—waiting instead for the forty acres and a mule they understood they had been promised by the Yankees. The Ku Klux Klan was formed with the ostensible purposes of providing protection for whites and of trying to establish some kind of economic order utilizing black labor, but too often the Klan provoked and carried out lawless and senseless persecution of black persons, who felt (often with much justification) that they were in effect being returned to slavery. It was not until Federal occupation troops were sent to Mississippi (more than a year after the end of the war) that non-violence became even a *possible* mode for trying to settle the enormous and difficult problems resulting from defeat in war, the destruction of the means of production, the freeing of the slaves, and the arrival of Northern carpetbaggers (some of whom were idealists dedicated to helping black people but too many of whom were unscrupulous opportunists willing to do anything that promised a personal profit).

454:4 **a new foe whose means we could not always fathom but whose aim we could always dread** 'a new foe' = not just (or even mainly) the Northern carpetbaggers who had descended, vulture-like, to scrounge for ways to turn a profit from the South's defeat—they were contemptible but at least understandable—but the much more difficult to fathom Northerners who professed to be idealists and who seemed to be trying to overturn the South's social order by arranging for ex-slaves to be in positions of authority over whites

454:8 **it was more than that which Father and the other men were doing** From other Faulkner books we know that Col. Sartoris was at this time organizing and leading the local unit of the Ku Klux Klan (or a Klan-like group).

454:15 **I aint a nigger any more. I done been abolished** Before the War 'niggers' were considered (or at least were customarily treated) as if they were less than fully human; they had "no rights that a white man need respect" (this from a pre-War decision by Chief Justice Taney of the U.S. Supreme Court); now they do (or soon will) have rights—the legal right to vote, for example; thus 'niggers' have 'been abolished.' See entry for 457:39//234:24 about the voting of black people. But that isn't all: consider also Ringo's meaning of 'folks' at 326:19//11:7: Do they eat the same thing in Tennessee 'that folks eat,' and Hubert Beauchamp's meaning in *Go Down, Moses* (1942) when, after the War, he says about his young-looking 'illicit hybrid female' cook: "They're free now! They're folks too just like we are!" (303)

454:23 **Uncle Cash that druv the Benbow carriage twell he run off with the Yankees two years ago** 'druv' = drove; 'twell' = until; Loosh had gone off in the summer of 1863, so if Cash had left at the same time, it would be about two years ago.

454:25 **Marshal of Jefferson** The Town Marshal had traditionally been the inept relative of someone in authority, for it was a relatively low level position—putting belligerent drunks in jail overnight, catching stray dogs, etc. The Sheriff would take charge of any important or difficult situation. That Col. Sartoris would make an issue over such an unimportant office shows how determined whites were to keep black people from holding *any* position of authority.

454:31 **a patent** an official authorization

454:32 **Republicans** the political party of Lincoln and Grant, thus identified in Southern minds with pro-black-rights party of the victorious North

454:33 **This War aint over. Hit just started good** The military struggle between North and South may be over, but the antagonism between North and South over economic and cultural differences and jealousies and the human struggle between races are gaining in intensity.

454:38 **nigger voting tickets** tickets already marked in favor of Cash Benbow, so black persons (most of whom, like Cash himself, could not read or write) could simply be given one of the tickets to deposit in the voting box

455:18 **I have come to appeal to them once more** 'them' = Col. Sartoris and Drusilla; 'appeal to them' = ask once again that they get married

455:27 **smell like dead roses** Doubtless Aunt Louisa kept a sachet of compressed rose petals in her handkerchief drawer. Attar of roses is more pungent than sweet, but it did serve as a perfume that could be made from the plants of one's own garden.

456:2 **after a year, I suppose I cannot call it surprise** Aunt Louisa could mean that by now she has known for a year that Father and Drusilla have been together (she has known this since Drusilla stopped by Hawkhurst to tell her about it the previous July or August), or she could mean that she knows now that Father and Drusilla have by now been together for at least a year (since about January of 1864, in fact). Either or both of these meanings would work.

456:3 **So Father came out too** 'too' = as Drusilla had run out of the cabin to get away from Aunt Louisa in the previous paragraph. They both leave because they know what Aunt Louisa is going to say and they don't want to have to listen to it.

456:4 **the spring and ... the big beech** Faulkner in his other books several times associates beech trees with springs.

Whether it is true that springs really are often found at the base of beech trees, I don't know, but I have had one beech tree with spring in Faulkner's Lafayette County pointed out to me.

456:11 **Father and I slept in the cabin with Joby and Ringo** which means that Aunt Louisa has gotten Drusilla out of the cabin with Col. Sartoris and she is now with Aunt Louisa and Louvinia in the ladies cabin

456:13 **getting the timber out** working at the sawmill, turning out lumber for the house—not dragging logs from the woods, which has already been done

456:16 **the election would never be held with Cash Benbow or any other nigger in it** Col. Sartoris has worded his objection so it seems he is opposing the chance of an illiterate black person becoming the town's law enforcement officer, but his *real* objection is to the idea that black people are going to be allowed to vote.

456:35 **Aunt Louisa went behind her back and chose a game she couldn't beat** Aunt Louisa didn't go behind Drusilla's back. She simply by-passed Drusilla and her wishes and appealed directly to Col. Sartoris's honor as a gentleman, demanding that he marry her daughter whose reputation he had compromised by his association with her. Col. Sartoris had no other option but to agree. Drusilla was not part of the decision-making process. This was at a time and place where many (if not most) upper-class marriages were arranged by parents and almost none took place without at least parental consent.

457:24 **They have beat you, Drusilla** 'They' = the women. In this skirmish in the War Between the Sexes, the women have won. Col. Sartoris and Drusilla will have to get married— whether they want to or not.

SECTION THREE

458:8   **Madeira**   a sweet imported wine—the wine of choice for festive occasions in the pre-war South

458:15   **a reception could be held for a bridal couple at any time, even ten years later**   Yes. A wedding and a reception do not have to be on the same day. The same is true for a burial and a funeral service.

458:25   **Aunt Louisa made Drusilla put on Father's big riding cloak**   to cover up her bridal gown, so she would not be announcing to the entire countryside that she was finally marrying Col. Sartoris—nearly two years too late

458:26   **wreath**   a bridal crown of flowers

458:27   **curried and brushed**   brushed first with a curry-comb, a stiff wire brush (which is normal), and then with a softer brush (which is not normal and which would be done only for a very special occasion)

458:38   **They kilt um**   Like Ringo saying (337:23//31:1) 'We shot the bastud, Granny! . . . We kilt him!'

459:27   **the derringer**   a small pistol with at least two barrels, one above the other, therefore capable of rapidly firing at least two shots

459:30   **I dont know how long it was**   how long they waited to listen for possible additional shots. Perhaps the repetition of this sentence immediately after the next following sentence is the result of Faulkner's deciding to change its position without indicating clearly it was to be deleted from its former position.

459:32   **nigger that was Mrs Holston's porter**   The Holston House was the hotel in Jefferson. A porter is a man who carries things—in this case, luggage.

460:5   **I let them fire first**   To let one's opponent fire first obviously requires considerable nerve, but once that has happened, firing in retaliation would be hard to criticize. We are never told whether the Burden who shot first missed

Col. Sartoris on purpose or whether he was just a bad shot. If the latter, he must have been a truly bad shot, since he and Col. Sartoris were in the same room.

460:9 **Does any man here want a word with me about this** Literally: Does anyone question my actions? In practical terms: Is there anyone here who believes my killing the Burdens was a dishonorable act and who is willing to say so to my face (which would be to challenge me to a duel)?

460:16 **I hereby appoint Drusilla Hawk voting commissioner** If you are tempted to ask by what authority does Col. Sartoris appoint Drusilla the new voting commissioner, you should also ask by what authority had the Federal government appointed the Burdens as voting commissioners for a local Mississippi election. The answer in both cases is, of course, 'might makes right' and 'stop me if you can.'

460:23 **Like hell you will** go alone to the sheriff. Some of us will go with you to testify to your honorable role in the shooting.

460:26 **Dont you see we are working for peace through law and order** As far as we can tell, Col. Sartoris is not being consciously ironic in saying this. Bayard makes no comment on it. Faulkner gives no sign that he does not also agree (even when "Skirmish at Sartoris" was published separately as a short story). But in the next story, "An Odor of Verbena," it will be clear that Bayard does not approve—to the degree that he is willing to pay with his life, if necessary, to show his disapproval of using violence to accomplish even a good objective.

460:28 **make bond** appear before a Judge and put up money to be forfeited if he should run away. He has killed two men and there will have to be at least some kind of official investigation.

460:35 **I reckon she and I both remembered at the same time** that Drusilla and Col. Sartoris had not gotten married

460:38 **women dont ever surrender: not only victory, but not even defeat** if they never surrender, they never have to acknowledge either your victory or their defeat; it may sound like chop logic, but there is a difference between saying "You win" and "I lose," a difference avoided by saying neither

460:39 **that's how we were stopped** 'stopped dead still' (see five lines earlier)

461:5 **You** *forgot?* To Aunt Louisa this is no doubt the surest sign yet that Drusilla has relinquished her womanhood, for what woman would possibly not get married because she *forgot?*

461:11 **Your bridesmaids of murder and robbery** ['Your groomsmen' in pre-1991 Vintage texts.] Aunt Louisa is getting carried away a bit with this characterization.

462:4 **Drusilla would call their names out** 'George Wyatt has voted, Amodeus McCaslin has voted,' etc.

462:7 **You needn't bother to count them . . . They all voted No** This is not a rigged election. Pre-marked ballots provided by the candidates with the voter requesting which one he wanted was the way *all* elections were held in the U.S. in the mid-nineteenth century. The secret ballot was not adopted by Mississippi until 1890.

462:13 **this time even Father could not have stopped them** 'them' = the men of Col. Sartoris's troop; 'this time' = in contrast to 460:39//239:18 when Aunt Louisa and the other ladies came out on the porch and did stop them as they rode up with the ballot box; 'stopped them' = stopped them from giving the Rebel Yell—as they do as they ride away

462:17 **Yaaaaay, Drusilla! Yaaaaaay, John Sartoris! Yaaaaaaay!** The Rebel Yell here is a cheer ('congratulations' and 'best wishes') for the wedding which they know will shortly follow (469:9//253:10). It is for both Drusilla and Col. Sartoris because both were fellow soldiers in their troop.

CHAPTER VII
An Odor of Verbena

The present action of "An Odor of Verbena" takes place during two days in October 1873, eight years after "Skirmish at Sartoris." Bayard is now twenty-four, shortly after his September birthday.

Title: **An Odor of Verbena** Verbena (ver-BEAN-uh) is a flower. There are many varieties; some have no smell at all. The verbena usually in the South has a strong and pleasant smell of lemon. It was frequently used as a sachet (crushed verbena leaves in a small cloth bag to place in drawers where linens were stored—to keep them smelling fresh).

SECTION ONE

463:1 **Coke** pronounced 'COOK'; a traditional text for a student reading law, by Sir Edward Coke (1552–1634), interpreting Sir Thomas Littleton's fifteenth-century work on the English Common Law (Eaton 54; Bledsoe 26)

463:4 **I should have known** that Prof. Wilkins was about to tell him that his father had been killed—although that this is what this means does not become clear until the next page

463:5 **presentiment** premonition, a feeling that something is about to happen

463:7 **I had lived in his house for three college years now** Bayard had been staying at the Wilkins' for the 1870, 1871, and 1872 college years and had just returned to Oxford to begin his final year, the term beginning September 1873.

463:8 both he and Mrs Wilkins called me Bayard in the house After three years they felt close enough to Bayard to call him by his first name, not 'Mr. Sartoris' (as it would then have been customary for them to call any adult, non-related male they had not known since he was a child). In public, of course, the Wilkinses still would refer to him as 'Mr. Sartoris.'

463:9 he would no more have entered my room without knocking than I would have entered his—or hers It was a rigid rule of etiquette *never* to enter a room with a closed door without first knocking and being given permission to come in.

463:12 one of those gestures with or by which an almost painfully unflagging preceptory of youth ultimately aberrates 'unflagging' = never letting up; 'preceptory of youth' = one who teaches moral lessons to children ('preceptory' is a Faulkner coinage, adding a 'y' to 'preceptor,' a synonym for teacher); 'aberrates' = deviates drastically from what would be expected, goes haywire

463:14 Bayard. Bayard, my son, my dear son At roughly the same time Faulkner was writing *The Unvanquished* he was also working on another Civil War novel, *Absalom, Absalom!* (1936). The title *Absalom, Absalom!* echoes the despair of a father in 2 Samuel 18:33: "Would God I had died for thee, O Absalom, my son, my son!"

463:22 although it was October, the equinox had not occurred The autumnal equinox occurs each year on or about September 22, when the sun passes over the equator, marking the first 'official' day of autumn. That makes record keeping easy, but it bears little relation to perceived reality. The older, informal, commonsense way of counting the seasons was to say that autumn began whenever the stifling summer weather broke. That would almost always be sometime in September or October, but on exactly September 22 only by coincidence. In any event, the autumnal equinox was said to have occurred whenever summer perceptibly changed to fall. Winter began when it started to get really cold, etc.

464:8 **Your boy** 'Boy' was the word for one's black personal servant. Simon was Col. Sartoris's 'boy' during the war and Joby (even though older than Col. Sartoris) was his 'boy' before the war. Ringo is now Bayard's 'boy.'

464:8 **in the kitchen** A Southern black person, from adolescence on, under all circumstances and no matter how close to the family nor how distinguished as a person, *always* in a white person's house waited or ate in the kitchen, never in the parlor or diningroom. That Ringo, who as a child shared everything (including a breast and a bed) with Bayard, now waits in the kitchen tells us quite a bit about how things have changed since 'time had slipped up on us while we were . . . too busy to notice it' (342:28//39:23).

464:8 **It was not until years later that he told me** This lets us know that Bayard is telling the story of *The Unvanquished* an unspecified number of years after the events had occurred. We learn a few lines later that he is twenty-four at the time of the present action. Thus *The Unvanquished*—or at any rate "An Odor of Verbena"—is the story of Bayard's *remembering* what happened when he was a boy and young man—subject to the distortions and 'improvements' (intentional and unintentional) which time and memory (and the desire to tell a good story) inevitably cause.

464:10 **Judge Wilkins** Bayard knew him at the University as 'Professor' Wilkins. Later he became, for Bayard, 'Judge' Wilkins (as he already is for Col. Sartoris—see 476:40// 266:13).

464:16 **forty miles** Faulkner's fictional Jefferson is based on his actual home town, Oxford, Mississippi, but there is at least one major difference between the two: Oxford is the home of the University of Mississippi, and Jefferson has no University. Faulkner consistently describes Oxford as being a separate town forty miles from Jefferson, but he never says in what direction; however, since Sartoris is four miles north of Jefferson on the rail line, and since Bayard says, 'we didn't have to pass through Jefferson either [in addition to not having to pass through Oxford] (477:17//267:1), if one uses the map of Yoknapatawpha County Faulkner drew for inclusion in *Absalom, Absalom!* (1936), the only way to reach Sartoris without passing through Jefferson would be from the northeast.

464:18 **what I knew, what I knew now I must have believed and expected** that Father's reliance on violence was sooner or later going to get him killed

464:20 **heard nothing in the feet** Bayard heard Professor Wilkins approaching down the hall but it was not until he flung open the door that Bayard realized he had anything unusual to report.

464:27 **deep-barrelled** large, round chest

464:27 **mare who looked exactly like a spinster music teacher** Horses, like dogs, can and sometimes do look like people (or like kinds of people), but it's up to you to supply the image of the music teacher.

464:28 **a basket phaeton** a light, relatively sedate buggy with wicker seats, intended mainly for town use, often the choice of women

464:32 **livery stable** a business which boards and rents horses and carriages and buggies—a pre-automobile Hertz or Avis

464:33 **Good for me** The accent is on 'good': the incongruity of Prof. Wilkins's offering his wife's mare was 'good for me'—'like being doused with a pail of cold water would have been good for me' (464:29//245:21).

465:3 **He followed me** 'He' = Prof. Wilkins, not Ringo

465:5 **like a laboring delayed woman** like a pregnant woman whose baby is past due and who is having a hard time accomplishing the delivery

465:9 **not ten years recovered from the fever** not ten years since the end of the war, with the implication that although one may have gotten over the fever stage of the illness, a full recovery has not yet been achieved

465:11 **we must pay Cain's price in his own coin** Cain killed his brother, Abel (this we learn in Genesis). The war is over but we are still killing our fellow men—which is to say, our brothers.

465:17 *Who lives by the sword shall die by it* "All they that take the sword shall perish with the sword," Matthew 26:52.

465:19 **toward which I walked, had to walk** toward where Mrs. Wilkins is waiting at the foot of the stairs; his reason for walking there is not to make his manners (say goodbye to her) but because he is now 'The Sartoris' and has to go by where Mrs. Wilkins is waiting in order to go home, presumably to do what must be done

465:22 **almost the last battle nine years ago** The last major battles of the war were in late fall of 1864, the last battles of any kind in spring 1865. The last battle would have been about nine years ago, the 'almost last' ones about nine and a half.

465:23 **The Sartoris** how the head of the Sartoris family (which is now Bayard, the oldest living male) would be referred to. This is a way of speaking ('The McCaslin,' 'The MacIvor') made popular by Sir Walter Scott that comes from a legitimate Scots tradition which is the heritage of many early Mississippi families.

465:27 **she was a woman and so wiser than any man** which is Faulkner's main point (or one of his main points) in the previous story, "Skirmish at Sartoris"

465:28 **gone on with the War for two years after they knew they were whipped** The two truly decisive battles of the Civil War, Vicksburg in the West and Gettysburg in the East, both disastrous Confederate defeats, occurred on July 4, 1863. The war continued for two years after that, but it was understood that there was scarcely any realistic chance that the South might still win. The South continued fighting

mainly because of a hope that the Union forces would eventually grow tired of a prolonged war and would permit the
South to go its own way.

465:32 **your Aunt Jenny** Col. Sartoris's younger sister, Virginia Sartoris Du Pre, who now lives with the Sartorises

465:35 **I lied even to her** by giving as an excuse that he
might have many things to attend to at home and not saying
what he is really thinking—which is that, after tomorrow,
she might not consider him honorable enough to be still welcome in her house

465:39 **what, despite myself, despite my raising and background (or maybe because of them) I had for some time
known I was becoming** What had he known for some time
he was becoming? How despite himself? How despite his
raising and background? How because of himself? How because of his raising and background? To find the answers to
these crucial questions, and discover the moral center of *The
Unvanquished*, we need to read on.

466:4 *if I am going to do what I have taught myself is right or
if I am just going to wish I were* if I have the resolve to act
according to how I believe I *should* act—that violence is not
the way to deal with any problem, not the way to respond to
any provocation, even when it is my father who has been
killed and I will be expected to punish his killer—or whether
such an idea/wish is one I will abandon when pressured by
others (as I know I will be) to act as 'The Sartoris' is *expected*
to act

466:12 **he had changed even less than I had since that day
when we had nailed Grumby's body to the door of the old
compress** It was an idea held by many white Southerners
that black and white children developed roughly at the
same rate until about age fourteen, at which point, while
white children continued to develop physically, mentally,
and morally, black children advanced only physically. (See
note on 'Your boy' above, 464:8//212:23.) Ringo was clearly
ahead of Bayard when they were fourteen (the time of "Ri-

poste in Tertio") but Bayard seems ahead of Ringo now that they are twenty-four. It is a matter worth thinking about whether Faulkner (or Bayard, who is telling the story) subscribed to the idea of black arrested development, or whether Bayard's passing Ringo can be explained by an environment which offered them strikingly different and unequal opportunities. Bayard is at the University, studying to be a lawyer. Ringo is Bayard's personal servant. To be the body servant of a wealthy or important white man was *the highest position* a black male was permitted to attain in the post-slavery South. This situation remained almost literally true (except for black people who went to a city and became barbers or undertakers for others of their race) until World War I and did not substantially change until after World War II—at least not in the South. As the saying had it, a 'nigger job' should never involve anything more valuable or complicated than a lawn-mower or a scoop shovel, as for the apprentice firemen in *Light in August* (1932). Society made *no* provision for a black person with Ringo's intelligence and abilities.

466:24 **maybe it was more than just weariness and so I would never catch up with him** maybe the wisdom/world-weariness borne of generations of slavery—a heritage which was not Bayard's and which produced a resignation Bayard could never know

466:31 **my mare Father had given me three years ago** when Bayard first went to the University in September 1870

466:32 **could do a mile under two minutes any day and a mile every eight minutes all day long** therefore a very good mare

466:39 **the Book** the Bible

466:40 **His blind and bewildered spawn which He had chosen above all others to offer immortality** Mankind—for only to humanity (even though imperfect) did God offer the promise of eternal salvation

467:5 **But I did not tell him** I did not tell him I did not intend to kill Redmond

467:8 **faced without warning and made to deliver like by a highwayman out of the dark** 'highwayman' = highway bandit; 'to deliver' = to hand over one's money and valuables. The point of Faulkner's comparison is that a highwayman gave his victims a choice that simply by-passed their principles—he offered a proposition they couldn't refuse: 'your money or your life.'

467:10 **only the young could do that** only the young can act according to what they believe is right when their belief goes against 'blood and raising and background'

467:11 **gratis** without having to pay a price for it

467:22 **this time and maybe last time** Maybe this will be the last time he will ride this road between Jefferson and the University—not because he thinks he might be killed the next day but because, if he acts as he intends to act the next day, maybe he 'forever after could never hold up his head again.'

467:22 **who would not die (I knew that)** Of course, it's obvious that Bayard wasn't killed, but how could he believe he *knows* he will not be killed at this point? Certainly Bayard realizes that it is possible that Redmond might kill him. But Bayard has a very good reason to know he will not be shot by Redmond, because at this point he does not intend to face Redmond *at all*. That is the decision which he is afraid will result in his losing everyone's respect.

467:23 **but who maybe forever after could never again hold up his head** See previous entry.

467:29 **I rather think it was the same quality** Ringo was able to get a good horse from the livery stable not because the proprietor recognized the genuineness of his grief and felt sorry for him but because Ringo had learned years ago (see "Raid" and especially "Riposte in Tertio") how to do whatever was necessary.

467:32   **too long and too close association with white people**
Bayard (and Faulkner) seem to be saying that, in retrospect,
it was a *mistake* for Ringo to have been permitted to be so
close for so long with whites; that, given the circumstances
of the time and place, Ringo's close association with whites
has not prepared him very well to live as a black person
must live.

467:37   **bushwhack**   to attack without warning, as from ambush; more generally, a Civil War term for any hit-and-run
guerrilla action

467:37   **Like we done Grumby**   Bayard's killing of Grumby
(even though he eventually did shoot Grumby in the back)
cannot fairly be described as 'bushwhacking' him. Bayard
gave Grumby every chance to act in an honorable manner.
For Ringo to refer to it now as 'bushwhacking' has to be a
deliberate attempt to irritate Bayard, to describe the incident
in the worst possible light. We are to understand that Bayard's and Ringo's easy relationship has seriously deteriorated
in the eight years since the war.

467:38   **But I reckon that wouldn't suit that white skin you
walks around in**   Ringo's bitterness is clear. Their 'common
enemy, time' (321:15//4:8) has indeed overtaken them.

467:40   **there was plenty of time still for verbena**   There had
not been a frost yet; verbena was still blooming.

468:1   **although I would have to reach home before I would
realise there was a need for it**   a need for verbena, not a
need for time. Since Bayard does imagine that Drusilla will
be waiting for him with a sprig of verbena in her hair
(468:25//252:9), the need for verbena which he does not yet
realize must not be Drusilla's need for it but his own. And
since Drusilla had said 'verbena was the only scent you could
smell above the smell of horses and courage' (469:23//
253:26), and since certainly Bayard is not thinking at this
moment about horses, the sentence here must be an indirect
way of saying that it would not be until he had reached home
that he would realize he would have a need for courage. Re-

member that, at the present moment, he does not intend to face Redmond when he gets home (see entry at 467:22// 250:15).

468:4 **gauntlets** long gloves with flaring, protective cuffs

468:5 **coaxed and ordered beds** carefully laid out and tended beds of flowers

468:5 **odorous old names** Obviously the *names* of the flowers don't smell, but the names do have an aura about them (see 468:14-15//253:15–16) which operates like a suggestive and pervading fragrance, an aura of association as distinct as an odor. Compare the leathery smell of a luxury sedan with the plastic of an economical family car.

468:8 **Indian Summer** a short, unseasonably warm spell after autumn has definitely arrived

468:11 **before I became a man and went to college** before I became twenty-one. Bayard started at the University in September a few days after his twenty-first birthday.

468:13 **five more just for the tonguing, the music** Many fox-hunters claim the best part of the hunt is to listen to the sounds (the music) made by the hounds. The idea is as old as Shakespeare: "My love shall hear the music of my hounds" (*A Midsummer Night's Dream* 4.1.106).

468:14 **possum** the singular and plural form of 'opossum,' a small (about the size of a cat), furry, carrion-eating animal—hunted more for the sport than for any other reason, although they can be roasted to produce what possum-lovers call an incredibly rich meal

468:17 **trains which had no longer belonged to Mr Redmond for a long while now and which at some instant, some second during the morning Father too had relinquished** a way of saying that the railroad became Bayard's at the moment of his father's death

468:22 **parlor** livingroom—the more formal livingroom in a house which has more than one

468:22 **in his regimentals** in his military dress uniform, complete with sabre and decorations

468:23   **all the festive glitter of the chandeliers, in the yellow ball gown**   Col. Sartoris is dead, his body lies in the parlor, yet the scene as Bayard imagines he will find it (and as he does in fact find it) has an atmosphere conspicuously inconsistent with mourning. Why is this? Drusilla does not consider the occasion one for mourning. Her thoughts are not on what happened to John yesterday but with 'passionate and voracious exaltation' (481:2//273:12) on what she assumes Bayard will do tomorrow—when he will 'be permitted vengeance,' when he will take on 'what they say is an attribute only of God's' and 'be permitted to kill.' Drusilla considers the occasion more like Easter than like Good Friday.

468:25   **the two loaded pistols**   two smooth-bore pistols specifically intended for formal duels

468:27   **room arranged formally for obsequy**   room set up for a formal funeral

468:31   **the two hands shoulder high, the two identical duelling pistols lying upon, not clutched in, one to each**   offering as if presenting ceremonially

468:33   **the Greek amphora priestess of a succinct and formal violence**   This is a difficult (and famous) passage. A priestess presides over and charges with emotional (and to a certain extent sexual) meaning some kind of sacred and/or esoteric ceremony—in this case one which celebrates violence. It is a 'formal' violence because it will be acted out according to a known, traditional ritual. It is a 'succinct' violence because its intended end, death, will be swift and sure. The priestess is a 'Greek' priestess in the sense that the rite she is energizing is pagan, not religious, certainly not Christian. She is an 'amphora' priestess (and here the meaning is idiosyncratically Faulkner's) because of the peculiar-to-Drusilla way she holds her arms—'the two arms bent at the elbows, the two hands shoulder high'—this because 'amphora' is the word for a kind of ancient Greek vase which has two prominent matching curved handles, rising (like curved arms) almost to the neck of the vase.

SECTION TWO

468:38   **I was twenty then . . . four years after . . . the evening
when Father and Drusilla had kept old Cash Benbow from
becoming United States Marshal**   Bayard was twenty the
summer before he entered the University, when he and Drusilla walked in the garden. If he was twenty that summer, he
would be twenty-one after his birthday in September when
he started at the University. That was the summer of 1870.
But (see 469:3//253:2) summer of 1870 would be closer to
five (not four) years after the election (in August 1865, when
he was fifteen), more than five (not four—see 469:18//
253:20) years after the War was over in April 1865 when he
was fifteen, and definitely more than five (not four—see
469:37//254:15) years after he had killed Grumby in February 1865 when he was fifteen. If for all three of these
Faulkner had written 'five' instead of 'four,' there would be
no problem. As the text stands, the times specified will not
mesh. This doesn't affect a normal reading of the story (the
times given are *about* right), but it does stymie a conscientious chronology-maker.

469:2   **which Father decided I should have**   Bayard entered
the University when he became twenty-one but it was to
study law which his father decided he should do. Thus Bayard's saying he had become a man at twenty-one (468:11//
251:19) must have been intended at least partly ironically.

469:5   **United States Marshal**   "Skirmish at Sartoris" said
Cash Benbow was running for Town Marshal. Here it says
he was kept from becoming United States Marshal. Town
Marshal is not an important post—a kind of minor-offense
watchman paid by town funds. A United States Marshal is
quite a different kind of Marshal. He is the local voice of the
Federal government's authority, and in the confused and
violent period shortly after the war that was indeed an important position. As Town Marshal, Cash could hardly have
done much damage if he proved incompetent. As United

States Marshal, an unqualified person could have been disastrous. Apparently between writing "Skirmish at Sartoris" and "An Odor of Verbena" Faulkner changed his mind about which kind of Marshal Cash was trying to be, and then forgot in revising to make the two accounts consistent.

469:6 **Mrs Habersham herded them into her carriage and drove them back to town** for Drusilla and Col. Sartoris to get married

469:8 **made him sign Father's peace bond** co-sign Col. Sartoris's pledge not to run away before the deaths of the Burdens had been investigated and a decision whether or not to indict him had been made

469:13 **the house was the aura of Father's dream just as a bride's trousseau and veil is the aura of hers** and as verbena is the aura of the role Drusilla has created for herself

469:23 **she said verbena was the only scent you could smell above the smell of horses and courage** I take Drusilla's word for it that verbena can mask the smell of horses. Courage has no smell. Neither does 'the will to endure,' really, but Bayard told us in "Ambuscade" (325:36//11:9–10) that that was how his soldier-hero father smelled to him as a boy. Since smells appear to be something Faulkner comes back to (Drusilla's hair smells like rain—on 445:4//212:27 and again on 469:36//254:14), since the present story is called "An Odor of Verbena," and since verbena plays a role in the story at important moments, it is probably worth remembering that Drusilla has said here that verbena can be smelled above courage, even if we don't know at this point what she might mean by that. For Drusilla, who rode in the troop of Col. Sartoris, it might seem entirely reasonable to mix the literal smell of horses with the figurative smell of courage.

470:13 **Father the next day sent some money** He tried to pay with money for a life he had taken, and he sent this money to the man's family by messenger instead of going himself. It is no wonder the wife threw the money in his face.

470:17 **Colonel Sutpen** Thomas Sutpen, the man *Absalom,*

Absalom! (1936) is mainly about. Pages 470-471//255–256 give a short summary of Sutpen's life.

470:19 **the regiment deposed Father after Second Manassas** No. Second Manassas was 31 August-1 September 1862. As explained at 353:6//56:19, if we take the Second Manassas date literally, Father could not have returned to Mississippi to form his unit of irregular cavalry by summer of that same year, 1862. There would be no discrepancy if we accept that Faulkner was thinking of Second Manassas as being a year after First Manassas (which it essentially was) and do not pin down Second Manassas to its actual date.

470:22 **underbred** neither born of good family nor well brought up and educated

470:38 **the night riders** Ku Klux Klan, although the Jefferson version may not necessarily have had that particular name

470:38 **carpet baggers** The South's contemptuous term for northerners who came to the South after the War, carrying all their worldly goods in satchels made of carpet, scrounging for a way to make a profit from the post-War chaos. Southerners saw them as vultures, out-of-work scavengers who were prepared to get out of town at a moment's notice, and who regularly had to.

471:22 **They were northerners, foreigners** A foreigner was anyone who was not a southerner.

471:28 **close implacable head** 'close' means hair cut short; 'implacable' is from a Latin verb, placare, which means to quiet, to soothe, to appease, to assuage, to reconcile. With a negative prefix (im) the meaning would be directly opposite—unwilling to be quieted, refusing to be soothed, etc. (Flanagan 431)

471:33 **I had one once** Yes, she described her war-destroyed dream at some length in "Raid" (387-388//114–115).

471:35 **There are not many dreams in the world, but there are a lot of human lives. And one human life or two dozen——** Drusilla is a spirited and in many ways admirable young woman. Bayard has always been attracted to her and I think Faulkner intends that we should find her attractive and sympathetic too. But what Drusilla is saying here—her easy writing off of human life—is monstrous. As Bayard had thought at 466:39//249:15: 'if there was anything at all in the Book, anything of hope and peace for His blind and bewildered spawn which he had chosen above all others to offer immortality, *Thou shalt not kill* must be it.'

472:3 **the next time I was twenty-four** 'the next time' = the second time (that we are told about) that Bayard walked with Drusilla in the garden. He was not really twenty-four at the time of this second walk; he was twenty-three and would not be twenty-four for another week-or-so, until his birthday in September. By the time he returned to the University in September he had had his birthday and was twenty-four, but he was not twenty-four when he walked with Drusilla in the garden in August. Also, when he walked with her in the garden the first time, when he says he was twenty, it was only three years ago, not four (we know this, because he has been at the University only three years). Faulkner is counting Bayard's age two different ways in these two scenes. It makes sense that Bayard would say he was twenty during the first walk, because he is trying to say that he was younger then—ready to voice his ideas about his father but not ready to stand up for them—but after the second walk when he is almost twenty-four he does stand before and confront his father after supper.

472:6 **It was just last summer, last August** This is being said from the point of view of the following October, the time-present of the story.

472:6 **Father had just beat Redmond for the State legislature** Elections in Mississippi apparently were held in late August.

472:19 **which permitted him to stand as much as he did from Father, to bear and bear and bear until something (not his will nor his courage) broke in him** What eventually broke was simply Redmond's willingness to continue to put up with Col. Sartoris's 'ruthless dictatorialness and will to dominate.' Enough was enough.

472:22 **Redmond had not been a soldier, he had had something to do with cotton for the Government** In *Requiem for a Nun* (1951) Faulkner says Redmond was a northerner, a carpetbagger. Perhaps that is how the town later remembered him.

472:26 **not having smelled powder** was not a soldier

472:26 **He was wrong** 'He' = Col. Sartoris

472:33 **paying the workmen and the waybills on the rails at the last possible instant** 'waybills' = bills for construction materials received. See 469:31//254:7: 'gold coins borrowed on Friday to pay the men on Saturday, keeping just two cross-ties ahead of the sheriff as Aunt Jenny said.'

472:36 **buy or sell, naming a price** one way of dissolving a partnership: the partners agree on what would be a fair price (fair to the seller, fair to the buyer) for half of the business; then each has the opportunity to buy out the other's half at the agreed-upon fair price

472:39 **at least Father claimed that Redmond did not believe he could raise it** The implication of this 'at least' clause is that Bayard may suspect that Redmond *did* realize that Father could raise it but didn't care, preferring to sacrifice money for peace of mind. If true, Col. Sartoris's tale of business acumen is a good deal less heroic.

473:2 **that's what started it** 'it' = that series of actions, beyond just words, by which the hostility between Col. Sartoris and Redmond manifested itself and intensified—Father taunting Redmond by blowing the train whistle as the first train passed Redmond's house, his running against Redmond for the State legislature, goading him at every opportunity, until Redmond finally shot him

473:8 **named for Aunt Jenny, with a silver oil can in the cab with her name engraved on it** This is Bayard's mild joke. The purpose of Col. Sartoris's railroad was to give Jefferson rail access to the eastern seacoast. The Sartoris line joined the Memphis and Charleston which, despite its name, led to Richmond, Virginia. It was customary in early railroading days to name locomotives and cars for their ultimate destination. Jenny Du Pre's name was really Virginia and that is doubtless the name Col. Sartoris gave to his locomotive and engraved on the oil can.

473:15 **the pilot** a plow-shaped bumper (to toss aside anything unfortunate enough to be on the track) with small wheels at the front of a steam locomotive, so-called because it "directs" the locomotive down the tracks

473:20 **he ought to let Redmond alone . . . there aint any use in making a brave man that made one mistake eat crow all the time. Cant you talk to him?** It will be important to remember over the next six or so pages that this suggestion by George Wyatt is what Bayard's and Drusilla's talk in the garden is about.

473:24 **eat crow** be publicly humiliated

473:27 **he would have listened, but he could not have heard me** He was too preoccupied with and too fixed on his own agenda to pay attention to any suggestions for a change in his actions from Bayard.

473:32 **after that train ran into Jefferson, he had no chance against Father** The coming of the railroad to an inland town automatically made that town an important shipping center for the surrounding countryside. Small towns on the railroad quickly grew; small towns bypassed by the railroad died out. The man responsible for bringing the railroad to a town would be seen as a local benefactor.

474:3 **This from you?** 'This' = what George Wyatt had told Bayard—that Father 'ought to let Redmond alone . . . Cant you talk to him?' (473:20//260:13).

474:3 **from you? You? Have you forgotten Grumby?** Drusilla is pointing out that it is hardly consistent for Bayard, who once pursued Grumby relentlessly for two months until he was able to kill him, to now be considering suggesting to his father that he ease up on the man who is his antagonist, Redmond.

474:5 **I never will forget him** Whether Drusilla understands his meaning here or not, Bayard is certainly saying that after more than eight years he still has not been able to get his killing and dismembering Grumby out of his mind, and he is afraid he never will be able to erase that memory. Unlike Drusilla who regards Bayard's Grumby experience as an act of justified vengeance and even heroism, Bayard has by now come to think of it as an act of violence (and even barbarity) which he is not proud of.

474:6 **There are worse things than killing men, Bayard. There are worse things than being killed** Drusilla may be right, but there are not *many* things worse than these two, and (except perhaps in defense of family, country, or honor) it would be hard to say what these 'worse things' might be. Surely to prolong a squabble between Col. Sartoris and Redmond would not be one of them. Because this is the first time Bayard has shown Drusilla expressing explicitly such a fanaticism in support of violence—apparently for *any* violence, not just that in support of a noble cause—it could be easy for us not to take in the import and implications of what she is saying, but Bayard has had a good idea of her feelings for some time. That is why he expected her to be in her ball gown when he reached home at the end of Section One (see entry for 468:24//252:8).

474:8 **Sometimes I think the finest thing that can happen to a man is to love something, a woman preferably, well, hard hard hard, then to die young because he believed what he could not help but believe** Consider how similar this is to Aunt Louisa's letter about 'the highest destiny of a Southern woman—to be the bride-widow of a lost cause' (448:33// 219:17). We understood this idea to be dramatized nonsense when Louisa wrote it, but is Drusilla's version of it here any more in touch with reality? Also, since it is too late for Col. Sartoris to die young, it must be Bayard that Drusilla

has in mind to do the dying this time. It is not clear whether
Bayard put all of these pieces together on this evening in the
garden, but he does later—at least by the time he goes to
town to face Redmond. Bayard very much admired Drusilla
when they were both younger. I think readers were meant
to admire her too—her honesty and spirit—but at least by
the time of the final days in "An Odor of Verbena" Drusilla
has gone over the edge. She is no longer fully sane.

474:11 **was what he could not (could not? would not) help
but be** The words in parentheses represent Drusilla's self-
correction: 'could not' implies inability, 'would not' implies
choice. Her hero is not a product of accident, but of self-
determination.

474:12 **she was looking at me in a way she never had before.
I did not know what it meant then and was not to know
until tonight** By 'tonight' Bayard means the night he was
called back from the University, the night Drusilla became
hysterical when she kissed his hand and sensed he was not
going to kill Redmond, the night he lay awake all night going
over in his own mind the events of his life which led up to
that present moment. What it was that he did not understand last August in the garden but does know 'tonight' is
not exactly clear. The whole matter of what did Bayard
know about Drusilla's state of mind and when did he know it
he presents to us with mixed signals. He must have understood much of her alliance with violence—her worship of it,
in fact—before reaching home after his father's death, for
otherwise he could not have expected her to be waiting for
him like a priestess in ball gown, as if for a celebration. On
the other hand, if he had by August fully understood that
she had passed beyond the edge of sanity, he would hardly
have kissed her as he did—and been so affected by their
kisses.

474:21 **Kiss me, Bayard** Why does Drusilla unexpectedly
and suddenly want Bayard to kiss her? Is it a delayed giving
in to a long-standing attraction? No, the reason is quite dif-

ferent, much more calculating on Drusilla's part. They have been talking about George Wyatt's idea that Bayard suggest to his father that his father restrain his violence, 'let Redmond alone.' He was asking Bayard to say, in effect, that his father ought to 'do a little moral housecleaning' (477:10// 266:24). But if on the day Bayard was to say this he had just kissed his father's young wife, would Bayard be in a moral position to offer advice to his father about his father's moral conduct?

474:23 **And eight years older than you are. And your fourth cousin too. And I have black hair. Kiss me, Bayard** a series of irrelevancies, reasons which have nothing to do about whether they should or should not kiss. At least we learn from them that Drusilla is Bayard's fourth cousin, which could tell anyone who understands how degrees of cousinship work just what relation Granny must have been to Aunt Louisa (or to her husband).

474:28 **now it was she who said, "No."** Drusilla holds back at this point, though Bayard is starting to cooperate, because she doesn't want him to be able to excuse his behavior afterward by saying that she kissed him; he will have to admit that he kissed her.

474:33 **the woman of thirty, the symbol of the ancient and eternal Snake** A 'woman of thirty' is no longer a puppy-like, inexperienced, post-adolescent twenty-year-old, nor is she yet old enough to have begun to go downhill in physical attractiveness. Her ideas and interests are adult (she would prefer champagne to ice cream, making love in a bed to making out in a buggy) and she now has the knowledge and experience and skills to know how to go about getting what she wants. In short, a woman of thirty is a woman at the height of her power as an attractive, interesting, seductive, sexually-compelling woman. She is the incarnation of Eve, that conscienceless temptress of men who exists (at least potentially) in every woman just by the fact that she is a woman. The 'ancient and eternal Snake' is the snake of the

Garden, the one that instructed and corrupted Eve. So the woman of thirty as the symbol of the eternal Snake combines the associations we have with Eve, with the snake as corrupter of Eden, with a fully alive and mature and knowing and powerful woman. Whatever all of these add up to applies to Drusilla as she is seen at this moment by Bayard.

474:35 **I realised then the immitigable chasm between all life and all print—that those who can, do, those who cannot and suffer enough because they cant, write about it** Those who can't do are the ones who write (i.e., they write about that which they haven't themselves experienced and so can give only their guesses as to what whatever they are describing must be like), and Bayard is now discovering that they didn't get it right—at least not about what it is like for a man to kiss and be kissed by a 'woman of thirty' like Drusilla. Bayard's only source of knowledge about such things has been what he has read in books (one of Balzac's was actually titled 'A Woman of Thirty') and he is learning that what he has read is inadequate to the present situation.

474:39 **inscrutable** Her look does not reveal whatever she is feeling or thinking or scheming.

474:40 **watched her arms rise with almost the exact gesture with which she had put them around me as if she were repeating the empty and formal gesture of all promise so that I should never forget it, the elbows angling outward** This makes the third time Bayard has told us Drusilla has made this unusual 'amphora' gesture.

475:17 **live on Government reservations** live on military pensions, in county poorhouses or old folks' homes, maybe simply in a world which is so hemmed in by government interference that a 'free' life (like the one they knew during the war) is no longer possible

475:23 **Now I must tell Father** What must he tell his father? That he had kissed his father's wife? Or tell him what George Wyatt had asked him to, that his father should quit badgering Redmond, stop provoking further violence? At this point the story doesn't let us know which of these Bayard means, but Col. Sartoris's response when Bayard does tell him (476:37//266:9) makes it almost certain that it is about the violence that Bayard tells him.

475:24 **Yes . . . You must tell him. Kiss me** Again Drusilla is pressuring Bayard—this time so he will not be able to minimize his actions afterward by saying they kissed only once. Drusilla is indeed demonstrating that she is a 'woman of thirty.'

475:27 **each time both cumulative and retroactive** Each kiss draws strength from those which went before, each kiss adds strength to those already experienced.

475:27 **immitigably unrepetitive** different each time, not just the same old kiss over and over

475:28 **each wherein remembering excludes experience, each wherein experience antedates remembering** This is not one of Faulkner's more successful wordings. Here is another version of the same idea in one of his most famous passages—from *Light in August* (1932): "Memory believes before knowing remembers. Believes longer than recollects, longer than knowing even wonders" (487). The cumulative effect of a repeated experience is greater than the sum of its occasions, expanding exponentially as memory is multiplied by anticipation.

475:29 **the skill without weariness, the knowledge virginal to surfeit** She kisses well, without at all tiring of the game (as one would think anyone would tire who had had enough practice to be able to kiss so well)—but in fact she hadn't had any practice at all and was simply doing what any woman (any daughter of Eve) knows how to do by the time she becomes a 'woman of thirty.'

476:9 **Drusilla, in the yellow ball gown** this time for the celebration dinner for Col. Sartoris's winning the election

476:10 **gave me one fierce inscrutable look** Raising this question: Do you still plan to tell your father after dinner about what George Wyatt said?

476:17   **forensic**   formal, argumentative, not conversational

476:19   **him who was anything and everything except a lawyer**   Yes, Col. Sartoris's temperament was much more in tune with a slogan of the 1920's: 'direct action beats legislation.'

476:30   **that transparent film**   the nictating membrane, present in the eyes of some animals (dogs, for example), which sometimes is drawn across the eyeball. Col. Sartoris obviously is not so equipped. The idea is that he seems to be able to shut out that part of the world which he does not want to see (or be bothered with).

476:31   **carnivorous**   meat-eating

476:32   **ruminant**   a gentle, non-meat-eating animal; peaceable, non-aggressive

476:35   **I said again, "Father," then I told him**   Told him what? Everyone, so far as I am aware, has assumed that Bayard tells his father that he and Drusilla had kissed, but I do not believe that is right. Col. Sartoris's response would make no sense if the subject were kissing.

476:38   **this time I knew it was worse with him than not hearing**   'This time' as opposed to 473:27//260:20 when Bayard said he could have talked with his father before he entered the race for the election: 'I could have talked to him and he would have listened, but he could not have heard me.' But by now, 'this time,' it was 'worse with him than not hearing.' By now 'it didn't even matter,' which is to say that Col. Sartoris is by now so completely caught up in his own ideas and plans that it doesn't make any difference to him what anyone else (including his son) thinks about him or his plans. He knows what he wants to do and he knows how Bayard will fit in his plans. Nothing else is important to him. As Wyatt had said: 'I know what's wrong: he's had to kill too many folks, and that's bad for a man' (473:21//260:13). He now admits others to his world only 'to reply now and then . . . with that courteous intolerant pride' (476:15//265:10).

476:39   **You are doing well in the law, Judge Wilkins tells**

me If Bayard had told his father he had just kissed his wife (or his wife had just kissed him), this response by Col. Sartoris would be literally incredible, an absolute non-sequitur. He might as well have replied by talking about the price of cotton.

477:7 **pettifogging and doubtless chicanery** both mean the same: trickery, sharp practice

477:10 **now I shall do a little moral housecleaning** This is Col. Sartoris's understated, ironic way of referring to his previous behavior—like a man with a hangover saying he got a little drunk the night before. It happens that his proposed new behavior does go along with George Wyatt's suggestions, but I think we are to understand that Col. Sartoris arrived at this idea by himself, not because of Bayard's talking with him (nor for the same reasons Bayard and Wyatt would have offered).

477:12 **Tomorrow, when I go to town and meet Ben Redmond, I shall be unarmed** More than a few readers have cited this line to show how corrupt Col. Sartoris has become: When he is shot by Redmond he *is* armed; he has his derringer. So, the argument goes, he has grown so corrupt that he wasn't able to keep even for one day his resolve not to carry a gun. This argument is, of course, nonsense. It springs from what is demonstrably a misreading of the text. Col. Sartoris is not shot the following day. He is not shot until about two months later. For all we know he did not carry his derringer the next day. As for why he may later have decided to begin carrying it again, see entry for 489:9//287:7.

SECTION THREE

477:17 **we didn't have to pass through Jefferson either** 'either' = as they had not had to pass through Oxford. Then it was because Ringo had already gotten Bayard's horse and a fresh one for himself, so they did not have to stop at the

Oxford livery stable. This time it is apparently because the road from the University to Sartoris does not necessarily go through Jefferson. See 464:16//245:6 for speculation on the location of Oxford vis-a-vis Jefferson.

477:21 **drawing room** the larger, more formal livingroom in a house which has two; the less formal one, where the family usually sits, was called the parlor

477:28 *it will have to begin tonight. I wont even have until tomorrow in which to begin to resist* Bayard's intention is not even to go into town to face Redmond, let alone kill him. He knows Wyatt and others of his father's old troop and Drusilla and Ringo will not approve of his decision and will try to shame him into behaving as he is expected to behave. When he sees the troop waiting outside the house, he knows he will have no respite but will have to begin resisting their pressure tonight.

477:29 **a picquet** the military term for soldiers acting as sentries, lookouts

477:33 **curious vulture-like formality** like vultures sitting in a row on a tree limb, waiting patiently for a feast they know will soon come

477:37 **It was all right** Redmond shot Col. Sartoris fairly, according to accepted rules: he shot him from in front and Col. Sartoris was armed.

478:8 **We'll take this off your hands** One of us will face (and kill) Redmond for you, if you don't want to do it yourself. This is a polite offer and would be carried out if it were accepted, but Wyatt has no expectation that Bayard might accept. When Bayard says 'I reckon I can attend to it,' Wyatt says 'I reckon we all knew that's what you would say.'

478:22 **unctuous** excessively polite

478:22 **voracious** hungry, ready for blood

478:31 **postulated** not just assumed, but created, orchestrated, and stage-managed

478:32 **like another actor** Bayard is referring to himself, as if he were just another actor in the scene Drusilla is stage-managing.

478:35 **Roman holiday** a spectacle for the masses, centering on someone's having been (or about to be) hurt. The term comes from the gladiatorial contests of ancient Rome. In Faulkner's sentence, 'Roman holiday' is not a clarification of 'death' immediately preceding in line 34//19, but of 'scene' in line 31//15—that scene with leading actors and chorus which Southerners regularly enact whenever a death has occurred.

478:35 **engendered by mist-born Protestantism** derived from the harsh religion of the Scottish highlands

479:4 **gear** a horse's equipment (harness, bridle, saddle, etc.)—in this case, a chain attaching the bit to the bridle

479:5 **My aunt and my—Drusilla** Drusilla is his step-mother, but he realizes 'step-mother' is appropriate only technically for his relation to her—certainly it is not how he usually thinks of her—so he hesitates over what to call her before his father's old troop. He settles for what they called her when she rode with them—'Drusilla.'

479:9 **Tomorrow?** Wyatt is asking if Bayard will take care of the matter at hand by facing Redmond tomorrow. When Bayard answers that it will be 'tomorrow,' he means he will do tomorrow what he is going to do, although it will not be what Wyatt expects.

479:22 **just clay** just a body—now a dead one. 'For dust thou art, and unto dust shalt thou return' (Genesis 3:19).

479:28 **frigate** warship

479:28 **Fort Moultrie** off the coast of Charleston, South Carolina, where the first shots of the Civil War were fired

479:29 **Tennessee Junction** where Col. Sartoris's north-south railroad joins the main east-west Memphis and Charleston line

479:37 **Uncle Bayard** This is a different Bayard Sartoris—John's and Jenny's brother. He was killed by a Federal cook during the war as the result of a prank—he was trying to liberate some anchovies from the camp of Union General Pope. John and Bayard are the traditional names for Sartoris males. We learn from other Faulkner books that our present Bayard will have a son named John, and this John will have twin sons named John and Bayard. Such repeated names within a family can be confusing to readers new to Faulkner, but they do accurately reflect both Scots and Southern naming practices.

479:37 **fanlight** a decorative curved window above a door—made of relatively small pieces of glass

480:8 **unsentient** appearing not to have normal human feeling

480:10 **Hadn't you better go to bed now?** Jenny is addressing this to Drusilla. Jenny has a good idea of what is likely to happen if Drusilla and Bayard talk that night, and she is trying to forestall it.

480:14 **plumes** An officer's dress uniform often included a feather on his hat.

480:15 **that irrevocable difference which I had known to expect yet had not realised** that alteration in appearance which I had intellectually understood death would cause but which, until I saw Father's dead body, I had not fully accepted

480:22 **beneath the invisible stain** The blood of the men he had killed had of course been washed away in a literal sense, but, like Lady Macbeth, in a metaphorical and more important sense he could never be cleansed of the blood he had shed.

480:27 **appendages** attachments to the body—in this case: the hands

480:36 **dying fall** the cessation of a sound so emotionally charged that it seems to resonate even after fading (See 428:31//162:2 above.)

481:6 **what they say is an attribute only of God's** to pass final judgment and then, when it is called for, to administer death

481:9 **you have fired them** not that he has fired these two particular duelling pistols before but that he has already fired (and therefore embraced) 'triggers quick as retribution' when he killed Grumby

481:10 **slender and invincible and fatal as the physical shape of love** Pistol barrels do have an unmistakably phallic hardness and shape and manner of functioning. What is striking is that Drusilla, woman of the generally sexually-prudish nineteenth century, would at this moment of high tension think of the 'shape of love' with such a conspicuously masculine image—and that she would speak of it in that way to a young man. Clearly Drusilla has by this point *internalized* many male attitudes. When she said to Louvinia seven years earlier 'We went to war to hurt Yankees, not hunting women' (453:23//227:13), we noted (and smiled at) the masculine orientation of her words, but we understood them then as her exasperated (and justified) reaction to her mother's petty assumptions about her motives for being with Col. Sartoris's troop, not as an expression of a serious realignment of her conception of her sexual identity. It appears now that such a realignment must have already been well underway. As for why Drusilla describes the shape of love as 'fatal,' see 471:32//257:15: 'A dream is not a very safe thing to be near, Bayard. I know. I had one once. It's like a loaded pistol with a hair trigger: if it stays alive long enough, somebody is going to be hurt.' She is referring, of course, to the life she had expected to live with her fiancé and which the War destroyed.

481:11 **Again I watched her arms angle out and upward as she removed the two verbena sprigs from her hair . . . putting one of them into my lapel** again the amphora gesture—as Bayard imagines she will be waiting (468:31// 252:16), and again as she did after she and Bayard had kissed in the garden: 'the rigid curiously formal angle of the bare arms . . . as she removed the verbena sprig and put it into my lapel' (475:6//263:7).

481:17 **it will not fade** The smell from the sprig of verbena will continue to be strong.

481:19 **abjure** formally swear never to use again

481:25 **the fire of heaven that cast down Lucifer** 'Fire of heaven' is Faulkner's echo of Milton's "Paradise Lost" when Christ threw Satan (Lucifer) down from heaven: "Him the Almighty Power / Hurled headlong flaming" (Book I, ll. 44–45). Drusilla's idea is that Bayard, like Milton's Christ, will overpower the evil one (Redmond), and the gun she is giving him (like Milton's cannon) is the flaming instrument with which he will do it.

481:31 **bent and kissed it** consecrating it to a sacred purpose

481:33 **fierce exultant humility** 'fierce' because violently charged, 'exultant' because she identifies with what she expects the hand she is kissing will do the next day, 'humility' because it is Bayard, not herself, who is privileged to carry out the retribution

481:36 **damned forever of all peace** Drusilla has passed the point of emotional no-return: i.e., anyone who has gone as far as she has in idealizing violence can never go back emotionally to the tamer values most of civilized mankind has agreed to honor and live by.

481:38 **clairvoyance** intuition

481:39 **the laggard brain** the sluggish, slow-to-react intellect (compared to direct, instant clairvoyance)

482:6 **one of those rubber rings women seal fruit jars with** thin, pink lips, framing a round, open void

482:8 **He's not—** Drusilla senses/knows (from kissing Bayard's hand) that that hand is not going to shoot Redmond.

482:34 **Now it was Aunt Jenny who said "Bayard" twice before I heard her** 480:32//272:27: 'Drusilla must have spoken twice before I heard her . . . her voice . . . with a passionate and dying fall: "Bayard".'

482:35 **You are not going to try to kill him. All right** Jenny, Col. Sartoris's sister, is telling Bayard that she does not oppose Bayard's decision not to try to kill Redmond.

482:38 **Dont let it be Drusilla** Don't let the disapproval of Drusilla pressure you into doing what you do not believe is right.

482:38 **a poor hysterical young woman**   This is a very mild way to describe Drusilla's condition—a euphemism, in fact. Drusilla is mad, insane at least on the subject of violence, and Jenny and Louvinia both know it. Note how they have been watching her, ready to lead her away should she lose control of herself.

482:39 **dont let it be him**   Don't let what you might imagine would be the disapproval of your father pressure you into doing what you do not believe is right.

482:40 **dont let it be George Wyatt and those others**   And don't let Wyatt and the others determine what you will do.

483:4 **I must live with myself, you see**   If I don't face Redmond tomorrow, I can never *know* that my reason for not facing him is really an honorable one (refusing to take part in and so continue the pattern of violence and killings) and not at least partly a cowardly one (not wanting to risk getting killed myself).

483:13 **now it could begin**   the panting—his grieving for his father

483:26 **weeping the facile tears which are the white man's futile trait and which negroes know nothing about**   A white person's tears are futile because they are the easy (facile) and learned response to situations in which tears are considered appropriate. Thus they are essentially sentimental and even phony. But a black person's tears spring from emotions that are actually felt, emotions that are real. At least that is what Bayard appears to be telling us.

483:35 **the tragic mute insensitive bones**   As man has taught himself to do so much more with his hands than they were intended to do (480:28//272:54), so man's bones can bear much more than they were intended to bear.

SECTION FOUR

483:40 **whip-poor-wills**   night singing birds

484:2 **drowsy moony fluting**   the lazy, non-imitative night

singing of a mockingbird, which does indeed sound like
a flute

484:6 **I still lay on the bed (I hadn't undressed)** Apparently
Bayard had not slept at all, thinking about what he should
do (and not do) the next day, and going over in his mind
everything we have read so far in "An Odor of Verbena"
(and perhaps everything we have read so far in the whole
book).

484:12 **Soon they would begin to arrive** for Col. Sartoris's
funeral in the afternoon

484:14 **they too would wait first to see what I was going to
do** 'they' = the funeral-attendees; 'too' = everybody else,
because from Bayard's point of view *everybody* will be waiting
and watching to see what he is going to do

484:15 **So the house was quiet when I went down** Even in
the Sartoris household everyone is keeping out of Bayard's
sight until he indicates what he plans to do.

484:18 **I didn't look in to see** Bayard doesn't look in the
parlor because he doesn't want to come face to face with his
father, perhaps afraid that his father would not approve of
what he plans to do (or not do).

484:20 **I saw Joby watching me . . . Loosh looked up at
me . . . Ringo didn't look at me at all** Louvinia must have
told in the quarters what had happened between Bayard and
Drusilla last night. Joby and Loosh are curious about what
Bayard is going to do, but Ringo avoids Bayard's eyes because he is afraid he knows what Bayard intends to do.

484:21 **Loosh** Many ex-slaves in the first flush of freedom
left their former owners to find a better life. Loosh apparently found nothing out there for him, and so, like many
others, he had little choice but to return to work for the
family which had once owned him.

484:22 **Betsy** Bayard's mare

484:22 **curry comb** a wire brush used to groom horses

484:32 **I had not had to pant in some time now but it was
there, waiting** 'it' = his need to pant, to give expression to
his 'regret and grief, the despair' at his father's death

484:33   **a part of the alteration**   'the alteration which is death'
(479:21//235:8)

484:34   **as though by being dead and no longer needing air
he had taken all of it . . . along with him**   Since Col. Sartoris
was dead, and since the house was so completely his ('the
house was the aura of Father's dream,' Drusilla had said—
469:13//253:15), and since, being dead, he no longer had
need of any of it ('it' = the dream which was 'compassed and
claimed and postulated between the walls'), it was as though,
like a long-distance mover, he had taken everything in the
house along with him—including even the air which, being
his, was his to take away.

485:2   **Are you going now?**   Bayard originally had intended
not even to go to town—simply to let the matter with Redmond drop. We know this because he had at first thought
that he *knew* he would not be killed (467:22//250:15). But
after his meeting with Drusilla last night, he has decided that
he will at least go to town to meet Redmond, although not
shoot him. Jenny appears to have figured out that this is the
decision he has come to.

485:3   **Yes, thank God, without pity**   not like Mrs. Habersham's saying 'You poor child' (451:26//225:11)—which
Bayard didn't want to hear then even from a stranger and
certainly doesn't want to hear now from Jenny, which Jenny
is wise enough to understand

485:3   **You see, I want to be thought well of**   Bayard on
483:4//276:24 gave one reason for going to face Redmond:
he has to be able to live with himself. Now he gives a second
reason: honor depends at least partly on how one is thought
of by others.

485:7   **Maybe if she knew that I was going. Was going to town
anyway**   Maybe if Drusilla knew I was at least going to face
Redmond (even if she knew I intended to do nothing more)
she would understand that I am not a coward and that I
must have some other reason for how I have chosen to act.

485:9   **"No," she said. "No, Bayard."**   Jenny's 'no' does not
mean that she is saying Bayard's just showing courage would

not be enough for Drusilla, that she requires an act of vengeance, but that Bayard should not allow Drusilla's wishes to
determine for him how he is going to act.

485:10 **So I mounted the stairs** 'So' = in order to see Drusilla before he leaves, even though he knows in advance that
seeing her will do no good

485:32 **so it would not start yet** 'it' = the panting

485:35 **Even if you hid all day in the stable** I would still
think well of you (see 485:3//280:6).

485:38 **blockade runners** The South had almost no manu-
facturing. Except for what they were able to capture from
Union troops, the Confederates' main source for guns and
ammunition was Europe. England remained officially neutral during the war but its sympathies lay mainly with the
South, so the Confederacy was able to buy most of what it
needed from England, paying in cotton, with British ships
providing the transportation. At first there was little the
North could do to stop this trade, because the North had a
very small navy. At the beginning of the war the Northern
Secretary of the Navy personally owned more ships than the
entire U.S. Navy. During the four years of the war the North
added (by building and by purchase) over 600 ships to its
Navy. The purpose was to gather a force that could intercept
and capture the ships bringing supplies to the South. Since
there were only three Southern ports on the Atlantic capable
of receiving cargo-carrying vessels (Wilmington, Savannah,
and Charleston) the Northern navy was able to concentrate
its fleet outside these harbors to form an effective blockade—one able to detect and stop cumbersome trans-ocean
cargo-carriers. The British and Southern response was to
have the ocean vessels deliver their cargoes to the British
islands of Bermuda or the Bahamas off the coast, and then
transfer the cargo to a specially built fleet of smaller and
much faster ships designed to avoid detection and to outrun
pursuit, able to slip through the blockade at night. These
ships (and the men who manned them) were called blockade

runners. Profits from blockade running were great; a ship could pay for its cost if it managed two successful voyages. It is estimated that 8000 ships attempted to run the blockade and that only 1500 were captured or destroyed.

485:38 **Charleston** one of the Southern ports where the blockade runners brought in their cargoes

485:40 **heroes in the sense that David Crockett or John Sevier would have been to small boys or fool young women** romantic adventurers of the kind hero-worshiping stories are told about, regardless of any serious cause they may or may not have served—like Daniel Boone or Robin Hood. Davy Crockett was a famous American frontiersman, later a Congressman from Tennessee. John Sevier (suh-VEER) was an Indian fighter, first Governor of the Independent State of Franklin, and eventually first Governor of Tennessee.

486:7 **before he changed his name** Most of the blockade running ships were British-owned and many of their officers were on leave from the British Navy. Since blockade running was legally considered piracy and since England was techni-cally a neutral in the American Civil War, these officers adopted assumed names so, in case of capture, their iden-tities would not embarrass either their country or their families.

486:8 **a vocabulary of seven words** Obviously this is a hu-morous exaggeration. The point is that he did not do much talking nor did he need to in order to get what he wanted.

486:10 **I'll have rum . . . across the champagne, to whatever ruffled bosom or low gown** The blockade runner had the rum, the woman had the champagne, bosom, and low gown.

486:12 **No bloody moon, Bayard** Blockade-running ships were constructed and operated so as to be able at night to slip through the ring of Federal ships guarding the harbors. The ships rode very low in the water, were painted blue-gray, used only anthracite (smokeless) coal, and, in short, did everything possible to make themselves difficult to be seen or heard. If the night was truly dark, a blockade runner could pass within 100 yards of a Federal ship and not be detected. But not all nights were completely dark, and in full moonlight the chances of a blockade runner being seen were enormously greater. Since there was too much cargo to be brought in to wait for the two or three moonless nights of each month, the blockade runners had to risk trips during times of considerable moonlight. All they could hope for was a cover of clouds obscuring the moon at the moment they ran the blockade. Thus 'no bloody moon' was a wish for favorable circumstances—a toast to 'good luck.'

486:18 **General Compson** This is not the husband of the Mrs. Compson of "Retreat," "Raid," and "Skirmish at Sartoris." Mrs. Compson's husband is considerably older and has been crazy for some time. This General Compson who lifts his hat to Bayard is related, of course, but a different man. He will shortly become Governor of Mississippi. We learn all of this, piece by piece, from various other Faulkner books.

486:23 **looked me full in the face for one moment, the sullen determined face, the eyes rolling at me defiant** Ringo, like Drusilla, believes Bayard should kill Redmond and he realizes Bayard does not intend to do that.

486:27 **the new courthouse** the rebuilt one, since the Yankees burned the original during the war

486:28 **not yet noon so there were only women on the street** The merchants and professional men were inside their stores and offices, it not yet being time to close to walk home to dinner.

486:29 **at least not the walking stopped sudden and dead in midwalking . . . that not to begin until we reached the square** The women either did not know why Bayard was coming to town that morning, or did not recognize him, or did not by their actions indicate that they knew about what was soon to take place. It would not be until he reached the square where men would be waiting who knew why he was there that Bayard would see signs of repressed tension because of the upcoming confrontation.

486:32   *If I could only be invisible* ... **But I could not**   in effect
wishing for himself no bloody sun (instead of no bloody
moon)—but that was not possible

486:34   **the Holston House**   the Jefferson hotel

486:35   **saw the row of feet along the gallery rail come suddenly and quietly down**   Spectators had gathered on the
gallery of the hotel to be on hand (but not to interfere) at
the moment of truth. When Bayard arrives in the square,
the men come to respectful attention, for they expect that
in another few minutes either Bayard or Redmond will
be dead.

487:1   **the still circumspect eyes**   of the men watching from
the gallery of the Holston House. 'Circumspect' means 'dis-
creet but attentive.'

487:7   **"No you aint." So I walked on**   Ringo has no choice
but to accept Bayard's insistence on facing Redmond alone—
partly because Ringo is black and can't persist in arguing
with a white, but mainly because Col. Sartoris was Bayard's
father, not Ringo's, and it is Bayard's responsibility (and
privilege) to deal with Redmond.

487:11   **I moved in a cloud of verbena as I might have moved
in a cloud of smoke from a cigar**   The book begins with
Bayard and Ringo behind the smokehouse throwing dust as
imitation smoke to create a smoke-screen that shielded them
from reality, they are interrupted by the arrival of an idealized, dust-covered Col. Sartoris on his smoke-colored horse,
Bayard is later unable to see the effect of his shot at the Yankee because of the smoke caused by firing the musket, and
now, at the end of the book, he finds himself enveloped in a
cloud of verbena as if it too were a cloud of smoke—as if it
might also shield him from reality, from 'fact and doom.'

487:22   **already fumbling the pistol into my pocket**   like
Prof. Wilkins trying to offer Bayard a pistol before he left
the University

487:23   **the same thing seemed to happen to him that happened to Drusilla last night when she kissed my hand**

Wyatt too sensed that Bayard did not intend to shoot Redmond.

487:29 **Is your name Sartoris** See 354:26//59:9 (when Buck tells thirteen-year-old Bayard that all he has to say is 'I'm John Sartoris' boy') and 379:32//101:23 (when Drusilla greets Bayard at Hawkhurst by saying 'Hello, John Sartoris') and 445:23//213:22 (when Buck says 'Aint I told you he is John Sartoris' boy?'). Now George Wyatt is pressing Bayard to show once again he is Col. Sartoris's son by acting as Col. Sartoris would have acted. All of these zero in on what has come to be Bayard's problem. At twenty-four Bayard isn't sure he *wants* to be 'John Sartoris' boy,' if that means he must try to be in all ways like his father. He does not want to deny his father and his heritage, but he is *Bayard* Sartoris, not young *John* Sartoris. As he thought before riding home from the University (466:3//248:1): *'this will be my chance to find out if I am what I think I am or if I just hope; if I am going to do what I have taught myself is right or if I am just going to wish I were.'*

487:37 **I should have knowed you wouldn't do anything that would keep John from laying quiet** Ringo had said, when he and Bayard fastened Grumby's hand to Granny's grave, 'Now she can lay good and quiet,' to which Bayard had said 'Yes' (444:7//211:14).

487:40 **remember: he's a brave man** Yes, Redmond is brave. He has been waiting to give Bayard his chance to shoot him since yesterday morning, but that is a long time for even a brave man to have to wait to be killed, so his nerves are likely to be on edge by now and his actions may not be completely rational.

488:4 **when suddenly I said it without having any warning that I was going to: "No bloody moon"** wishing himself good luck, knowing he will need it to survive the next five minutes

488:12 **enclosed in the now fierce odor of the verbena** Bayard acknowledges that Jenny's good luck wish for him (the moonless darkness of the blockade runner) is out of the question, yet feels protected by an enclosing 'cloud of verbena' (487:12//283:23). The point seems to be that while Bayard cannot have the precise good luck talisman wished for him by Jenny, he does have one (which proves equally effective) provided for him by Drusilla: courage.

488:12 **Then shadow fell upon me** He has entered the shadow of the building from the hot sunshine, but given the context, there is no doubt a suggestion here of 'the valley of the shadow of death' (the 23rd Psalm).

488:16 **the heavy bewildered boots of countrymen approaching litigation** The boots are heavy but it is not the boots which are bewildered; it is the countrymen. To attach 'bewildered' to 'boots' says something about the countrymen's uneasy steps in their unaccustomed climb to a lawyer's office.

488:21 **freshly shaven and with fresh linen** There are several ideas involved here: Redmond expects to be dead in a few minutes. The religious catch-phrase warns one in the face of impending death to "prepare to meet thy Maker." So Redmond shaves and puts on fresh linen. Also, Redmond's waiting for Bayard to return from the University and to come to town to meet him is the honorable act of an honorable man under a traditional honor code designed to resolve what are called 'affairs of honor.' In such a serious and formal situation one should surely present himself with as much dignity as possible.

488:39 **I could see the foreshortened slant barrel and I knew it would miss me though his hand did not tremble** At such close range Redmond could not possibly miss him, yet the angle at which he held the pistol indicates that Redmond had reached the same conclusion that Bayard had: violence had gone on for too long and I refuse to continue it—even if my refusal costs my own life.

489:1 **the pistol in the rocklike hand** When Bayard shot Grumby: 'the pistol was level and steady as a rock' (443:26// 210:16).

489:2 **Maybe I didn't even hear the explosion** When

Grumby shot at Bayard: 'I reckon I heard the sound, and I reckon I must have heard the bullets . . . but I dont remember it' (443:3//209:16).

489:3 **I remember the sudden orange bloom and smoke as they appeared against his white shirt** When Grumby shot at Bayard: 'the next second there were two bright orange splashes, one after the other, against the middle of the gray coat' (442:38//209:10).

489:8 **it was done then** The whole business of Redmond having shot Bayard's father and Bayard subsequently calling Redmond to account by facing him in a duel-like confrontation is now over, finished forever, for one of the features of the old Southern honor code—perhaps the feature which most accounted for how long the code continued to be influential in a world which was rapidly becoming less and less preoccupied with honor—was that any dispute was considered *settled*, without possibility of being reopened or subject to further action, once the two principals had faced each other and allowed each other the opportunity of a shot. It made no difference whether either or both were killed or wounded or emerged unscathed. Once the confrontation had taken place, the matter in dispute, whatever it was, was considered to have been honorably resolved. Thus feuds which might have continued generation after generation were stopped at their beginning. Another meaning contained in this line is that the series of shootings or attempted shootings or avoided shootings around which *The Unvanquished* is structured is now, finally, at an end: Bayard's and Ringo's shooting at the Yankee soldier, the shooting of Granny, Grumby, Col. Sartoris, and the two Burdens. But this time Bayard and Redmond, by their independent decisions not to continue the violence, decisions for which they were willing and expecting to pay with their lives, have broken the pattern and, perhaps, ended it.

489:11 **I knew too what it was to want air when there was nothing in the circumambience for the lungs** Bayard had

experienced the feeling earlier that morning (see 484:32//
279:19).

489:20 **He was brave; no one denied that** brave in that he
had waited for Bayard to come to kill him, knowing he was
not going to try to stop him, and brave again when he walked
down the stairs and through the crowd, knowing that the
men there (Wyatt and the six others from the old troop and
no doubt many more) would like to kill him, because they
believed for the moment that he had now killed Bayard too.
The reason the men allowed Redmond to walk away is that,
according to the honor code, it was not their affair. Once
Bayard and Redmond had faced each other, whatever the
outcome proved to be, the issue under dispute was over—
settled forever. The situation was much like Aunt Louisa going behind Drusilla's back and arranging with Col. Sartoris
for the marriage; Drusilla had no role in the decision; here
Wyatt and the others have no role (except as witnesses) in
resolving the Redmond-Sartoris dispute.

489:29 **went away from Jefferson and from Mississippi and
never came back** Even though he knows Jefferson will remember him as being honorable and brave, nevertheless he
knows there is no longer a place for him there now, for he *is*
the one who killed Col. Sartoris, and Col. Sartoris was Jefferson's hero.

489:33 **the flat of the pistol** the side of the pistol

489:39 **rapport for violence . . . which in George's case was
actual character judgment** so completely attuned to violence that he understands by instinct the people who involve
themselves in violence

490:7 **ratiocinative** reasoning

490:10 **got up this morning aiming to do what you did**
What Bayard did which so impresses Wyatt was to present
himself before Redmond, as if for a duel, without bringing
a gun. The only reason Bayard is still alive (and the only
reason Redmond is still alive) is that *both* had reached the
same decision not to participate further in violence, and nei-

ther of them could have known (or even reasonably have suspected) that the other had arrived at that same conclusion. Both expected to die, and both were willing to uphold what they considered right by paying with their lives.

490:19 **ride out there in time for the—** in time for the funeral

490:20 **I couldn't do that either** I couldn't make myself eat, and it turns out I couldn't make myself go to the funeral either.

490:29 **Maybe you're right, maybe there has been enough killing in your family** Maybe so, but we learn from other Faulkner books that Bayard's refusal to kill on this day is not something Yoknapatawpha County will choose to remember and make part of the Sartoris legend. Uncle Bayard's stealing the anchovies, Col. John's wartime successes and his shooting of the Yankee carpetbaggers—these and other violent but ultimately self-destructive exploits are what the Sartorises are remembered for. Bayard's equally courageous gesture leading *away* from violence may have impressed Faulkner but it did not, in the long run, impress the people Faulkner wrote about.

490:35 **raised their hats and I raised mine** They are acknowledging that, in their eyes, Bayard has acquitted himself honorably on this morning, and he is acknowledging that they have done so.

490:37 **the carriages and buggies would begin to leave the square soon** for Sartoris, for the funeral

491:7 *Now it can begin again if it wants to* 'it' = the panting

491:8 **I went to sleep** While Bayard sleeps, two important things happen: Drusilla goes away on the train, and Col. Sartoris's funeral is held with his only son a few hundred yards away but not in attendance.

491:15 **flag station** a place on a railroad line which is not a usual stopping place but where a train can be signaled to stop if there is something or someone to pick up

491:16 **Ringo brought his hat full of water from the creek**

but instead I went down to the water myself   At the beginning of the book, when Bayard and Ringo were twelve, they carried a leaking water bucket between them, needing to join forces 'against a common enemy, time,' but now, when they are twenty-four (the common enemy having operated for twelve years) Bayard rejects Ringo's offer of a hatful of water and goes to the creek himself. That one was white and the other black may not have made any difference to them when they were children, but obviously the closeness which existed then has altered by now.

491:22   **again the moon like the rim print of a heel in wet sand**   'again' = as at 467:15//250:6: 'a thin sickle of moon like the heel print of a boot in wet sand'

491:26   **I had not looked at him again. I had started to before I left the house but I did not, I did not see him again**   Bayard had not looked at his father because he did not wish to be reminded that his father might not have approved what he was going to do. Certainly it is not what his father would have done under similar circumstances.

491:34   **the corporeal shape**   the form of the physical body

492:6   **Then she didn't—**   She didn't say anything about the way I handled the meeting with Redmond? She didn't say she could forgive me for not acting as she thought I should act?

492:13   **I knelt beside the chair**   as beside Granny's chair in "Ambuscade," this time less for protection than for solace, although perhaps the two are not entirely different

492:22   **Oh, damn you Sartorises! . . . Damn you! Damn you!**   All male Sartorises seem so determined to do what *they* think is right (or sometimes just what would be fun) and they give no thought to those others who live with them, love them, and sometimes are left behind and alone.

492:33   **the pillow on which it lay—the single sprig of it**   Although it is possible that Jenny has placed the verbena on Bayard's pillow, since she knows its significance and has already articulated her pride in Bayard, it seems clear that it was Drusilla who put the verbena on his pillow before she left.

492:37 **that odor which she said you could smell alone above the smell of horses** At another point (469:23//253:26) Drusilla said verbena could be smelled above the smell of courage, too. Surely whatever the message is that the verbena on Bayard's pillow is intended to convey, it must have more to do with courage than with horses. This final cryptic sentence, so typically Faulknerian, calls for some kind of interpretation which goes beyond literal meaning. Here's how Faulkner responded to a questioner in an undergraduate course in contemporary literature at the University of Virginia: "the sprig of verbena meant that she [Drusilla] realized that that [facing Redmond unarmed] took courage too and maybe more moral courage than to have drawn blood, or to have taken another step in an endless feud of an eye for an eye" (Gwynn, *University*, 42).

CHRONOLOGY

When Faulkner wrote and published the magazine stories which, revised, make up the chapters of *The Unvanquished*, he did not pin down when each story took place. They were seven related but separate stories set at unspecified times during and after the Civil War. Bayard was obviously younger in the first stories than in the later ones, but that is pretty much all we were told about when each story was supposed to have occurred. When Faulkner revised the stories to make them into a novel, he made an attempt to make his fictional timetable consistent from chapter to chapter and with events of the War which have known dates, but he was not especially conscientious in doing this. The result is that it is now impossible to construct an internally consistent chronology for *The Unvanquished* which matches all details of Faulkner's text and all dates of real historical events, but we can come very close—close enough so that the few inconsistencies are hardly troublesome.

If we begin with the text's one specific date, 14 August 1863 on the U.S. Army repossession order in "Raid," and work forward and backward from that, noting what we are told about Bayard's age in each story, remembering that his birthday is in September, realizing that he followed the nineteenth century custom of overstating his age in the month-or-so before his birthday (see entry for 355:29//54:5), then we can arrive at a chronology which fits Faulkner's fictional story and the progress of the real War.

AMBUSCADE
1862 summer: Bayard 12

We know "Ambuscade" takes place during a summer, because the first line of the text tells us so. We know it was the summer of 1862, because that is when the Union Army first reached north Mississippi. (See entry for 322:21//5:7 for further explanation of why the year of the story must be 1862 and not 1863.) We know Bayard was twelve at the time, because he says so five times during the story.

RETREAT
1863 summer: Bayard 13

We know "Retreat" takes place during a summer, because even at six in the evening it was hot enough for the rosin to be cooking out of the front steps. We know it was 1863, one year after "Ambuscade," because the silver buried in "Ambuscade" had been buried for a year. We know Bayard is thirteen, because he tells Buck McCaslin he is fourteen and Ringo corrects him and says they won't really be fourteen until their birthdays in September.

RAID
1863 August: Bayard 13 (one month before he is 14)

"Raid" takes place a month-or-so after "Retreat"—just long enough afterward for Granny to learn where the Union Army which took her silver had gone. We know "Raid" occurs in August of 1863, because that is the date on the Union Army repossession order. We know Faulkner must have thought about and intended 1863 as the right year, because when he was revising he changed his original magazine date from 1864 to 1863. We know Bayard is still thirteen, because his birthday which will make him fourteen won't be until September.

From the above we can determine that Bayard and Ringo were born in September 1849—fourteen years before their upcoming September 1863 fourteenth birthday.

RIPOSTE IN TERTIO
1864 October–December: Bayard 15 (became 15 in September)

"Riposte in Tertio" takes place *more* than one year after the August 1863 "Raid" trip to Hawkhurst. We know it is more than a year later because several mule swindling transactions are said to have occurred in April, May, and July, and the mule swindling operation could not have begun until *after* they got the original Union repossession order in August 1863. We know Bayard is fifteen—just past fifteen in October—because he says so three times.

VENDÉE
1864–1865 December–February: Bayard 15

"Vendée" follows immediately after "Riposte in Tertio," from December 1864 to February 1865. These dates have to be right, since Col. Sartoris and Drusilla are home from the war at the end of the story and the war itself is all over but the surrendering, an event which formally took place in Virginia in April 1865, but the fighting in Mississippi had for the most part ended several months earlier. The text doesn't specifically say Bayard is fifteen but he has to be, since he was fifteen in the preceding story, "Riposte in Tertio," and is still fifteen in the succeeding one, "Skirmish at Sartoris."

SKIRMISH AT SARTORIS
1865 spring–August: Bayard 15
"Skirmish at Sartoris" begins not long after "Vendée" ends, in the same year, 1865. We know this because we are told that Louisa's second letter arrived just before Christmas in 1864 and it did not take her long after that to learn where Drusilla was and to come to Sartoris to arrange the marriage. "Skirmish at Sartoris" tells us twice that Bayard is fifteen. Since the story ends at election time, earlier than his September birthdate, the year would have to be still 1865, the month August (election month). (See introductory note to "Skirmish at Sartoris" for further discussion of the timing of this first post-war election.)

AN ODOR OF VERBENA
1873 October: Bayard 24 (just became 24 in September)
The text explicitly tells us that the time of the present action in "An Odor of Verbena" is October, when Bayard is twenty-four. Since October is after Bayard's September birthday, and he was born in 1849, the year has to be 1873, eight years after "Skirmish at Sartoris."

There are two significant discrepancies in the above chronology:
1 Col. Sartoris could not have been demoted from command of his regiment *in the summer after Second Manassas*—as Bayard says he was (353:6//50:11). By Second Manassas (September 1862) Col. Sartoris was back in Mississippi and had already formed his second group. If we can allow Faulkner to mean instead that Col. Sartoris fought in Virginia with his first regiment for more than a year, including at *First* Manassas, and then was demoted and came home, there is no problem.
2 Faulkner gives us (on 420//149 and 447//189) two different accounts of when Granny died in relation to when Louisa's second letter came. In the first, she was still alive and Bayard and Ringo read the letter when it arrived; in the second, she had already been killed and Bayard and Ringo

did not read the letter until a month or two later. There is no way to resolve this inconsistency.

There are a number of small discrepancies (perhaps as many as fifteen—which are identified in the line-by-line notes), but none is likely to put off a close reader or even a Civil War scholar.

BIBLIOGRAPHY

Angle, Paul M., and Earl Schenck Miers. *Tragic Years, 1860–1865: A Documentary History of the American Civil War.* 2 vols. New York: Simon and Schuster, 1960.

Aresty, Esther B. *The Best Behavior.* New York: Simon & Schuster, 1970.

Balzac, Honoré de. *Les Chouans.* 1829. Trans. George B. Ives. Philadelphia: Barrie, 1898.

Beeching, Cyril Leslie. *A Dictionary of Eponyms.* London: Clive Bingley, 1979.

Benét, William Rose. *The Reader's Encyclopedia.* New York: Crowell, 1948.

Bettersworth, John K. *Mississippi in the Confederacy as they saw it.* Baton Rouge, LA: Louisiana State UP, 1961.

Blair, Arthur H. *Faulkner's Military World.* Diss. U of North Carolina, 1975.

Bledsoe, A. S. "Colonel John Sartoris' Library." *Notes on Mississippi Writers* 7 (Spring 1974): 26–29.

Blotner, Joseph. *Faulkner: A Biography.* 2 vols. New York: Random House, 1974.

Boatner, Mark M., III. *Military Customs and Traditions.* New York: David McKay, 1956.

Bok, Sissela. *Lying.* New York: Pantheon, 1978.

Botkin, B. A. *A Treasury of Southern Folklore.* New York: Crown, 1949.

Bowen, Catherine Drinker. *The Lion and the Throne: The Life and Times of Sir Edward Coke.* Boston: Little, Brown, 1957.

Brasch, James D., and Joseph Sigman. *Hemingway's Library: A Composite Record.* New York: Garland, 1981.

Breckinridge, Scott D., and Scott D. Breckinridge, Jr. *Sword Play.* New York: A. S. Barnes, 1941.

Brewer, Ebenezer Cobham. *Brewer's Dictionary of Phrase and Fable.* Rev. Ivor H. Evans. New York: Harper & Row, 1963.

Brooks, Cleanth. *William Faulkner: The Yoknapatawpha Country.* New Haven, CT: Yale UP, 1963.

Brown, Calvin S. *A Glossary of Faulkner's South.* New Haven, CT: Yale UP, 1976.

Brown, May Cameron. *Quentin Compson as Narrative Voice in the Works of William Faulkner.* Diss. Georgia State U, 1975.

Bruce, D. D., Jr. "Play, Work, and Ethics in the Old South." *Southern Folklore Quarterly* 41 (1977): 33–51.

Bryson, Frederick Robertson. *The Point of Honor in Sixteenth-Century Italy: An Aspect of the Life of the Gentleman.* New York: Columbia U Publications of the Institute of French Studies, 1935.

Buck, Polly Stone. *The Blessed Town.* Chapel Hill, NC: Algonquin, 1986.

Calkin, Homer L. "Elk Horn to Vicksburg." *Civil War History* 2 (Mar. 1956): 7–9.

Campbell, John C. *The Southern Highlander and His Homeland.* New York: Russell Sage Foundation, 1921.

Cash, W. J. *The Mind of the South.* 1941. New York: Knopf, 1970.

Cash, William M., and Lucy Somerville Howorth, eds. *My Dear Nellie: The Civil War Letters of William L. Nugent to Eleanor Smith Nugent.* Jackson, MS: UP of Mississippi, 1977.

Catton, Bruce, ed. [Ezra H. Ripple]. "A Civil, and Sometimes Uncivil, War." *American Heritage* 15 (October 1964): 51–61.

———. *Grant Moves South.* Boston: Little, Brown, 1960.

Chafetz, Henry. *Play the Devil.* New York: Clarkson N. Potter, 1960.

Chekhov, Anton. *Letters on the Short Story, the Drama, and Other Literary Essays.* Ed. Louis Freidland. New York: B. Blom, 1964.

Chestnut, Mary. *Mary Chesnut's Civil War.* Ed. C. Vann Woodward. New Haven, CT: Yale UP, 1981.

Claiborne, J. F. H. *Mississippi, as a Province, Territory, and State.* 1880. Baton Rouge, LA: Louisiana State UP, 1964.

Clancy, Tom. *Patriot Games.* New York: Berkley Books, 1988.

Clark, Robert Denning. "How to Fire a Civil War Musket." *Civil War Times Illustrated* 2 (Dec. 1963): 36–37.

Clark, Thomas D. *Pills, Petticoats, and Plows: The Southern Country Store, 1865–1915.* Indianapolis, IN: Bobbs-Merrill, 1944.

Cochran, Hamilton. *Blockade Runners of the Confederacy.* Indianapolis, IN: Bobbs-Merrill, 1958.

Cohen, J. M., and M. J. Cohen. *The Penguin Dictionary of Quotations.* New York: Penguin, 1960.

Cohn, David L. *Where I Was Born and Raised.* Notre Dame, IN: U of Notre Dame P, 1967.

Connell, Richard. "The Most Dangerous Game." *O. Henry Memorial Award Prize Stories of 1924.* Garden City, NY: Doubleday, Page, 1925.

Cooke, John Esten. *Stonewall Jackson.* New York: Appleton, 1866.

Cunnington, Dr. C. Willett. *Feminine Attitudes in the Nineteenth Century.* 1935. New York: Haskell, 1973.

David, Paul, et al. *Reckoning with Slavery.* New York: Oxford UP, 1976.

Dohan, Mary Helen. *Our Own Words.* New York: Knopf, 1974.

Dolan, J. R. *English Ancestral Names.* New York: Clarkson N. Potter, 1972.

Dollard, John. *Caste and Class in a Southern Town.* New York: Doubleday Anchor, 1957.

Donald, David. *Divided We Fight.* New York: Macmillan, 1952.

Doyle, Bertram Wilbur. *The Etiquette of Race Relations in the South.* Chicago: U of Chicago P, 1937.

Drago, Edmund L. "How Sherman's March Through Georgia Affected the Slaves." *Georgia Historical Quarterly* 57 (Fall 1973): 361–375.

Dumas, Alexandre. "The Ambuscade." Chapter 25. *The Forty-five.* 1848. Philadelphia: University Library Association, n.d.

Dunbar, Seymour. *A History of American Travel.* New York: Tudor, 1937.

Dwyer, Bil. *Dictionary for Yankees and Other Uneducated People.* Highlands, NC: Merry Mountains, 1971.

Eaton, Clement. *A History of the Old South.* New York: Macmillan, 1967.

Eby, Cecil D. "Faulkner and the Southwestern Humorists." *Shenandoah 11* (Autumn 1959): 13–21.

Edson, H. A., and E. M. Fairchild. "Word Lists: Tennessee Mountains." *Dialect Notes* 8 (1895): 370–377.

Ewing, Elizabeth. *Dress and Undress.* New York: Drama Book Specialists, 1978.

Faulkner, William. *Absalom, Absalom!* 1936. *Faulkner: Novels 1936–1940.* Ed. Joseph Blotner and Noel Polk. New York: Library of America, 1990.

———. "Carcassonne." 1931. *Collected Stories of William Faulkner.* New York: Random House, 1950.

———. *Flags in the Dust.* New York: Random House, 1973.

———. *Go Down, Moses.* 1942. New York: Vintage, 1973.

———. *The Hamlet.* 1940. *Faulkner: Novels 1936–1940.* Ed. Joseph Blotner and Noel Polk. New York: Library of America, 1990.

———. "Never Done No Weeping When You Wanted to Laugh." Ed. Gail M. Morrison. *Mississippi Quarterly* 36:3 (Summer 1983): 461–474.

———. *The Reivers.* New York: Random House, 1962.

———. *Requiem for a Nun.* New York: Random House, 1951.

———. *The Sound and the Fury.* New York: Random House, 1929.

———. Tapes of interviews, classes, and speeches. Alderman Library, U of Virginia.

———. "The Tall Men." 1941. *Collected Stories of William Faulkner.* New York: Random House, 1950.

———. *The Unvanquished.* 1938. *Faulkner: Novels 1936–1940.* Ed. Joseph Blotner and Noel Polk. New York: Library of America, 1990.

Fiske, John. *The Mississippi Valley in the Civil War.* Boston: Houghton Mifflin, 1900.

Flanagan, John T. "Faulkner's Favorite Word." *Georgia Review* 17:4 (Winter 1963): 429–434.

Follmer, Don. "A Gun, a Dog, and a Good Horse." *Voice of the Tennessee Walking Horse.* 20:8 (Aug. 1981): 32, 55–56.

Foote, Shelby. *The Civil War: A Narrative.* New York: Random House, 1958.

Fuller, Claud E., and Richard D. Stewart. *Firearms of the Confederacy.* Lawrence, MA: Quarterman, 1944.

Fuller, Edmund. *Thesaurus of Anecdotes.* New York: Crown, 1942.

Funk, Charles Earle. *Heavens to Betsy and Other Curious Sayings.* New York: Harper, 1955.

Funk, Wilfred. *Word Origins.* New York: Grosset & Dunlap, 1950.

Gates, Arnold. "Of Men and Mules: A Modest History of Jackassery." *Civil War Times Illustrated* 23 (Nov. 1984): 40–46.

Gentry, Claude. *Private John Allen.* Decatur, GA: Bowen, 1951.

Gordon, Caroline. *None Shall Look Back.* New York: Scribners, 1937.

Gorn, Elliott J. "Black Spirits: The Ghostlore of Afro-American Slaves." *American Quarterly* 36 (Fall 1984): 549–565.

Gray, Richard. *The Literature of Memory.* Baltimore, MD: Johns Hopkins UP, 1977.

Green, Harvey. *Fit for America.* New York: Pantheon, 1986.

Greene, Francis Vinton. *The Mississippi.* New York: Scribners, 1882.

Gwynn, Frederick L., and Joseph L. Blotner. "William Faulkner on Dialect." *Virginia Spectator* (Winter & Spring 1958).

———. *Faulkner in the University.* 1959. New York: Vintage, 1965.

Haardt, Sara. "The Etiquette of Slavery." *American Mercury* 17 (May 1929): 34–42.

Hamilton, William Baskerville. *Holly Springs, Mississippi, to the Year 1878.* M.S., U of Mississippi, 1931.

Harris, Joel Chandler. "Ambuscade." *Tales of the Home Folks in Peace and War.* Boston: Houghton Mifflin, 1899.

Hartje, Robert G. *Van Dorn: The Life and Times of a Confederate General.* Nashville, TN: Vanderbilt UP, 1967.

Hawkins, E. O. "Jane Cook and Cecilia Farmer." *Mississippi Quarterly* 18:4 (Fall 1965): 248–251.

Held, Robert. *The Age of Firearms.* New York: Harper & Row, 1957.

Hemingway, Ernest. *Death in the Afternoon.* New York: Scribners, 1932.

Henry, Robert Selph. *"First with the Most": Forrest.* Indianapolis, IN: Bobbs-Merrill, 1944.

Hergesheimer, Joseph. *Swords and Roses.* New York: Knopf, 1929.

Higgins, Frances Caldwell. "Life on the Southern Plantation During the War Between the States." *Confederate Veteran* 21 (1913): 17–20.

Hildebrand, J. R. "Machines Come to Mississippi." *National Geographic* 72 (Sept. 1937): 263–318.

Hirshberg, Jeffrey. "Regional Morphology in American English: Evidence from DARE." *American Speech* 56:1 (Spring 1981): 33–52.

Hopley, Catherine Cooper. *Life in the South from the Commencement of the War.* 2 vols. 1863. New York: Augustus M. Kelley, 1971.

Horn, Stanley F. *The Army of the Tennessee.* Norman, OK: U of Oklahoma P, 1941.

Hundley, D. R. *Social Relations in Our Southern States.* New York: Arno, 1973.

Hunsberger, I. Moyer. *The Quintessential Dictionary.* New York: Hart, 1978.

Hunter, Edwin R. *William Faulkner: Narrative Practice and Prose Style.* Washington, DC: Windhover, 1973.

Ingram, Forrest L. *Representative Short Story Cycles.* The Hague: Mouton, 1971.

Johnson, Charles S. *Shadow of the Plantation.* Chicago: U of Chicago P, 1934.

Kane, Harnett T. *Plantation Parade.* New York: Morrow, 1945.

Kendrick, Benjamin Burks, and Alex Mathews Arnett. *The South Looks at Its Past.* Chapel Hill, NC: U of North Carolina P, 1935.

Kerr, Elizabeth M. "The Women of Yoknapatawpha." *University of Mississippi Studies in English* 15 (1978): 61–82.

Killion, Ronald, and Charles Waller, eds. *Slavery Times When I was Chillun Down on Marster's Plantation.* Savannah, GA: Beehive, 1973.

Knapp, David, Jr. "The Rodney Church Incident." *Journal of Mississippi History* 32:3 (Aug. 1970): 245–249.

Lamb, Robert Byron. "The Mule in Southern Agriculture." Berkeley, CA: U of California Publications in Geography, 1963.

Lee, Stephen D. "Index to Campaigns, Battles and Skirmishes in Mississippi from 1861 to 1865." *Publications of the Mississippi Historical Society* 8 (1904): 23–32.

Letwin, Shirley Robin. *The Gentleman in Trollope: Individuality and Moral Conduct.* Cambridge, MA: Harvard UP, 1982.

Lewis, Lloyd. *Sherman: Fighting Prophet.* New York: Harcourt, Brace, 1958.

Litwack, Leon W. *Been in the Storm So Long.* New York: Knopf, 1979.

Long, E. B. *The Civil War Day by Day.* Garden City, NY: Doubleday, 1971.

Lytle, Andrew Nelson. *Bedford Forrest and His Critter Company.* New York: Minton, Balch, 1931.

Martin, William. *Back Bay.* New York: Pocket Books, 1979.

Massey, Mary Elizabeth. *Ersatz in the Confederacy.* Columbia, SC: U of South Carolina P, 1952.

Matloff, Maurice. *The Civil War.* New York: Promontory, 1982.

McAlexander, Hubert, Jr. "General Earl Van Dorn and Faulkner's Use of History." *Journal of Mississippi History* 39 (Nov. 1977): 357–361.

McCain, William D. "Nathan Bedford Forrest: An Evaluation." *Journal of Mississippi History* (Oct. 1962).

McClellan, Elisabeth. *History of American Costume 1607–1870.* New York: Tudor, 1969.

McDermott, John Francis, ed. *Before Mark Twain.* Carbondale, IL: Southern Illinois UP, 1968.

McGinnis, R. J., ed. *The Good Old Days.* Cincinnati, OH: P. & W., 1960.

McKee, James W., Jr. "Congressman William Barksdale of Mississippi." *Southern Miscellany,* Frank Allen Dennis, ed. Jackson, MS: UP of Mississippi, 1981.

McKern, Sharon. *Redneck Mothers, Good Ol' Girls and Other Southern Belles.* New York: Viking, 1979.

McNeily, J. S. "Barksdale's Mississippi Brigade at Gettysburg." *Publications of the Mississippi Historical Society* 14 (1914): 12–13.

McPherson, James M. *Battle Cry of Freedom.* New York: Oxford UP, 1988.

McWhiney, Grady. "The Revolution in Nineteenth-Century Alabama Agriculture." *Alabama Review* 31 (Jan. 1978): 3–32.

Meier, August, and Elliott Rudwick. *From Plantation to Ghetto.* New York: Hill & Wang, 1976.

Mencken, H. L. *A Mencken Chrestomathy.* New York: Knopf, 1956.

Mitchell, Margaret. *Gone With the Wind.* New York: Macmillan, 1936.

Mizener, Arthur. *A Handbook for Use with Modern American Short Stories.* New York: Norton, 1966.

Moore, John Hebron. *The Emergence of the Cotton Kingdom in the Old Southwest.* Baton Rouge, LA: Louisiana State UP, 1988.

Murray, Albert. *South to a Very Old Place.* New York: McGraw-Hill, 1971.

Myrdal, Gunnar. *An American Dilemma.* New York: Harper & Row, 1962.

Nilon, Charles H. *Faulkner and the Negro.* Boulder, CO: U of Colorado Studies in Language and Literature, 1962.

Odum, Howard W. *The Way of the South.* New York: Macmillan, 1947.

Ownby, Ted. "The Defeated Generation at Work: White Farmers in the Deep South, 1865–1890." *Southern Studies* 22:4 (Winter 1984): 3–9.

Payton, Geoffrey. *Webster's Dictionary of Proper Names.* 1970.

Pearson, Alden B., Jr. "A Middle-Class Border State Family During the Civil War." *Civil War History* 22 (Dec. 1976): 318–336.

Perry, Thomas Edmund. *Knowing in the Novels of William Faulkner.* Diss. U of Rochester, 1974.

Peterkin, Julia. *Roll, Jordan, Roll.* Indianapolis, IN: Bobbs-Merrill, 1933.

Phillips, Ulrich Bonnell. *Life and Labor in the Old South.* Boston: Little, Brown, 1929.

Price, William H. *The Civil War Handbook.* Fairfax, VA: Prince Lithograph Co., 1961.

Putzel, Max. "Faulkner's Trial Preface to *Sartoris*: An Eclectic Text." *Papers of the Bibliographical Society of America* 74 (1980): 375.

Rainwater, Percy L., ed. "The Civil War Letters of Cordelia Scales." *Journal of Mississippi History* (July 1939).

Randall, J.G., and David Donald. *The Civil War and Reconstruction.* Lexington, MA: Heath, 1969.

Randolph, Vance. *Ozark Superstitions.* New York: Dover, 1947.

———., and George P. Wilson. *Down in the Holler: A Gallery of Ozark Folk Speech.* Norman, OK: U of Oklahoma P, 1953.

Raven, Simon. *The Decline of the Gentleman.* New York: Simon & Schuster, 1962.

Rhodes, Carolyn Avery. *An Analysis of the Effectiveness of Faulkner's Use of Folklore.* M.A., Stephen F. Austin State College, 1963.

Ripley, Warren. *Artillery and Ammunition of the Civil War.* New York: Van Nostrand Reinhold, 1970.

Roard, James L. *Masters Without Slaves.* New York: Norton, 1977.

Roebuck, Julian B., and Mark Hickson, III. *The Southern Redneck.* New York: Praeger, 1982.

Rose, Willie Lee. *A Documentary History of Slavery in North America.* New York: Oxford UP, 1976.

Ross, Stephen M. *Fiction's Inexhaustible Voice*. Athens, GA: U of Georgia P, 1989.

Rowland, Dunbar. *History of Mississippi: The Heart of the South*. Chicago: S. J. Clarke, 1925.

Savory, Theodore H. "The Mule." *Scientific American* 223 (Dec. 1970): 102–109.

Schick, I. T., ed. *Battledress: The Uniforms of the World's Great Armies, 1700 to the Present*. Boston: Little, Brown, 1978.

Silver, James W., ed. *Mississippi in the Confederacy as Seen in Retrospect*. Baton Rouge, LA: Louisiana State UP, published for The Mississippi Department of Archives and History, 1961.

Simkins, Francis Butler, and James Welch Patton. *The Women of the Confederacy*. Richmond, VA: Garrett and Massie, 1936.

Sitterson, J. Carlyle. "The Transition from Slave to Free Economy on the William J. Minor Plantation." *Agricultural History* 17 (October 1943): 216–244.

Skaggs, Merrill Maguire. *The Folk of Southern Fiction*. Athens, GA: U of Georgia P, 1972.

Smith, E. A. "Early Recollections of Oxford." *Oxford Eagle* 31 Mar. 1910.

Smith, Fabia Rue, and Charles Rayford Smith. *Southern Words and Sayings*. Jackson, MS: Office Supply Company, 1977.

Smith, Frank E. *The Yazoo River*. New York: Rinehart, 1954.

Smith, Minnie Holt. "Letter." *Oxford Eagle* 8 Nov. 1923.

Smith, Norah. "Sexual Mores and Attitudes in Enlightenment Scotland." *Sexuality in Eighteenth-Century Britain*. Ed. Paul-Gabriel Bouce. Totowa, NJ: Barnes & Noble, 1982.

South Carolinian, A. "South Carolina Society." *Atlantic Monthly* 39 (June 1877): 670–684.

Stein, Jean. "Paris Review Interviews." 1956. *William Faulkner: Three Decades of Criticism*. Ed. Frederick J. Hoffman and Olga W. Vickery. New York: Harcourt Harbinger, 1963.

Stephens, Robert O. "Language Magic and Reality in *For Whom the Bell Tolls*." *Criticism* 14 (Spring 1972): 151–164.

Stevens, William Oliver. *Pistols at Ten Paces*. Boston: Houghton Mifflin, 1940.

Stewart, George R. *American Place-Names*. New York: Oxford UP, 1970.

Stone, Alfred Holt. "Mississippi's Constitution and Statutes in Reference to Freedmen, and Their Alleged Relation to Reconstruction Acts and War Amendments." *Publications of the Mississippi Historical Society* 4 (1901).

Stone, Kate. *Brokenburn: The Journal of Kate Stone 1861–1868.* Ed. John Q. Anderson. Baton Rouge, LA: Louisiana State UP, 1972.

Stoneback, Harry R. *Faulkner's Use of Dialect.* M.A., U of Hawaii, 1966.

Street, James, Jr. *James Street's South.* Garden City, NY: Doubleday, 1955.

Stroud, George M. *A Sketch of the Laws Relating to Slavery.* 1856. New York: Negro University Press, 1968.

Sydnor, Charles S. *Slavery in Mississippi.* Baton Rouge, LA: Louisiana State UP, 1933.

———. "The Southerner and the Laws." *The Pursuit of Southern History.* Ed. George Brown Tindall. Baton Rouge, LA: Louisiana State UP, 1964.

Taylor, Joe Gray. *Eating, Drinking, and Visiting in the Old South.* Baton Rouge, LA: Louisiana State UP, 1982.

Thigpen, S. G. *Next Door to Heaven.* Kingsport, TN: Kingsport Press, 1965.

Thompson, Edgar T. *Plantation Societies, Race Relations, and the South: The Regimentation of Populations.* Durham, NC: Duke UP, 1975.

Thornton, Weldon. "A Note on the Source of Faulkner's Jason." *Studies in the Novel* 1 (Fall 1969): 370–372.

Tucker, Glenn. "[Forrest]: Untutored Genius of the War." *Civil War Times Illustrated* 3 (June 1964): 6–9, 35–37, 49.

Vance, Rupert B. *Human Geography of the South.* Chapel Hill, NC: U of North Carolina P, 1935.

Walkley, Christina, and Vandra Foster. *Crinolines and Crimping Irons.* London: Peter Owen, 1978.

Wasson, Ben. *Count No 'Count.* Jackson, MS: UP of Mississippi, 1983.

Watkins, Floyd C., and Charles Herbert Watkins. *Yesterday in the Hills.* Athens, GA: U of Georgia P, 1973.

Weaver, Richard M. *The Southern Tradition at Bay.* New Rochelle, NY: Arlington, 1968.

Wecter, Dixon. *The Saga of American Society.* New York: Scribners, 1937.

Wheeler, Richard. *Voices of the Civil War.* New York: Crowell, 1976.

White, B.F., and E.J. King. *The Sacred Harp* (facsimile of 1859 edition). Nashville, TN: Broadman P, 1968.

Wicker, Tom. *Unto This Hour.* New York: Berkley Books, 1985.

Wiener, Jonathan M. "Female Planters and Planters' Wives in Civil War and Reconstruction: Alabama, 1850–1870." *Alabama Review* 30 (April 1977): 135–149.

Wiley, Bell Irvin. *The Plain People of the Confederacy*. Chicago: Quadrangle, 1963.

———. *Southern Negroes 1861–1865*. New Haven, CT: Yale UP, 1938.

———., and Hirst D. Milhollen. *Embattled Confederates*. New York: Harper & Row, 1964.

Wittenberg, Judith Bryant. *Faulkner and the Transfiguration of Biography*. Lincoln, NE: U of Nebraska P, 1979.

Wolk, Allan. *The Naming of America*. Nashville, TN: Thomas Nelson, 1977.

Woodward, C. Vann. *The Strange Career of Jim Crow*. New York: Oxford UP, 1966.

Woodward, W. E. *The Way Our People Lived*. New York: Dutton, 1945.

Wright, Richardson. *Hawkers and Walkers in Early America*. Philadelphia, PA: Lippincott, 1927.

Wyatt-Brown, Bertram. *Southern Honor: Ethics and Behavior in the Old South*. New York: Oxford UP, 1982.

Wyeth, John Allan. *That Devil Forrest*. 1899. New York: Harper, 1959.

Yarwood, Doreen. *Costume of the Western World*. New York: St. Martin's, 1980.

Young, Stark. *So Red the Rose*. New York: Scribners, 1934.

Young, Thomas Daniel. "Pioneering on Principle, or How a Traditional Society May Be Dissolved." *Faulkner, Modernism, and Film*. Ed. Evans Harrington and Ann J. Abadie. Jackson, MS: UP of Mississippi, 1979.

Zall, P. M. *Abe Lincoln Laughing*. Berkeley, CA: U of Calif P, 1982.

Zogbaum, Rufus Fairchild. *Horse, Foot, and Dragoons*. New York: Harper, 1888.

INDEX